N GRAY · FRANK GIFFORD · AL CARMICHAEL · TOM NICKOLOFF

RON MIX · HAL BEDSOLE · WILLIE BROW̶ ̶FERTIG · BII

OGGE · JOHN McKAY · JOHN VELLA · SAM ̶ ̶ALLAN

MATTHEWS · FRANK JORDAN · PAUL McDONALD · KEITH VAN H

DAN · JEFF BREGEL · REX MOORE · MARK CARRIER · JOHN JACK

PADAKIS · JOHN ROBINSON · CARSON PALMER · KEVIN ARBET ·

AN BING · AMBROSE SCHINDLER · BILL GRAY · JIM HARDY · GO

ALAKIS · MARV GOUX · JON ARNETT · C. ROBERTS · MONTE C

TIM ROSSOVICH · RON YARY · ADRIAN YOUNG · MIKE BATTLE ·

OD McNEILL · MANFRED MOORE · J. McKAY · RICHARD WOOD

Y FOSTER · JEFF BROWN · MICHAEL HARPER · TIM GREEN · STEV

OD MARINOVICH · SCOTT ROSS · DERRICK DEESE · MATT GEE ·

NART · BRANDON HANCOCK · TOM MALONE · MARIO DANELO ·

GRAY · FRANK GIFFORD · AL CARMICHAEL · TOM NICKOLOFF

RON MIX · HAL BEDSOLE · WILLIE BROWN · CRAIG FERTIG · BII

OGGE · JOHN McKAY · JOHN VELLA · SAM CUNNINGHAM · ALLAN

MATTHEWS · FRANK JORDAN · PAUL McDONALD · KEITH VAN H

DAN · JEFF BREGEL · REX MOORE · MARK CARRIER · JOHN JACK

PADAKIS · JOHN ROBINSON · CARSON PALMER · KEVIN ARBET

WHAT IT MEANS TO BE A TROJAN

WHAT IT MEANS TO BE A
TROJAN

SOUTHERN CAL'S GREATEST PLAYERS
TALK ABOUT TROJANS FOOTBALL

STEVEN TRAVERS

FOREWORD BY PETE CARROLL

TRIUMPH
BOOKS

This book is available in quantity at special discounts for your group or organization. For further information, contact:

Triumph Books
542 South Dearborn Street
Suite 750
Chicago, Illinois 60605
(312) 939-3330
Fax (312) 663-3557
www.triumphbooks.com

Printed in U.S.A.
ISBN: 978-1-60078-211-4
Design by Nick Panos
Editorial production and layout by Prologue Publishing Services, LLC
All photos courtesy AP Images unless otherwise indicated

*To all of the Trojans, past and present, who have made
Southern Cal the greatest university in the world*

CONTENTS

"FIGHT ON"

The USC Fight Song

Fight On for ol' SC
Our men Fight On to victory.
Our Alma Mater dear,
Looks up to you
Fight On and win
For ol' SC
Fight On to victory
Fight On!

Music and Lyrics by Milo Sweet and Glen Grant

FOREWORD

What It Means to Be a Trojan

Growing up as a kid in the '60s and '70s and loving football, I could not help myself—I loved USC football! It could have been the great teams, the great players, the Coliseum, the many championships, or the Rose Bowl spectacles. The pageantry was awesome! The Cardinal and Gold, Traveler, the sounds of the irrepressible Trojan Marching Band, and the beautiful cheerleaders in any combination could have been enough to enrapture a young, impressionable fan like me. There was something more to the connection than those tangible aspects of the Trojan experience. It was something more profound than the obvious. There was a style and grace and an air of confidence that was unique. In those days I couldn't have explained it; I just dreamed of being a part of it.

I witnessed it firsthand as a fan at the Coliseum in 1969 when 'SC was playing archrival UCLA for the conference championship. My high school friends and I traveled from the Bay Area to the Southland to see one of the great classic matchups in college football. As luck would have it, our less-than-stellar connections awarded us seats seven rows from the top of the Coliseum just below the old clock. In the closing moments of a highly contested game, USC quarterback Jimmy Jones threw a strike to Sam Dickerson for the game-winning touchdown, in the extreme opposite corner of the end zone. Through the haze and the darkness we couldn't see a thing but the 'SC faithful cheering wildly, with the news of the catch working its way to even the far-reaching corners of the Coliseum. The Trojans had won, and my schoolboy dreams had been validated…how could you not love Trojan football and USC?

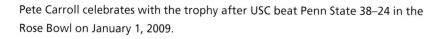

Pete Carroll celebrates with the trophy after USC beat Penn State 38–24 in the Rose Bowl on January 1, 2009.

Many years later, having served as a football coach at this great university, I now know precisely what it is that separates the Trojan experience from any other. It is the collection of all the incredible elements that stand together to define the "spirit of Troy." The pride and the passion that come along with being a member of the Trojan family is legendary in Southern California and around the world. I will forever be grateful for the opportunity to realize a dream and represent all those who have come before us. Being able to partake and share with our fans the essence of the spirit of Troy is a true honor of a lifetime, and for that I will always be grateful.

Fight on!

—Pete Carroll

USC STATS

First game:	November 14, 1888, vs. Alliance Athletic Club (Trojans win, 16–0)
Home stadium:	Los Angeles Memorial Coliseum (built 1923)
Stadium capacity:	93,607
All-time record:	766–303–54 (.717)
Postseason bowl record:	31–16
National championships:	11 (1928, 1931, 1932, 1939, 1962, 1967, 1972, 1974, 1978, 2003, 2004)
Conference titles:	38
Heisman Trophy winners:	7 (Mike Garrett, O.J. Simpson, Charles White, Marcus Allen, Carson Palmer, Matt Leinart, and Reggie Bush)
All-Americans:	154
Colors:	Cardinal and Gold
Fight song:	"Fight On"
Mascot:	Traveler
Marching band:	The Spirit of Troy

Four photos courtesy Getty Images

EDITOR'S ACKNOWLEDGMENTS

Thanks to Pete Carroll, the greatest coach in football. Thanks to Tom Bast, Natalie King, Mitch Rogatz, Adam Motin, Mindi Rowland, Fred Walski, Bill Ames, Josh Williams, Adam Rifenberick (president of Press Box Publicity), Alex Lubertozzi, and all the great folks at Triumph Books, Random House Publishing, and Prologue Publishing Services for having faith in me with what is now my seventh book with them.

Thanks also to Lori Perkins, Mary Ann Naples, and Ian Kleinart. Thanks to Lloyd Robinson of Suite A Management in Beverly Hills. He is a fine Trojan. Thanks to Tim Tessalone, Paul Goldberg, and Dave Tuttle with the USC sports information office. Thanks to three all-time great, late Trojans who granted me interviews in 2000 when I covered the Trojan sports beat for a magazine: John McKay, Marv Goux, and Rod Dedeaux. Thanks to my friend, the late, great Bud "the Steamer" Furillo. Thanks to my friend, the late Craig Fertig. Thanks to Anthony Davis. To Loel Schrader: your words were so touching, full of generosity and spirit. May God bless you and keep you.

Thanks to the interviewees who participated and tell their stories of what it means to be a Trojan in the pages of this book.

Thanks to Ryan Kalil, Bob Schmidt, Riki Ellison, Lynn Swann, Keyshawn Johnson, Tony Boselli, Carson Palmer, Scott Ware, Mike Salmon, Pete Beathard, John David Booty, Mike Garrett, and Matt Grootegoed.

Thanks also to Bill Bordley, Tom Seaver, Bill "Spaceman" Lee, Rich McKay, Jeff Cirillo, Barry Zito, Jeff Trepagnier, Angela Williams, Mark Prior, Mike Gillespie, and Chad Kreuter.

A special mention for my friend, the late Mickey Meister. Also, to Mrs. Cindy McCain, a great Trojan.

I want to mention the following people: John Hall, Art Spander, Dwight Chapin, Garry Paskwietz, Linda McCoy-Murray, Don Andersen. Liz Kennedy, Jose Eskenazi, Lori Nelson, and Danielle Harvey.

Thanks to Doug Caravalho, Anthony "Bruno" Caravalho, Ken Flower, Terry Marks, Keith Ferrante, Linda LeBlond, Dale Komai, Cynthia Christian, Marni Lovrich, Nick Racic, Keith Matsuoka, Mark Wleklinski, Rob and Melanie Pedrick, Meribeth Farmer, Massimo Ristorante, Joe Enloe, Tony Russo, Gordon Pitts, Valerie Callejas, Cecil Brown, Rosemary DiSano, Teresa Verbeck, Professor Dan Durbin, Kerry McCluggage, Sebastian Twardosz, Tina Orkin, Pete Arbogast, Jim Starr, Dennis Slutak, Harvey Hyde, Chuck Hayes, Sergeant Gary Andrade, Marie McGlashan, Spiro Psaltis, Jim Connor, Jack Brannan, Bob Troppmann, Al Endriss, Skip Corsini, Mark Jackson, and Cheryl Kalil.

Thank you to Mike Lewis, and the Trojan Football Alumni Club. Thank you to two great Trojans, Bruce and Heath Seltzer.

Of course, my thanks as always go out to my daughter, Elizabeth Travers; my parents, Don and Inge Travers; and to my Lord and Savior, Jesus Christ, who has shed his grace on thee, and to whom all glory is due!

INTRODUCTION

Nobody embodies the magic, the charisma, the spirit, and the excitement of what it means to be a Trojan more than head coach Pete Carroll. This is quite a statement, considering the likes of John "Duke" Wayne, Rod Dedeaux, Frank Gifford, Bill Sharman, Jesse "Big Daddy" Unruh, Norman Topping, John McKay, Marv Goux, George Lucas, Tom Selleck, Tom Seaver, Bill Lee, Bob Seagren, C. Christopher Cox, Sam "Bam" Cunningham, Patricia Nixon, John Naber, Marcus Allen, Ronnie Lott, John Robinson, Randy Johnson, Cindy McCain, Dr. Steven Sample, and Mike Garrett are just a few of those who have also embodied what it means to be a Trojan. But Coach Carroll has taken it to a new level. He is the "Prince of the City" in Los Angeles, a man who could be mayor, maybe even governor as Paul "Bear" Bryant might have been in Alabama, had he chosen to try. This is a man who has attained the respect previously reserved for such luminaries as Jimmy Stewart, Vin Scully, and John Wooden.

So, for me, watching Pete Carroll rise to this level has been a particular thrill ride. You see, the first time I ever heard of Pete Carroll was my freshman year at Redwood High School in Marin County, a leafy suburb of San Francisco, located just north of the Golden Gate Bridge. The tradition at Redwood was to hang photos of baseball, football, and basketball captains in the boys' locker room. One would look up and see the visage of young sports heroes of previous years. I noticed that Carroll graced not one but three photos on that wall. He was pictured as captain in his football, basketball, and baseball uniforms. I immediately deduced that he must be a special athlete and leader. For young athletes like myself, guys like Pete Carroll were something to aspire to, to emulate.

Bob Troppmann was still coaching football at Redwood when I arrived there. He had been there since the school opened for business in 1958 and had built it into a Bay Area power. Coach Troppmann, as it turned out, was an old family friend. My father, Donald Travers, had been a great track and cross country coach at Lowell and Balboa High Schools in San Francisco. Coach Troppmann had come out of the Marine Corps, gotten his teaching credential, and was a young teacher/coach at Lowell when he met and befriended my father.

By the time I entered Redwood, my dad had become an attorney, and Coach Troppmann had moved across the bay to Marin. He was a genuinely nice, approachable man, and I often sought him out for knowledge of one kind or another. One of my first questions concerned Pete Carroll, who impressed me for having captained three varsity teams. Coach Troppmann just smiled when reminded of Carroll, who had since gone onto the University of Pacific on a football scholarship, made all-conference as a defensive back, and was a promising young coach, moving up the ranks. The affection and indeed admiration Coach Troppmann felt for Pete Carroll was obvious even then.

Over the years, I asked many of the coaches at Redwood who had mentored Pete Carroll about him. Jess Payan, Phil Roark, Dick Hart, Al Endriss; all had positive words to describe Pete Carroll, but one story really stands out. Coach Endriss was a baseball legend, and in fact, in my junior year he was named National High School Coach of the Year. In my senior year, we were the national champions of prep baseball.

Today Redwood has a new state-of-the-art facility, but in my day our field was considered one of the better yards in the area. Our center-field fence circled high over the adjacent track. Often track meets were held during baseball games, and a high home run might disrupt proceedings, but in Pete Carroll's day there was no fence. Extra-base hits slammed over the center fielder's head would land on the track and bound onto the football field, which served as the location for events such as the shot-put and the discus throw. A bounding outfielder would traipse into the midst of this scene, grab the ball, and throw it back to the infield, often amid much cursing and yelling.

My favorite Pete Carroll story somehow seems to symbolize the serendipity that is his life. He was roaming the center-field pastures when a long drive was hit over his head. Pete headed back for it, intent, concentrating on the ball. He ignored the cement cleft separating the track from the outfield grass, the running lanes a sort of "warning track" that he paid no attention to.

A relay race was in motion, and as Pete chased that ball down, a bevy of runners, maybe three or four tightly bound together, came sprinting around the turn, heading straight for Pete Carroll.

Nobody—not the runners, Pete, or the baseball—paid any attention to each other. A gasp went up, from the watching tracksters, from the baseball players shouting a warning, and the fans in the stands. Two locomotives were about to collide in a massive train wreck!

As quickly as it developed, it ended. Pete caught the ball, whirled, and made a Willie Mays–style throw back to the infield. The track runners continued to kick down the stretch. Everybody—the baseball outfielder, the runners, and the ball—had missed each other by inches, all as if choreographed like a beautiful ballet.

For some reason, this story is the story of Pete Carroll's charmed life. Good timing combined with skill. A little luck and a lot of focus. In the end, everything always seems to turn out just right with this man.

The story of Coach Carroll is what it means to be a Trojan.

Fight On!

The THIRTIES

NORMAN BING

END

1937

I WAS A WALK-ON and didn't play much. I was a premed major who just enjoyed playing a little on the 1937 team for Coach Howard Jones.

I played at Fairfax High School in Los Angeles. I played there in 1932 and 1933. I got out of USC in 1939. I was there four years. In 1935 I entered L.A. City College for a year. Then I started premed at USC and later moved to the business school in 1939.

I was not one of Jones' favorites. I was not to close to him, but we all enjoyed him. He played favorites. Everybody has his own opinion. Doyle Nave was a good friend and could throw like crazy, but Jones didn't care for him much. He didn't like the way he played, but he could pass very well. He won the Duke game for us.

Ray George and I were both good friends and chased the same girl. He married her. I was friends with Don McNeil and Tony Tonelli.

The UCLA rivalry was pretty damn big. We didn't have the armor plates like they have today, but as a consequence we'd not play as viciously. That was a big game just like today. Some days were good and some days were not. Most of the players came from the L.A. area, like today.

Jackie Robinson came after me with Kenny Washington to UCLA. They were star players. Washington could throw the ball the length of the field. Jackie did a good job, too. He was a shifty guy, Robinson. They had some big players.

Al Krueger was a damn good player for us. He was a big guy, and it was hard for guys to cover him. Pat Nixon, the future First Lady, was at USC when I was there, but I didn't know who she was. I never knew her. We had a fair number of famous people at USC, people who were in the movie industry. Before that we had Aaron Rosenberg from Fairfax High. Aaron went in the movies as a producer/director. He also helped us on spring training in high school. Homer Griffith was a good friend of mine.

I knew of Lou Zamperini, the trackman. He was a star, a very good star. He was one of the most accomplished guys of anybody in world history. He was fantastic, his character. He did great things during the war, and he was in the Olympics. He was shot down in the South Pacific and survived a lot of time on an island.

Rod Dedeaux was a student at USC in the 1930s and played baseball. I saw him one year before he died. He was a wonderful guy, all baseball. He did very well with the USC teams and won many national championships. He was the lowest-paid coach they ever had at USC. He worked for a dollar a year. He was a hell of a guy. I spent some with him at 50-year reunions; the last time was the year before he passed away, he sat at the football table. He was a millionaire with Dart Trucking.

Dean Cromwell was the best track coach in America. I knew some of the track guys. Cromwell was well thought of and well respected, very popular too.

What it means to be a Trojan: I was gonna be a dentist and went to the dental school. The atmosphere at 'SC was very close. It was just a great time, and being a Trojan continued my whole life to be a very great thing. We competed with UCLA. Half went to UCLA, portions went to USC. L.A. was a small town then. It was not as big as the mess we have now. You knew the fellows on other teams. The school today is like what I think of a county or town back then. You'd have interchangeable friendships with players, and it was not different from living in a community.

Most local high school players went to USC. A few went up to Stanford, Cal, or Washington, but in the main they came from the local area. USC would pick up fellows from the Midwest. It was a different atmosphere. Once you're a Trojan, you never forget it. My whole family—my wife, our kids— all went to 'SC. I helped start the Trojan Club of Orange County after the war. We met once a month during the football season. The coach came down to Newport Beach. The Orange County Trojan Club attracted top speakers;

they'd come out to a private house at Balboa Bay. It was very close with much camaraderie. Down in Balboa we had a good group; there were always a lot of 'SC people there, and they all came home from the service and knew one another. Once a Trojan, forever a Trojan. Even during the war, we'd run into each other.

I had a compadre in my class I was tight with. We'd run with the same girls. We practically all knew each other, we all married girls we knew. Like the last one I heard from, we had dinner with friends of ours in Newport. I knew his wife's folks at Fairfax High. They threw a cocktail party, and later we had a dinner party, so we had all these close friends and all had known each other forever. The camaraderie is still there. I reflect back on those days in school. I'm now 92. It was a wonderful time, and I appreciate all my life. I got a great education, got all I could get out of it. I want to compliment the staff and faculty; I had great professors, great personnel. It was a time of great memories.

Norman Bing was a walk-on for Coach Howard Jones in the mid-1930s and remains one of the oldest surviving players of that era.

AMBROSE SCHINDLER

QUARTERBACK

1936–1937, 1939

I GRADUATED FROM SAN DIEGO HIGH SCHOOL in February 1935. I played with Ted Williams in junior baseball. He went to Hoover High. I played for the Ryan Juniors, which was in a youth league in the city. That team was made up of high school kids who were going to the playgrounds. I played on the same fields with him. He pitched and I caught at different times together. My favorite player was Cotton Warburton, and I understood that he was Ted's favorite, too. Cotton had come out of San Diego High before me. He was my inspiration. He was so great. The best day of my life was after watching Cotton play in a high school game and finding out he was coming back for another year of high school football. He was there four years, a little guy, but he could sure run, so you were inspired by him. Harold "Hobbs" Adams was our high school coach. He coached both Warburton and me. Howard Jones hired Hobbs as an assistant coach at USC, and he brought me with him.

This was a fairly common practice in those days. Nibs Price, a high school coach from San Diego, started it. College football teams had always consisted of players trying out from among the student body, but after World War I the country became more mobile, and the concept of recruiting came into being. Suddenly teams did not consist generally of boys from the region, but rather a young man might be enticed to come to school even if he did not live near the campus.

The University of California at Berkeley had a large number of students come there for military training, so they were attuned to this situation, and Coach Andy Smith decided to turn his program into a national powerhouse. He hired Price because he had many contacts among the coaching fraternity in Southern California, which was a growing populace that Smith recognized as the place where most of the great athletes were coming from. One of those players was Brick Muller out of San Diego. Smith brought Price to Berkeley because he could bring Muller into school with him, but this practice was fraught with a new set of problems.

These recruits were prima donnas unlike average students, and Smith was a hard driver who conducted exhausting practice sessions. Muller and the Southern California contingent got fed up and decided to leave school. A meeting was held in the summer halfway in between, in Fresno, between Price and the players from Southern California in which it was agreed that the practice sessions would not be as strenuous. They all came back to school. Muller was the greatest player in the nation, and those teams were known as the Wonder Teams, up until then the best dynasty the country had ever seen.

Well, Howard Jones had decided to one-up Andy Smith and Cal. "Gloomy Gus" Henderson had built USC from a regional program to a national power by bringing in high school players from the Seattle area, which had been the best hotbed of prep talent for years. He ushered USC into the Pacific Coast Conference and won our first Rose Bowl over Penn State in 1923. Jones started the rivalry with Notre Dame, which gave us an edge over Cal and Stanford, making us a national power and the top program on the West Coast. Coach Jones also had an advantage in recruiting, which was the movie industry. John "Duke" Wayne had played for him before going into the movies, and Duke arranged for Trojan players to be extras in movies, attend Hollywood parties, and be around all those pretty actresses.

By the time I got to USC, this was the standard practice, and the program attracted the greatest players in America. I entered USC in February of 1935, right out of high school. It was mid-year, and, as I say, I went with my high school coach, who got his job as an assistant under Jones. It was never really spelled out for me, but I understand that he got the job by bringing me into school with him.

Cotton Warburton was at USC for three years before me. I attended at night at first. I had been on the track team in high school. A track meet was held at Southern Cal, and I participated and visited the campus in a slight

Ambrose Schindler, USC's starting quarterback in 1937, was moved to fullback by Howard Jones before the 1938 season in an effort to add backfield punch.

drizzle. The Tommy Trojan statue was getting wet a little bit, but it was an awesome sight, as the campus was turning from dusk to dark, so I could not have been there at a better time to be impressed. It was kind of plain otherwise, it was not much of a campus at the time. Coach Hobbs had all the connections. Hobbs had coached Cotton and had a good track record coaching in baseball, football, and track. So Hobbs had gotten to USC, and we were all together and were Sigma Alpha Epsilons. It was a great time, a great time in my life. I can't imagine anything being any better.

Even though USC was the school you wanted to play for, the football program had been down just a little bit before I got there. Cal and Stanford had gotten really jealous and accused us of cheating and academic impropriety, but it was all just a response to our surpassing them as a West Coast football power. We had won three national championships, and the 1931–1932 teams were probably the best teams ever, the famed Thundering Herd, but those freshmen up at Stanford had promised never to lose to Southern Cal again, and they never did, so they became known as "the Vow Boys." UCLA was getting better and better every year, so Coach Jones was determined to have his team get back to where they had been.

For me, it was a struggle. There was a lot talent, playing time was always hard to come by, and I broke my foot in a freshman game against Santa Ana High School. That set me back for a year and a half. All of my freshman year was gone, but it did not affect my varsity eligibility. Freshmen could not play varsity ball in those days. I became a starter in my sophomore year and started all the time I was at USC as long as I was healthy, but there was always competition at my position.

8

I was a tailback in a single wing offense. We lined up out of the huddle in a box formation single wing called the "Warner B." It was a designated single wing offense, and I always ran out of that formation. My varsity years were 1936, 1937—I was laid out in '38 with a broken ankle—and then 1939, I played my senior year. All in all, I was at USC for five and a half years.

I played against California in 1937. They were the most powerfully organized team I'd played against, and they were seniors. Stub Allison was their coach, and they had great players. There were great athletes like Vic Bottari and Sam Chapman, who went on to play outfield for Connie Mack's Philadelphia Athletics. Cal and Stanford made comebacks; they were determined to be national powers again, as Southern Cal had become. In 1937 Cal won the national championship, beating Alabama in the Rose Bowl, and in 1940 Stanford won the national title when they beat Nebraska in the Rose Bowl. Those were the last national championships each of those two schools won.

I got hit in the head against Cal. I was down, and a guy just swung his foot through my helmet, and I was goofy after that. We had a fierce competition with Cal and Stanford. Cal and Stanford never played an honest game in their lives, but there were a lot of shenanigans at that time. Cal would arrive in Los Angeles, and it would be 90 degrees, it hadn't rained in months, but the field would be a quagmire. The maintenance guy would come out all apologetic, "Oh, I must've forgot to turn off the sprinklers." But it would slow down Bottari and Chapman, you see.

It was always like that, rivalries between Northern and Southern California teams. Later the Candlestick grounds crew did the same thing to slow down Maury Wills of the Dodgers. Gamesmanship, all part of the sport of it, you see. But it was also an evolving time in the relationship between USC, Cal, and Stanford. And then UCLA became our biggest rival. They were just a little commuter school, first in downtown, then in Westwood, where at first people said nobody would travel that far just to go to school. But they played in our stadium, the Coliseum, were integrated, and quickly built themselves into a competitive team by doing that.

We had been integrated way ahead of almost everybody, what with Brice Taylor making All-America back in the 1920s, so these games between the integrated Bruins and Trojans in front of huge crowds at the Coliseum were just visual statements that were more powerful than any speeches.

Jackie Robinson and the Bruins tied us 0–0 in 1939. In 1936 they'd tied us 7–7. These games were just intense struggles with everything on the line. That game started to even things between the two teams, and over the next couple of decades UCLA was at least as strong as USC. Robinson was a great player, and his wife, Rachel Robinson, was a student at UCLA then. She still talks about the rivalry, which she compares to the Dodgers-Giants rivalry. But Jackie met his match in terms of opposing coaches when they went up against Jones. As a matter of fact, we were getting ready to play them, and Jones was at the blackboard drawing up UCLA's offense and defense. He drew their offense versus our defense and shifted where he saw weakness in our defense. We asked, "What about that, Coach?" and Jones saw weaknesses, but covered up the hole, and we outclassed them by overshifting them on our defense to offset their power. Robinson was on that '39 team, but when they were driving toward the end, for some reason they did not go to him. It cost them a chance at winning the game.

Kenny Washington, who also was a great sprinter in track, played for UCLA. Woody Strode was a big wide receiver, and we didn't have anybody who was tall enough to cover him, but they weren't able to get the ball into his hands as much as they would've liked. Jones just outcoached them, but they put the ball in the air, and that scared the living daylights out of Jones. Afterward, he just hid in his office like he was hiding from their passing.

I'd had some injuries—I think maybe I'd been hurt in '37, too—but we were the Coliseum "visitors," and I didn't play. So I was sitting outside with the lockers right behind us at tunnel six. I was on crutches, and I decided to walk up the tunnel to avoid both teams from rushing up past me. So I walked across the track, entered the tunnel, and started up. Then somebody said to stick around, and all hell broke loose. Kenny Washington broke through with the ball twice and scored two touchdowns in 45 seconds. Oh, man!

But we won in the Rose Bowl two years in a row. You know, we beat those southern teams, we beat Notre Dame, but our most difficult competition was in the conference. So the big argument going on at that time was, where's the best football being played? Before World War II it was determined that the best players were out west, and there were all kinds of theories, ranging from the sunshine, the vitamins in our fresh fruit, the gene pool of pioneers, to more athletic men and women coming out to Hollywood. The world was taking notice of American football. Adolf Hitler was alarmed that America had the most rugged athletes playing football, and that would make us formidable in war, and he sure would've been smart to have played that hunch.

I was hurt in 1938, and when we played Duke in the Rose Bowl, we were heavy underdogs. Those guys had not only not lost a game, but nobody had even scored a point on them. They would punt on third down just to pin opponents down. They would get turnovers and score off their defense and just overwhelm you. Nobody really gave us a chance. I didn't play in that game. I'd played two or three games early in the season, but I was injured with a broken foot, so I just decided to sit out and save my eligibility for 1939.

Well, we all know what happened. Duke led 3–0, and we couldn't move the ball against them at all, certainly not on the ground. That was how Howard Jones liked it on offense. He never liked putting the ball in the air, he never felt it was safe. But we went through several quarterbacks, and all were ineffective, so Jones was desperate. We had to put the ball in the air if we were going to have a chance.

Quarterback Doyle Nave was fourth-string; end "Antelope Al" Krueger was third-string, I think. In another offense, either guy would have started, they were great athletes—fast, and Nave could throw—but neither was entirely compatible with Jones' offense. But Duke was unprepared for Doyle's passing effectiveness. We were driving with a few minutes to go, and Doyle hit Al on several clutch passes until we were down near their goal line. Then he hit Al for a touchdown to win the game 7–3.

The place just went bonkers, and the press made the biggest possible deal out of it. For years, decades, this was said to be the biggest sports moment of the century, the biggest Rose Bowl game ever, and Doyle Nave was instantaneously elevated to national hero. Women wrote him letters, magazines featured him, and even though Southern Cal was a huge football power before that, it put us on the map. It was on the radio across the country. Norman Topping supposedly heard it on his deathbed, and it "miraculously" cured him, so the story goes. Braven Dyer made his name writing about that game.

Krueger was a demonstrative character. He and Doyle had great personalities, and this helped because they talked to reporters and expounded on what happened. It was all very colorful. They were both fun-loving guys, and the girls fell in love with them after that. They just had a great time at USC, we all did.

In a video Tom Kelly did some years ago, Krueger made these great descriptions of those catches. Doyle was sitting a little in front of him and would say, "Oh, every pass was right on the numbers," and in the back Al was gesturing and gesticulating like he had to dive and stretch out for every catch, and it was all great fun, typical of their personalities.

But as great as they were, neither really got better. Doyle never got better as a tailback, not in the kind of offense Howard Jones liked to run. Grenny Lansdell and I were ahead of him at tailback. The newspapers said Grenny and I were about equal. Doyle could not make three yards running in the single wing. He could throw and kick, but Jones liked us to run, and both Grenny and I were better runners. He would have been excellent in a better system for passing, but we were ahead of him.

Doyle as a person was sure of himself—he was athletic and confident in what he could do. Sometimes he felt he could do more than what he really could do. He was not as good a runner as Grenny or I, a good passer, but not a field general. This was the single wing, it was different then, a quarterback was not what he is today. Doyle was more oriented toward what we now think of as a "drop back" quarterback, whereby Grenny and I usually ran out of the formation but could on occasion throw short passes.

Krueger was a happy-go-lucky fellow, a great player, but not to the point where we would build an offense around him. He could execute his plays excellently, but the coaches did not develop an offense around him. He could get open against anybody who tried to cover him, though.

In 1939 I recognized that there was going to be a hell of a competition between myself, Grenny, and Doyle. Now Doyle was at first one up because of his Rose Bowl performance against Duke. Jones was influenced by the newspapers, because they all backed Doyle. Braven Dyer of the *Los Angeles Times* particularly advocated the modernization of football. The ball had been reduced in size, making it easier to throw. And it was a uniform-sized ball, whereas at one time balls might be one size in the West, another size in the South. Sammy Baugh was a throwing sensation; Don Hutson was an end who could catch any ball thrown at Alabama; and we had Doyle Nave. His performance against Duke had been considered a breakthrough.

It went against Howard Jones' natural instincts to throw the ball, but how could you argue against what Doyle had done? But when we tied Oregon in the opening game, boy, we all just thought that was the end of the world. How to overcome that? I don't recall much about that game. I'd say we were inexperienced, Doyle had hardly played in '38, aside from the last couple minutes of the Rose Bowl. So I was getting up and running, and Doyle did not make it. After that, Grenny and I got more playing time. Doyle certainly played a fair amount, but he did not emerge as the great star his Rose Bowl performance led so many to believe he was destined to become.

Well, we found our rhythm and just went on a streak. By season's end, there was not a better team in America. That was the year we went back to South Bend and walloped Notre Dame. In those days, we played the Irish at the end of the year whether at home or on the road. It could get cold in South Bend, and that was an advantage for them, but we beat them 20–12. We'd beat them 13–0 in Los Angeles the previous season, and the rivalry was very even, but USC never beat the Irish at Notre Dame again until O.J. Simpson in 1967.

The USC–Notre Dame rivalry is and always was exemplary of what college football is all about. To go back there and play against them, to be a part of that is an honor, it really is. I was a disappointment to Jones because I was a senior, but I was not playing as much as I thought I should. Doyle got a lot of time on the field, and Grenny was an All-American. I probably could have made a big success at any other school, but at USC that year there was more competition for playing time than the opposition provided in games. But I went in against Notre Dame, played well, and we won. I ran an end run in front of Coach Elmer Layden and made about eight yards. I decided to run it again and broke loose for 44 yards and a touchdown. Nobody was gonna catch me, so I thought of thumbing my nose at Layden. Some guy from 'Bama had thumbed his nose on about the 12, so I thought of doing the same thing. Then I thought it would be disrespectful, so I stuck my tongue out at him. Nobody saw it but me. I said to myself, *'SC doesn't do that.*

The West Coast had the best football teams at that time. We barely beat Washington 9–7, then tied UCLA 0–0, so when another unbeaten, untied, un*scored*-on southern team, this time Tennessee, came out to the Rose Bowl, we were not intimidated at all. We did not think of the national title before the game—it was not recognized, no group was authorized to do that. I was not playing to win that, just to win the game. The Associated Press had started up a poll in 1936, and there were a number of systems, the most recognized and respected being one devised by a Professor Dickinson based on strength of schedule and performance. It took into consideration the bowl games, and it was the most legit. But there wasn't the hype then as their is today, so our main concern was to win the game for the prestige of the university and the Pacific Coast Conference.

Coach Bob Neyland's Tennessee Volunteers were a fine team, but frankly we had a superior team, both in terms of our ability and our coaching. I felt I was the best quarterback on that team for field generalship, so I don't think we would have done as well without me, and I had earned the playing time, so I got in that game.

I threw a touchdown pass to Krueger, and as I say, in those days passing was not number one in 'SC's method of advancing the ball, especially when I was in the game. But Doyle was the inspiration for the idea of passing the football. Maybe not so much because of what Braven Dyer wrote, but he liked Doyle. Rather, Jones saw the way the game was changing and started opening things up.

The offense we designed meant that every pass was from the threat of a run. So we faked the run, dropped back one or two steps, then threw a pass under 10 yards. I was primarily a runner and only threw about two passes in that game. Essentially, we depended on running more and had to make it all look like I was running to help the passes.

I remember we had the ball on their 2-yard line. I went back to the huddle and thought to myself, *Here we are in the Rose Bowl.* I said to the guys, "Let's give 'em something to think about." After the snap, I faked two or

13

three steps and arched a perfect, beautiful pass. Al was not looking, but he just turned around, and it was there. We only needed two yards, and it was perfect.

Jones possessed tremendous ingenuity, but it was his application of the defense that made him great. He understood the game of football and understood defense, and his players were always strong on defense. He recruited good players who were strong on defense.

I felt we were better physically than our opponents. We had a first team and a second team. In the days of both-sides-of-the-ball football, you used to go with two teams, and our second team was as strong as our first. The second team with Joe Shell as our captain did most of the scoring, and Shell was really proud of that, made a big point of it.

Jones had adjusted to what he had because he had great players on that '39 team. They produced for him and they knew that. He never got beat badly. We never lost 40–0. Heck, that's just 'SC football over the years. Even in the rare times they're down, the Trojans almost never get beat 40–0. They lost like that to Notre Dame one year, and it was such a rarity they talk about to this day like it's a freak thing, which it was.

What does it mean to be a Trojan? I was happy I was able to go to USC and be successful in football. I had been well coached and could do what was required of me. I was so happy that other players were equally as skilled in football, on offense and on defense. I was very fortunate, and we could play with anybody. I figured we were as good as anybody we played, and we loved competition. We weren't afraid of Notre Dame or any team.

We had wonderful scholars there, and I had great teammates. We were recognized as a champion, and I was thrilled to death to play because of that. It was the best place I could possibly go to further my desire to be educated and get great coaching.

There is a sense of tradition there—it was strong then, and it's been maintained—and that's a big part of what it means to be a Trojan. Historically, USC never lost sight of the fact they are USC. They represent the great collegiate world of education and football, and are a vital part of the collegiate experience for undergraduates, as it should be. It was a perfect place to get an education, and we had great coaches to help us out.

USC was a place where all kinds of people came together. Patricia Nixon, the First Lady, was at USC when I was there. She was not yet married to Richard Nixon. They both lived in Whittier, and Nixon had a car, which was a little unusual in those days. But he had one because his father owned a grocery store, and he needed it to drive to the farmers' market in L.A. to buy groceries for the store. He would drive Pat on dates with other guys, like a limo service, and they'd go to the Coliseum to watch football games together.

USC drew good athletes. It was great to be part of that machine. The Olympic team in those days was like our track and swim team wearing red, white, and blue instead of cardinal and gold. In our leisure time, if you had money, you could do what you liked and really enjoy being a USC person, but it took money to be able to enjoy the social scene, to join a frat. It took money to maintain a wardrobe. You had to be a guy people wanted to associate with in order to be invited as a pledge.

But, as athletes, we were considered part of that in-crowd. John Wayne had played there, and even though he didn't come from money, he was invited to pledge a fraternity because he had a persona others wanted to be around. But he injured himself body surfing down in Newport Beach, and when he fell out of the first-string, he lost his scholarship. His fraternity brothers loaned him money, but the debts got too big after a while, so he left school and went over to Fox Studios and got into the movies. But he always maintained loyalty to USC. That's what it means to be a Trojan.

Ambrose Schindler was the star of USC's 14–0 victory over unbeaten, untied, unscored-on Tennessee in the 1940 Rose Bowl. His pass to "Antelope Al" Krueger secured victory and gave Coach Howard Jones his fourth national championship. He is a member of the Rose Bowl Hall of Fame.

The FORTIES

BILL GRAY

CENTER

1943

IT'S GETTING HARDER TO GET AROUND. I had to give up tennis when I twisted my back, I'm slowing down.

I was one of those guys who came in to the University of Southern California through a military program. I was with the Marines, and USC had a contingent of Marines. We were sent down there to Southern California, to Los Angeles, from Oregon, and I was allowed to go out for football.

The Pacific Coast Conference at that time was short because some of the schools didn't have enough guys to field football teams. Only schools that had a military contingent, Navy or Army Air Corps, or whatever, could play. I was in the Marine Reserves and played for Jeff Cravath, who was a fantastic coach and a great guy.

We got to play in the Rose Bowl. They weren't sure about the Rose Bowl because of wartime conditions. At the start of the war, it was kind of tough; but towards the end of the war, we kind of took over until the Japanese were not a problem any longer. We were no longer concerned about any military action by them.

I had previously played at Benson Tech and under Coach Lon Stiner at Oregon State. I was on the Oregon State team that beat Duke in the Rose Bowl in January of 1942. The game was switched from the Rose Bowl to Durham, North Carolina, because of Pearl Harbor. I was not allowed to play in that game, because I was a freshman.

Everyone at that time in college joined the military reserves, or they had to wait for the draft. Some of the guys were drafted, and that wasn't so great, because you had no choice what you would do, so we joined the Marine Reserves. I wasn't called up right away, because all the services had a great influx of these college kids due to the draft. If you waited too long, you got drafted.

I got into a great program and was sent to Quantico, Virginia. So that's how I got into the Marine Corps. I was at Quantico, and the football season was going to roll around the next year. The Marines wanted to do everything. The Navy had all kinds of horsepower, and the Marines just had a few guys. But a lot of us played football. We didn't play a lot of games, but we played Navy and we played Army.

They had service teams throughout the world. It was big for morale and for the entertainment of servicemembers. We beat Japan and Germany on two war fronts while playing sports—football, major league baseball—and they had to look at that and wonder how we did that. Here's these two countries putting every available resource into beating us in a war, and they're getting beat, both of them, by a country that still finds the time for sporting activity. Only in America!

19

It was kind of an offhand thing, in fact. They took Marines who were seniors first, but I was a sophomore, so I got to stay around and play for USC in 1943. A lot of the colleges at that time had V-12 programs. USC had one, and I was transferred to them. It was a special situation. We had barracks and took over the girls' dorms. Girls were not around. It was like we were just sitting around, and they decided to have football. It was almost intramural, but there were enough big teams, and the East Coast was loaded with ballplayers. To get back to how strong the U.S. was, here we were defeating Nazi Germany and imperial Japan while our service academies held back their football players and won national championships. What a morale boost for America, and you have to think the German and Japanese high commands looked at that and just thought, *We can't beat these people*, which they couldn't.

So we had baseball and recreation, and of course it was interesting. We had a guy like "Crazy Legs" Hirsch playing on military teams, and a lot of people came out to see him.

The T formation was just coming in, and I played with Sammy Baugh from TCU. I never saw a guy throw a football like Sammy Baugh. I never played in the T. In our offense, we had played the single wing. Clark Shaughnessy at

Stanford brought the T to the Pacific Coast Conference, and it took a long time to get in because people couldn't figure out how to handle that.

Sportswriters were writing about it, and a lot of teams were just starting it out, but nobody knew about it or how to run it to perfection. It gets kids to do the thinking, and it's a big change from the single wing to the T formation. This was right at the beginning of the war. The T was not that sophisticated, but it had just started.

I'd never scouted a T formation team until the seventh game of the season. We'd won every game by shutout, then we went to San Diego, and Navy beat us 10–7. That's interesting, they had college and pros in there. They had no eligibility problems. If you wore a uniform, you got in there.

We had pros and college kids from the Big Ten. Those guys were a mixture, and it was very, very special because it was football season, and it was entertainment for service people. It was special, the best thing about it was we got special treatment.

We beat Washington 29–0 in the 1944 Rose Bowl. They didn't want to bring a team out from the East, so they selected Washington, who'd won the Northern Division of the PCC. They played the northern schools. It wasn't the Pac-10 like now. It was a wartime arrangement. We drew 68,000 at the Rose Bowl, and they were very careful; there was a lot of security.

They were worried about a terrorist operation like later with 9/11. They wanted to do it, but they wanted to be very careful, so we had Navy, Army, and Air Corps personnel protecting the Rose Bowl. Southern California was a popular place for service schools, and a lot of guys fell in love with the area during the war.

I was assigned before the war to the First Division, Fifth Marines, and they were moving into China, in Peking. We were aligned with Chiang Kai-shek, who was fighting the occupying Japanese while Mao Tse-tung was in the hills waiting for the right time to try and take over. We beat the Japanese, and Mao took over later, but I never got into action. I was younger, so by the time I got into it, most of the heavy fighting was over. I was a lieutenant and had a platoon, but by the time I got in there, they'd moved back, and it was settled down. I missed most of the Marine action on the islands because I was so young. I had been in a replacement battalion at Quantico. If I'd been older, I'd have seen some real fighting. If they'd have casualties, they'd move us up.

I was happy when the war was over. I was in the Hawaiian Islands when the war was over and then went to Japan to repatriate the Japanese, to get everyone back to where they belonged. The Marines did that.

California in those days, when I got to USC, right after the war, was like Shangri-La. That's why California got a lot of people from Oregon, where it rains half the year. Guys would see California, and nobody could believe L.A. The sun was always shining, and it was something else. USC is in the middle of the city. I couldn't believe it, it was a beautiful school. Jeff Cravath was a famed player and outstanding coach. He was great.

What does it mean to be a Trojan? I think that was a great experience to be down there with those guys, on the field. We had great guys. It was rugged out there. Cravath was the toughest guy ever. He was the toughest, pound for pound, I ever saw or played for. We also had an assistant coach named Hubert Herd. I really liked that guy

It was better to play for a tough guy like Jeff Cravath than sweating it out against the Japanese in the middle of the Pacific. Several guys ahead of me were killed. We were right behind them. I was a second lieutenant. There were all kinds of jokes about second lieutenants. We were expendable, that's all I can say.

We were "China Marines," and that was a very special thing. That was Jimmie Doolittle and Pappy Boyington. I loved the Marine Corps. I was in Peking, China. Now it's called Beijing. What was interesting is we were cleaning out the Japanese and sending them back to Japan, and we had to make sure they got on their way safely. The duty of that fighting outfit, the First Division, was the very foundation of what later became a famed outfit, from way back to modern days.

Ralph Heywood was an All-American. After the war, I played for the Redskins. I'd been a center but later I was a linebacker with the Redskins.

Bill Gray was one of Jeff Cravath's "Marine Trojans," who attended USC because the military sent him there for training. He was an All–Pacific Coast Conference center for the team that beat Washington in the 1944 Rose Bowl, and he later played for the Washington Redskins.

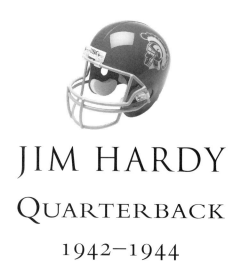

JIM HARDY

QUARTERBACK

1942–1944

MY BROTHER, DON, ALSO PLAYED at USC, in 1943 and 1944, then after the war in 1946. He was an All-Coast end. We came out of Fairfax High School. Los Angeles prep football was outstanding then, far better than it is today. Football in the CIF–Southern Section is superior to the L.A. City Section, but at that time it was outstanding. A lot of guys from city schools went on to play at USC or other Division I schools.

Life in L.A. was much different. L.A. at that time was what I like to call a "little pueblo." It didn't have the congestion, crime, and dirty, unkempt streets that there are today. The atmosphere was much clearer. I can remember walking to school in the morning, and I could see the Hollywood sign in the Hollywood hills. The hills were not covered with homes like today. I'd go hiking up there. We'd race cars up the streets—wagon cars, not automobiles. It was much smaller in population, plus it was warmer and friendlier than it is today.

The movie industry influence has always been a big part of USC. The two "major league" items in L.A. were movies and the Trojans. At that time there were no Dodgers, Angels, Lakers, Kings, or Rams. UCLA had not yet "arrived." The only "major league" attraction in sports was the Trojans, and we played a great schedule. I can remember listening to the USC–Notre Dame game on radio, and they were winning national titles. USC was dominant under Howard Jones. Those were the glory days of the Thundering Herd.

Jim Hardy was an all-purpose star later elected to the USC and Rose Bowl Halls of Fame.

I wanted to go to USC from the time I was eight years old. As a kid, I rooted for them. If the Trojans lost, I was in tears. I remember kneeling down at night to say my prayers, saying, "Please make me a USC football player."

I also played baseball for Rod Dedeaux. He had outstanding teams. The last year I played, I was the only guy on the team not to play professional baseball. Five guys went to the big leagues, but football was my passion. I had baseball ability, and Rod said if I had committed to baseball as I did to football, I'd have played in the big leagues for 10 years. But all through high school and college, I was always the first to arrive and the last to leave football practice. I didn't do that to impress anybody, but I didn't have the same passion for baseball, which you have to have.

I was the batboy for the Hollywood Stars for years. They played at Gilmore Field where the Farmers' Market was. They'd have midget auto races and motorcycle races over there. Loyola played football there. It's where the CBS-TV studios are now. The football stadium was next door to the baseball field. There was the Pan Pacific Auditorium. Before they built Gilmore Stadium, other than the Farmers' Market at Third and Fairfax, there was a semipro baseball field. The Paramount and Twentieth-Century Fox semipro baseball teams played there on weekends during the Great Depression. On game days, the farmers would park their trucks and sell produce right out of their trucks. In 1934 or 1935, Mr. Gilmore set up the field with chicken wire and two-by-four bleachers. He owned the property; the family still owns the red adobe hacienda in the back. In the back of it was an oil field, and he told the farmers that if they'd rent space, he'd turn the stand into fruit stands. They accepted, and that's how the Farmers' Market grew. Nothing else was around it. There was no park yet, no stadium or the Pan Pacific. There was just the La Brea Tar Pits and open fields. When they built UCLA out in Westwood, people said nobody would go to school way out there. There was nothing between Western and the beach houses in Santa Monica.

Sam Barry gave me my scholarship to USC. He was the head basketball and baseball coach, and Howard Jones' number-one assistant football coach. My last year of high school, I broke my leg three days prior to the opening game. I didn't play any games all season, and my hopes of a scholarship were nil. But I was determined. I knew I could play and was determined to play as a walk-on at 'SC, so I paid my own tuition and books. I beat out all the others and played on the freshman team. We couldn't play varsity ball, but I beat out all the scholarship guys who were all-city, and at the end of the year there were three or four varsity games to play. They said to the freshmen, "Your season's over, forget football until next spring, unless you want to play on the scout squad." So I did.

We played a single wing, not the T formation. I played tailback on the scout squad and was whoever the opponent's star player was in the upcoming game. I did real well, night after night. The season and the semester ended, and I ran out of money.

I worked during the summer session to pay my tuition. Every month I made an installment on tuition, but at the end of the semester when it was time register, I had determined to go to junior college at Los Angeles City College because I had no more money. I came home one afternoon, and my mom said Coach Barry was on the phone.

Howard Jones had died the summer before my freshman year. They didn't have time to go out and search for a coach, so they appointed Barry as head coach in 1941. He'd been my coach when we scrimmaged the varsity. I couldn't believe he was calling me. He asked, "How come you didn't register?" I said, "I ran out of money." And he said, "Get down here tomorrow. You've got a scholarship." It was the biggest thrill in my life. I guess I would have gotten one had I been healthy my senior year of high school, but I can't say for sure. But I had confidence that I could play football. I had no trepidations.

Barry coached the team in 1941. Our star was Bob Robertson, a great player. He was a senior at that time. The war started in December 1941. He gave me a scholarship around the first part of January. Then, about two months later, he got called to the Navy, and in March before spring practice, we hired Jeff Cravath. He'd been at USF but had played at USC and been an assistant under Jones. Now, after I thought I'd impressed the coaches, I had to start all over again.

Cravath came in before spring practice in 1942. He had tremendous material. We had a lot of transfers during the war. Oregon dropped football. Washington State and Stanford dropped football. Their guys would come to USC, Cal, UCLA, or Washington, and we had a lot of good material. It was not difficult to win at that time, but in 1942, Jeff's first year, we had a mediocre season. I can't recall, I think we were 5–5–1. We had good material but did not have an outstanding season.

25

The next year we went to the T formation, but he didn't know how to run the T. We'd run the single wing. We'd line up in a T, then run out of a single wing. Contrast that with Frank Leahy at Notre Dame. When he switched to the T, he had Chicago Bears quarterback Sid Luckman and the creator of the formation at Stanford, Clark Shaughnessy (who had been hired by Chicago), come to Notre Dame for spring practice and teach them how to install the T formation.

We didn't do that. We retained the same coaches. Years later, when I was in the pros, Les Casanova wanted to change from the single wing to the T, and he asked the Rams to install the T at Santa Clara. I went up there and met Cas. He said, "There's a blackboard and chalk," and I drew up the whole offense in spring practice. By then I'd had great coaching and schooling in the T formation. I'd not had that at 'SC. I had on-the-job training, one season anyway.

We had officer candidates come in. Bill Gray came in from the Marines. We had transfers from Oregon State to USC. Eddie Saenz, who later played for the Redskins, came from Loyola. All the transfers from Santa Clara, Fresno State, and both Oregon schools came in under the Naval and Marine programs. It was not really a problem. Some resented not playing more, but they all became Trojans. Some didn't cotton to Cravath, but they became Trojans and certainly played like it. Nobody asked for anything.

The track star Lou Zamperini was a fabulous guy I've known since back then. He's an eccentric. I saw him a couple weeks ago. Even today, with Pete Carroll, I go to practice one day a week. I drive up there and I knew all the coaches—Don Clark, John McKay, all that group. A lot of players I knew. I know Pete but not the other coaches or players. I'm a Trojan and try to contribute moral support at spring practice and in the fall, and Lou is up there frequently. Pete encourages the old guys to come to practice. It's no secret day, no one watches to keep you out. If you're a Trojan, you get into practice. I see Zamperini once in a while, and I've known him over the years. His story is legendary. It's a miracle he's alive after what happened to him during World War II. He was a fighter pilot who was shot down in the South Pacific and had to survive for a long time until he was rescued. He's a smallish kind of guy with a slim build, as a miler would be, but maybe that's how he survived the hardship. I don't know what he doesn't do. He skis, he surfs.

He got out of school before I started, but his exploits were legendary before that. At the 1936 Berlin Olympics, he shimmied up a pole to take down the Nazi flag. That's a famous story about Zamperini.

We played Notre Dame my first two years with Sam and Jeff (1941, 1942). They beat us in South Bend, 20–18, in 1941. They had a national championship team in 1943. My senior year, 1944, we finished seventh in the AP poll. Stanford with Frankie Albert had won the 1940 national championship. They were coached by Clark Shaughnessy and beat Nebraska in the Rose Bowl. Speaking of which, I've seen every Rose Bowl since 1930 except for January 1, 1942, when Oregon State beat Duke in Durham, North Carolina. That game was moved from Pasadena for security reasons after Pearl Harbor. That's the only game I've missed since 1930. I saw Aaron Rosenberg, Grenny Lansdell; these were all my heroes growing up.

UCLA really started to come on in the late 1930s. In 1939 and 1940 they featured the likes of Kenny Washington and Jackie Robinson, some pretty good players, but they couldn't beat 'SC. They tied 'SC 0–0 in 1939, the year we beat Tennessee in the Rose Bowl for the national championship. Then in 1941, my freshman year, they tied the Trojans 7–7. In my sophomore year of 1942, they beat USC for the first time and played Georgia with Frank Sinkwich and Charlie Trippi in the Rose Bowl. Georgia won, but they had arrived at that time. The next year with the war on, we played UCLA twice and won both times. In the opening game of the 1943 season, we beat them 20–0, and in the last game of the season again, 26–13.

In 1944 they had a hell of a good team with Bob Waterfield, Jack Myers, and Jerry Shipkey. The rivalry was intense between good teams. We had them beaten in the opening game, leading 13–6 with about 35 or 40 seconds left to play, but I misread the clock. It was fourth down deep in our own territory. I thought there was 1:30 left. I punted beyond our coverage, and Johnny Roesch, a great halfback, ran it back 80 yards for a touchdown to make it 13–12. Waterfield kicked the extra point. It hit the crossbar and dribbled over for a 13–13 tie. I was the goat.

The last game of the 1944 season was for the Rose Bowl. There was a lot of pressure, but we had them 40–0 at the end of the third quarter, and Cravath took out the starters. UCLA made it 40–13. We played Tennessee in the Rose Bowl and beat them 25–0 to finish the season unbeaten.

From that last team, most of the guys are dead. John Ferraro, Jim Callanan, my brother, my center; all the guys are dead. Only a couple are left.

Don Doll, who used to be named Burnside, played in the NFL. Gordon Gray was a great player who started as an end. We had no wideouts in those days. In the 1944 Rose Bowl, he caught two touchdown passes as an end in a 29–0 win over Washington. I had a touchdown in the 1945 Rose Bowl win over Tennessee, 25–0. That's USC 54, opponents 0 in the 1944 and 1945 Rose Bowls!

Gordon weighed 190 pounds and could run like a deer. He was a gifted athlete. The next year I moved to halfback and started both ways. We were outstanding on offense and defense in 1944. I led the nation in interceptions as a safety with nine. On fourth downs I'd return punts. I was mediocre at that. Braven Dyer, a sportswriter with the *Los Angeles Times*, wrote an open letter to the coach saying we should use Gray, that "Hardy's standing around, use Gray." My nose was out of joint, but we played Washington in the first night game ever at the Coliseum. Gordon brought it back 70 yards. He was absolutely one of the all-time most unsung players we ever had.

Ralph Heywood was our captain and an All-American. He died. Other guys across the line all passed away. Bill Gray, who lives in Oregon, is still alive.

Pete Carroll is unreal. He knows Xs and Os, but he inspires you by walking into your living room and saying, "I want Junior to play for me." Parents hear him, and they say to Junior, "I want you to go to 'SC." Most coaches played favorites, but he makes you earn it or lose it on the practice field. Nobody grouses or gripes, because the guy ahead of you is the better player. I tell Pete, "If you were around then, I'd have loved to play for you."

Jim Hardy was All-PCC in 1944. He is a member of both the USC and Rose Bowl Halls of Fame. Drafted No. 1 by the Washington Redskins, he went to the Los Angeles Rams, where he starred for them before playing for the Chicago Cardinals and Detroit Lions until 1952. His brother, Don, also played for the Trojans.

GORDON GRAY

RIGHT HALFBACK

1943–1944, 1946–1947

I CAME OUT OF POLY HIGH SCHOOL in San Francisco. It's interesting how I ended up at USC; they hate 'SC in the Bay Area. The war was on, and I was 17. I was gonna be 18 in a couple months, and I had been advised to get into the officer training program, which was the V-1 program for the Navy. I went to St. Mary's on a scholarship, but I knew I'd be called in. I had room and board, books, and spending money, and played basketball in the spring. In July the Navy called me up. They sent me to USC, where they had an officers training program, and I played football.

Jeff Cravath was a good defensive coach, but lousy on offense. If he liked you, you were golden, but if not, you could do nothing right. In my first year I was an end, as I'd been in high school. My freshman year [1944], we went to the Rose Bowl. I made some fancy runs, catching passes, but I switched to halfback for my last couple years. I was All-PCC two times.

Jim Hardy was there my first two years. All four years I was there, John Ferraro was there. He was an All-America tackle and later entered politics. He was on the Los Angeles City Council for 34 years and was president of the council 27 of those years. Paul Cleary was an All-America end for us. Don Clark was our captain and a fine guard. It's hard to recall many of the others.

We played Notre Dame twice. In my junior year, we scrimmaged during a stop we made on the way to South Bend. We played in front of the biggest crowds—102,000 for UCLA and almost 105,000 for the 1947 Notre Dame game, the biggest crowd in the history of Coliseum.

We played in the Rose Bowl three times. In 1944 versus Washington, the war was on, so we split the Pacific Coast Conference into Northern and Southern Divisions. Washington was favored by four touchdowns. We beat them 29–0. We beat Tennessee 25–0. In the 1948 Rose Bowl, we played Michigan. They beat us 49–0. They were a great team, it was a toss between them and Notre Dame for the national championship. Michigan was the first team to have full platooning on both offense and defense. Fritz Crisler was the first to take advantage of the new rules. We played a lot of those Notre Dame and Michigan guys in Chicago for the College All-Star Game.

I did not play in the Rose Bowl versus Alabama after the 1945 season. I was on a destroyer. We had a weak team that year. USC had beaten highly touted southern teams with big reputations, so they wanted to prove themselves.

We knew a lot of the UCLA guys, more from high school and socially; but at game time, you hated them and they hated you. We had to live with those guys if they beat 'SC. They'd lord it over you all year, but we were the nice sweetheart guys if we beat them. They were obnoxious. The Notre Dame rivalry is entirely different from UCLA. Against Notre Dame, we wanted to be the best in the country—and you know, so do they—so you go for it. Against UCLA, it's more intense in a lot of ways because we live in the same city and see them all the time.

Sam Barry was an assistant football coach. He'd been the head baseball coach before going into the Navy, and Rod Dedeaux took over for him, but he was also the head basketball coach at a time when USC was one of the best basketball programs in the nation. The "triangle offense" was invented under Barry at USC, when Tex Winter was there, and he took it to Phil Jackson in Chicago and later Los Angeles. He'd played before the war but was still around when I came back. Alex Hannum, a basketball Hall of Famer, played for Barry. Bill Sharman, another Hall of Famer, was a freshman when I was a senior. He was a great baseball player and was with the Brooklyn Dodgers when Bobby Thomson hit the "shot heard 'round the world" in 1951, but went to play basketball with the Boston Celtics after that.

I ran track for one year and lettered in basketball, but was not allowed to play on the varsity because they started in October, and our season was never over until January 1. You couldn't come in that late and expect to play, but one year a team was formed for Cardinal and Gold. The Cardinal and Gold schedule was for those of us who'd played football and wanted to play basketball. We'd play in the preliminary to the varsity game.

What does it mean to be a Trojan? 'SC has a tremendous network, a system for you to obtain your first job, and through that system, all my life it has helped me. My associations with the university, and through those I knew there and afterward, and having played there with some name recognition, it could not have been better.

Rod Dedeaux was a great Trojan. I have great memories of him. I was flattered, I was the only one whose name he remembered. He called everybody "Tiger," but he remembered my name. I knew him in school and knew him in business. I was in the Rotary with him, and he was a hell of a guy. He never used a cane; he used a baseball bat made into a cane. Rod was a great businessman, building the Dart trucking empire. He coached for a dollar a year.

I sure remember all the cute girls on campus. I'm pretty close to the university, and I can see nothing has changed in that regard. All through the years, I've been on different groups, like the president's convocation, the community board of governors, the alumni association, and I was the past president of the Half Century Trojans. I'm still active.

When I was there, it was all Bovard Field; there was no track, no baseball field, no Heritage Hall. The track guys had to dodge the baseball players when a game and a meet were both on.

Pete Carroll impresses me. I met him in Mike Garrett's office. He shook my hand and he looked me in my eyes. He looks you right in the eye.

Gordon Gray was a four-year letterman, his career interrupted by one year in World War II. He was All–Pacific Coast Conference in 1944 and was drafted by the Los Angeles Rams in 1947.

The

FIFTIES

FRANK GIFFORD

HALFBACK

1949–1951

BEFORE BAKERSFIELD I LIVED in Hermosa Beach. I lived at 913 5th Street in Hermosa. When the war broke out, we went there, and my dad worked in the Long Beach shipyards. Honestly, Hermosa Beach hasn't really changed all that much since then. It was a beach town then and now. After the war, my family went to work in the Bakersfield oil fields.

Growing up in Bakersfield, in my senior year I was not qualified to get into Southern Cal academically. I never even thought about playing football at USC until my senior year. My coach at Bakersfield High School, Homer Beatty, had played at USC. That was a big thing. No one in my family had ever gone to school, but he said it was possible.

I changed my course curriculum, and he said if you have a good year, it's possible to go to USC. USC said to come on and check out the campus, that they'd changed their offense. I'd been used to the T, where I was a quarterback, but as a junior I was in the single wing. I could run, throw, and catch. I had a big year, and we won the San Joaquin Valley championship. But I still didn't get in academically. Coach Beatty said I needed to go to Bakersfield Junior College to make up classes in language and a few other things. I had one semester and made junior college All-American. I was recruited by everybody in the country. I was astonished. My family and I were oil workers. I lived with my sister and never thought of anybody else. In the second

Frank Gifford was one of USC's brightest stars in the early 1950s.

semester of my freshman year, I transferred from Bakersfield J.C. to USC. Others were trying to land me, but I was a Trojan.

Jeff Cravath was my coach. Some people said the game went by him, but my relationship with him was not about football. I met him and his wife, and our relationship was about personal things that involved other aspects of my life, financial things. My dad was not terribly successful in the oil business; it was not booming like it is today. His was a very personal relationship.

In the UCLA game in 1950, he had me playing defense. In my sophomore and junior years, we had bad years, and there were rumors that he'd be fired. UCLA was stomping us, and he came up to me and pointed out all these seagulls on a foggy day at the Coliseum.

"The buzzards are circling me, Frank," he said. We both laughed. He knew he was gone. He put his arm around me. He was from the Howard Jones days of the 1930s. For many reasons, I shouldn't have liked him because he played me on defense. I made All-Coast on defense, and he helped me a lot. A year later, the Giants drafted me for both offense and defense.

Jess Hill came in. He was much different and quite accomplished. Hill had run track and played football at USC. He played baseball for the New York Yankees. He was the track coach after Dean Cromwell, and later he was the athletic director during a time when USC athletics was probably more dominant than any school ever was. He wore a suit and a hat. He was reserved, dignified, and quite religious, a John Wooden type.

He knew he had to do something different. He didn't do that much coaching. He made sure we were in great shape and really made us run. That helped me a great deal. Later on, I ran a lot for the Giants. I'd not done that much at USC, but we did a lot of sprints. I liked Jess. He was not really that much of a football coach, he'd coached track and was more of an administrator. He delegated authority to his assistants. I was never the fastest guy around, but he helped me a lot through his track techniques.

In 1951 we were 4–0 and ranked No. 11. California was unbeaten and ranked No. 1. Pappy Waldorf's team had not lost a regular-season game in years and had been to three straight Rose Bowls. They'd been a big-time power and were really back.

The interesting thing about that game was I had a high school teammate from Bakersfield named Bob Karpe. He went to California and was an All-America tackle. He was on an academic and football scholarship up there. He'd been on the freshman football team at Cal when I was at Bakersfield

J.C. He tried to get me there. Pappy Waldorf wanted me, so that was the backdrop of that game. They were No. 1 in the nation, and Karpe was my best friend and cocaptain with Johnny Olszewski. They were loaded. They had Les Richter, one of the best guards ever. We were unbeaten going in, but nobody dreamt we could do anything against California.

The legend has it that we trailed 14–0 at the half and I "fired up" the team with locker room antics. I was not that kind of football player, but I got animated and ran around the room telling people, "We can win this game!" People made more out of it than it was. I just said we could do it, and others felt the same thing. We'd had a couple fumbles in the first half and were down 14–0, but by the second half we started kicking their butts. On the first play from scrimmage, I ran 69 yards for a touchdown. I threw and caught for touchdowns, and we won 21–14.

Midwestern teams dominated in the early 1950s, but just like everything else in the country at that time, travel and communications caused a mass population shift from coast to coast. On the West Coast, we'd get athletes who play sports all year round. If you live in Illinois or Michigan, six or seven months of the year you're stuck in the house or in a gym. The most dominant athletes in every sport come from California.

I've had a great career and a great life, but I go back to my experience at the University of Southern California, and it all started there. I'm a Trojan for life, and now my son, Cody, is at USC. *Fight On!*

In the pantheon of celebrity, few stars outshine the New York sports icon, legends including the likes of Babe Ruth, Lou Gehrig, Joe DiMaggio, Mickey Mantle, and Frank Gifford. "The Giffer" was an All-American at USC in 1951, a first-round draft choice of the New York Giants, an All-Pro, a member of both the College and Pro Football Halls of Fame, and a famous sportscaster who for years teamed with Howard Cosell and "Dandy Don" Meredith on ABC's *Monday Night Football.*

AL CARMICHAEL

RIGHT HALFBACK

1950–1952

I ARRIVED AT USC IN JANUARY 1950 from Santa Ana Junior College, where I had played in 1949. Prior to that, I had played at a small school, Gardena High.

There were no freeways when I was there. I got out of high school and entered the Marine Corps in 1946. I spent three years at the El Toro Marine base and went out for football. In 1946 I was in boot camp. I missed playing football for a year, but once in the corps, I decided to play and played for the Marine team that won a championship. So the local junior college scrimmaged us, and the coach asked me to go to school there after I got out of the Marine Corps. I played one semester, and USC came along. I had not made plans, but one thing came after another, everything fell into place—the guy upstairs led me on—and I was a Trojan!

Jeff Cravath was my coach in my first year. He reminded me of the Wallace Beery character from the movies. He had some of the same motions, his personality reminded me of Beery on screen. He was not a theatrical guy, it was not that so much, but his looks and stature, the way he carried himself was like Beery. He was not a comical guy, he was pretty tough.

I got to play a lot and started most of the games unless I had an injury, but he had the T formation, which I liked. The problem was that he was a little antiquated. He was something of a dinosaur when it came to teams changing offenses. He insisted on our wearing out-of-date equipment. He refused to let us wear low-cut shoes or newer equipment. Low-cut shoes were coming in, but he wouldn't allow any of that. We had to wear high-tops. He didn't want to "go with the crowd." Teams had plastic helmets, but he stuck with the old leather helmets.

He would get carried away in practice. We'd turn the lights on and practice late into the night. We left too much on the practice field. My big complaint was that we left most of the game plan in practice and were listless in the games. He was pretty restrictive with water and whatnot. We could drink water at the beginning of practice and at the end.

Frank Gifford was my teammate. Frank had different abilities and played different positions. Frank should have been the halfback on offense, but Cravath had him on defense. He won honors as an All-PCC defensive back, but then they let Jeff go. After that, the last two games were under an assistant. In 1951 we hired Jess Hill, and he went to the single wing. He knew more than Cravath, who had used the T formation. Hill had played single wing under Howard Jones. Giff moved to USC from Bakersfield. He'd been an All-American at Bakersfield Junior College. He was perfect for the position—a good runner who could throw, an excellent player, and smart.

The young Frank Gifford was very sociable and well liked. We all got along with him; nobody said anything bad about him. He blended in with the crowd and was real happy-go-lucky. He had no dark side. Frank came from an oil family in Bakersfield, and one interesting story he told was how he once volunteered to make care packages for welfare families, which they would put in front of the homes of the downtrodden. And one morning, Gifford's family received their own care package.

Later on, a lot of us worked on the movie studios in the summers. Frank was good-looking and smart. He got bit parts acting, and back at Bakersfield he had a five- or 10-minute radio show, and he sort of prepared himself for the future. In New York he got exposure in commercials. When he played for the Giants, they put him at defensive back at first, but he argued that he should be moved to offense. When he was, he made All-Pro.

But he played mostly on defense in my first year at USC, 1950. It was in my junior year, 1951, which was his senior year, when he got his real opportunity to play tailback at USC. Gifford surprised a lot of people. He had hidden abilities. Cravath would move a guy around to the wrong position. He didn't read individual traits like Jess Hill did. Hill *did* put the right people in place.

Al Carmichael (21) is all alone in the end zone as he cradles a pass from tailback Rudy Bukich to give USC a 7–0 victory in the Rose Bowl over Wisconsin on January 1, 1953.

Hill was a real gentleman, the complete opposite of Cravath. He wore double-breasted suits with a hat and was a mentor to his assistant coaches, like Don Clark and Joe Muha. Mel Hein was our centers coach. Hill had good assistants and let them do their thing. He orchestrated the whole thing, he was good at putting a team and staff together.

The 1952 team beat Wisconsin in the Rose Bowl 7–0. They had Alan Ameche. He was an All–Big Ten Conference guy and their big gun. They had a good defensive team, and people had them figured to beat us bad. The odds were that we'd put up a good game but not win, but our defense was one of the best in Pacific Coast Conference history, one of the best ever at USC other than the 1932 team. Spread out, we had given up something like five or six points per game on average. Nobody scored against our defense. That was the power of that team. We got in that game and held them defensively. We kept it in at midfield most of the game. It was mostly a defensive struggle.

I had an average game in the Rose Bowl. I caught a few passes. Jim Sears, God bless his heart, and Aramis Dandoy, had fine games. Rudy Bukich started throwing the ball and did a good job. He threw a 22-yard pass to me, which I caught for a touchdown. Rudy was the Most Valuable Player of that game.

Big Ten teams would be very conservative against USC. They really looked forward to that game. Ohio State would have USC players' names in their locker room. The approach to USC was different than other Pacific Coast teams, it was a different game plan than against a more freewheeling Pacific Coast team such as Stanford or UCLA. That's why you see a lot of low-scoring defensive struggles when the Trojans are the Rose Bowl representative, like some of those games with Michigan and Bo Schembechler. A similar game was the 1970 Rose Bowl, where Jimmy Jones broke up a low-scoring duel with a long touchdown pass to Bobby Chandler, not unlike Rudy catching me in the end zone for the only score.

41

The legacy of USC over the years has always been of a great football school. The teams were great in the 1920s and 1930s, and we have the heritage that they handed down. So we try to keep that spirit going when we represent the University of Southern California and the West Coast. I feel like we have to carry the banner wherever we go, to make a good showing and continue to be winners, with that reputation to point to. It was like that when I was there. We felt we had to build on what was before us, and now teams feel that need to carry on the traditions my teams established. I'm very proud to be part of this legacy.

We had some very strong conference rivals. UCLA was a dog 'n' cat fight. In 1951 at Berkeley, they had won a string of games, something like 28 regular-season wins in a row [37–0–1] under Pappy Waldorf. California was ranked No. 1 in the nation, and since the war ended they had established themselves as the conference powerhouse. Nobody thought we had a chance on their home field, and they had us down at the half 14–0. Frank got so fired up at the half, he was yelling and got us up, and in the second half we scored 21 straight to win 21–14.

This reestablished us as the power in the Pacific Coast Conference. They had taken away the banner from us as *the* national team from the West Coast. I remember Johnny Olszewski, their star halfback. We had a guy named Pat Cannamela, a linebacker. He's no longer with us, he went to the big football field upstairs years ago, and he tackled him. John later admitted he was taped from his hip to his ankle because he had a bad knee, and Pat gave him a little extra aside. The crowd went crazy, they thought he tore his leg up, but it was a clean hit.

Les Richter was an outstanding guard/linebacker for Cal whom I played against. We had a pretty good season. We won our first seven games, but lost the last three. Stanford's Bob Mathias ran a kick back in the last few minutes at the Coliseum and knocked us down 27–20. UCLA beat us, and then we lost to Notre Dame; all tight scores.

Frank Gifford was outstanding. In 1951 we played Army at Yankee Stadium in New York, and he had a great game, but it was played in a mud storm. It was a terrible day, and the stadium was empty except for 200 cadets at the 50-yard line. The game was shown on national television and was expected to be a huge event like the Notre Dame–Army games had been. I don't how the cameras avoided showing how small the crowd was. It rained hard and was so muddy they had to stop and start the game. But we won 28–6 in the cold.

Later, my 1952 team that beat Wisconsin to finish 10–1 had 15 players go in the 1953 NFL Draft, which is the most players ever in a single draft. I went in the first round, was drafted by and played for Green Bay.

Recently, I wrote a book of my own. It's a tabletop book called *106 Yards*, with a lot of pictures about my days in school, the Marines, junior college, and the NFL.

Al Carmichael played halfback for three years after a stint in the Marines. A first-round draft pick of the Green Bay Packers, he was a member of USC's 1953 all-time-highest class of 15 players drafted by the NFL. He played for the Packers and Denver from 1953 to 1961.

TOM NICKOLOFF

RIGHT END

1951–1953

I CAME OUT OF LOS ANGELES HIGH SCHOOL. They used that school in the TV show *Room 222* after I left. Jeff Cravath recruited me, but he didn't last. He got canned my freshman year. Jess Hill took over in 1951. Frank Gifford was an also-ran because of injuries. He didn't play a heck of a lot, but when Jess came in, they had Red Sanders across the road at UCLA. They thought the single wing would take over the world. We adopted it, and Frank became a superstar.

We played Cal in 1951, and at that time Cal had something like 25 or 26 consecutive wins in conference, maybe more, but they'd lost every year they went to the Rose Bowl. So we went to Berkeley in 1951. They were ranked No. 1, and it was 14–0 Cal at the end of the first half. But Frank had an outstanding day, and we won the game. To make a long story short, Frank was an absolute superstar and played in the NFL 10 years after he was a high draft choice.

I was an end. I never knew Cravath. He lived two blocks from my family's house in L.A., but I moved into school as a freshman, so I didn't see Cravath. I joined a fraternity and lived on campus, so I just came home to wash clothes on weekends.

Hill was my coach. He was a very great athlete in his own right. I mean, he was just a super baseball player and a track star. He relied on assistant coaches a great deal, and we had some really good assistant coaches. He was

Hot and heavy action from the early 1950s.

more of an administrator, in my opinion. He called the number signs and what have you, but he relied on his assistant coaches.

As for my teammate, Marv Goux, I can't say enough about "Marvelous Marv." Following the 1952 season, we went to the Rose Bowl and played Alan "the Horse" Ameche and Wisconsin. I was primarily an offensive end, but when they got down to the goal line, they put me in at defensive end. I was good size—6'3", 220 pounds—and they had a guy who was 5'9", 160. I'll never forget this play as long as I live. They went into a field-goal formation, and I told Marv I was going for the block, but Marv tackled the runner after getting past the block. He played an outstanding game. He was not much for size, but he could sure play. He was very special. I did have the pleasure of catching seven passes in the Rose Bowl, but there was nothing better than what Marv did. Al Carmichael caught the only touchdown in that game. He was a great running back, but it was a single wing, and candidly, in the single wing he didn't have a chance to shine. But he was the No. 1 pick of the Packers, and had a great football career.

The UCLA rivalry was very intense. I grew up near Wilshire and La Brea. I lived in that area and went to L.A. High and knew more UCLA freshmen than I knew at USC. A couple went to Cal or Army, but I knew their whole team. They had 29 players on their freshman team, and we had 40. We played in all-star games in high school.

Red Sanders walked on water. He did unbelievable things at UCLA and made good football players into great players. He had good players, but when they went to the single wing, they excelled. Paul Cameron was one player he made great. He made them all great. I came close to going there. I knew Ronnie Knox but not well. He was later. Cameron and Bill Stits were their big honchos.

We had a perfect season but lost to Notre Dame in 1952. We lost three years in a row to Notre Dame. The first year it was just a good game, but by far they had their best team in 1952. We should have been national champions. We were 9–0 going back to South Bend, and our heads were up in the sky. We had just beaten UCLA and were going to the Rose Bowl. The only detriment was that the field was frozen. I was offside twice in that game, the only times I was ever offside in 31 games and 300 minutes per year. We were thinking about something else, and they beat us 9–0. We blew it against them. We were far and away the best team, but we left our game at home.

I was highly drafted in the third round by the Rams. They had two ends at the time, Elroy "Crazy Legs" Hirsch and another guy. But I had an auto accident that ended my football career.

I got married and attended Southwestern Law School at night. I practiced law for 45 years. I had a small firm and had 14 people working for me, mostly defense work. My clients were about a dozen insurance companies. I specialized in offers and compromise.

45

I moved to San Diego in 1965. I put on luncheons twice a year and saw teammates, and that was the extent of my activity. I'd go to occasional events, but I didn't go to all the games. I followed the games but don't go a lot—one, two, or three a year, or the Rose Bowl.

In my humble opinion, Pete Carroll walks on water. He's a truly great coach. Every year he gets half a dozen pro offers from everybody under the sun, but I hope he stays where he is.

What it means to be a Trojan is that, coming out of high school, I had 10 offers, but thank God I was directed to USC. I was fortunate to end up there, and I never regretted that choice one little bit. I'm proud of the university and the people I remember and know up until this time. It's a wonderful tradition.

Tom Nickoloff starred in the 7–0 victory over Wisconsin in the 1953 Rose Bowl. The captain of the 1953 team, he was drafted by the Los Angeles Rams. Tom practiced law in Los Angeles and San Diego for decades.

SAM TSAGALAKIS

PLACE-KICKER

1952–1954

GRADUATED FROM MANUAL ARTS HIGH SCHOOL near the University of Southern California campus. Jon Arnett was behind me at Manual Arts and my roommate at USC. I was a walk-on. It was during the Korean War, and we'd either get drafted or try and go to school. My parents agreed to pay. I had to go to extension and get a C average, but I didn't get in as a kicker or anything.

I had friends who had scholarships, and they talked to Joe Muha, who had been a punter with the Eagles, about getting me a scholarship. I had kicked in high school, but I was kicking with street shoes. Jim Bluett was my high school coach. He was the best coach in the state and put out a lot of great athletes. Manual Arts and the other schools in the south-central L.A. area produced a lot of super players in baseball, football, and track, and he was a great human being. But I was lucky they let me come out at USC. Frank Gifford was a senior, and he could do everything. I started on the JVs, then the rest is history.

My claim to fame was a field goal I kicked with 14 seconds left to beat Stanford 23–20 in 1953 in front of a huge throng at the Coliseum. That knocked Stanford out of the Rose Bowl and sent UCLA in. The game was tied 20–20 when I went in. Bob Mathias was not on that Stanford team. He was there in 1951 and 1952, but they had their great quarterback Bob Garrett.

Sam "the Toe" Tsagalakis trots onto the field with his kicking board in a game against the University of Minnesota in 1953. *Photo courtesy of Getty Images*

I never had a scholarship, even *after* I kicked that field goal. I was named the Helms Athletic Foundation Hall of Fame Athlete of the Month for November of 1953 in a ceremony at the Biltmore Hotel downtown. Sam Balter, a sports announcer, came up to me and said, "I understand you don't eat at the training table. Why not?"

I just turned to Jess Hill and said, "Ask him." The next day, I was put on the training table, but I never had a scholarship. I never went to the hotel with the team on Friday nights. I'd just show up on Saturday. I wore my own sweatshirt, not the one issued by the team. I was on my own, and people looked at me kind of like an outsider. But that was all right.

So I had no grant-in-aid. I went to Jess Hill and Don Clark and said I needed to have a scholarship. They just said they went to the players who took the hits. Clark said, "You're not gonna get a scholarship." Years later, Jess Hill said, "I apologize for not giving you a grant-in-aid." But I got my degree, and being a walk-on was not a big deal. That was my team.

Sam Balter called me "the Toe," and they also called me "Sad Sam" because I always had my head down. Harley "Ace" Tinkham created the "Morning Briefing" for the *L.A. Times*. He gave me that name, "Sad Sam." Braven Dyer was a fine writer for the *Times*. I knew his son. He ran the Helms Hall trophies and stuff. Braven was a good guy, and the paper was just great back then. Any time I kicked a field goal, you'd think World War II was over—unbelievable headlines, front page, everything. I kept a scrapbook but don't know what happened to it. Not many kickers in those days won games like that. We beat Cal 10–0 in 1952. I kicked a field goal and the headlines read, "Trojans Win on Sam's Feet," or, "'SC wins on Jim Sears' arm."

Jim Murray was a great guy. I went to see him all the time. I worked for Blue Diamond. I was down in Pismo Beach, and he was there with his wife, and we spent some time together. He always remembered me. He was just a genuine guy and would go out of his way to do things for people. I probably met him later at USC. I'm the past president of the Trojan Club board and the football alumni group. I hosted a luncheon going back to 1984 every two years called "The Game Is On." It was my idea. Craig Fertig and Tommy Hawkins, a Notre Dame guy, cohost and switch wearing each other's letterman sweaters. It's a USC–Notre Dame dinner held the night before the game when it's played in Los Angeles. Pat O'Brien would come and do Knute Rockne routines. Nick Pappas was a big alum who was part of that.

We've had every Heisman Trophy winner from the two schools except Marcus Allen. Rodney Peete's there this year; he and Anthony Munoz. For Notre Dame, hopefully we'll get Joe Montana now that his son plays football for Bill Redell at Oaks Christian now.

Ronald Reagan was at our events back in the 1950s. He was there my sophomore year when we had a kickoff at the Biltmore in downtown L.A.

He was the guest speaker, and he was funny and great, and I remember thinking, *Goldarn, that guy should go into politics*. He flipped the coin at the USC–Notre Dame game and said, "Let's win one for the flipper."

Passions run high when the two schools play each other. One of the biggest robberies of all time was when Todd Marinovich played against Notre Dame at South Bend and they made a bad clip call on us.

USC–Notre Dame is the greatest rivalry going. I've always liked Notre Dame. I had a chance to kick back there in the snow. It's cold. I've gone back there since 1979. I never miss that game. I walk on that campus and I can just *feel* the Gipper, Rockne, Leon Hart, Johnny Lujack…

It's a shame they're on a downer. Two thousand and five was one of the best games when we won at the end. I don't want to lose to UCLA, but I respect Notre Dame and their tradition.

> Nicknamed "the Toe" after kicking a dramatic field goal to beat Stanford in the closing seconds of their 1953 game, Sam Tsagalakis remained active in Trojan alumni circles for many years, and is credited with starting "The Game Is On," a biennial luncheon featuring former Southern California and Notre Dame players held every even year in Los Angeles.

MARV GOUX

CENTER, LINEBACKER

1952, 1954–1955

USC ALWAYS HAD A GOOD RECORD in the area of civil rights. Brice Taylor was black, and he was our very first All-American, way back in the 1920s. I played with C.R. Roberts. He was a black running back on coach Jess Hill's team that traveled to Austin in 1956 to play Texas. The night before that game, Roberts was not allowed to stay in the same hotel as the USC team. Coach Hill took the whole team out of that hotel to keep them together.

The next day, there was tremendous abuse heaped on C.R. The fans yelled awful epithets and the Longhorn players abused him, but C.R. was a very competitive guy and used all of it to fuel his performance. He gained 251 yards *in the first half*. He was removed midway through, and we won 44–20. After the game, the Texas players shook his hand and acknowledged in effect that they were wrong. But the Texas fans continued to catcall him. They were not ready for change yet.

I was injured at Notre Dame. It probably prevented any chance I had at a pro football career, but it got me into coaching. I coached at Carpinteria High School for a year, but there were some problems there. I moved on to USC and was there with Don Clark and Al Davis, with John McKay, and with John Robinson until 1982. I was one of the gladiators in *Spartacus*, Stanley Kubrick's 1960 Roman Empire classic. Later I made speeches in the old "dungeon," and many have said I used Kirk Douglas' speech from *Spartacus*.

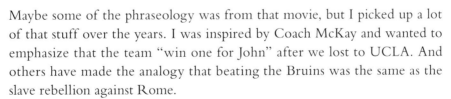

Marv Goux goes over schemes on the sideline with his coach during a September 1953 game. *Photo courtesy of Getty Images*

Maybe some of the phraseology was from that movie, but I picked up a lot of that stuff over the years. I was inspired by Coach McKay and wanted to emphasize that the team "win one for John" after we lost to UCLA. And others have made the analogy that beating the Bruins was the same as the slave rebellion against Rome.

When Sam "Bam" Cunningham led us to a 42–21 victory at Alabama in 1970, Jim Murray wrote in the *Los Angeles Times*, "Hatred got shut out." You know, at the time, I had my hands full. So did Coach McKay. We were talented but unable to build on that game. Our season was disappointing. The team was not as together as others, although talent-wise we were close. But it was only over time, the media bringing it up, old friends talking about it and asking about it, that I've come to see just what an incredible event it was. I made some strong statements about it at the time, but remember, no sooner did we win that game than we had to fly back to L.A. and get ready for the next one, and the one after that. Sports is hard to be involved in and see the big picture.

Sam was a big recruit, yes. He was built like a brick you-know-what. But we were loaded, and John McKay was not promising starting jobs to sophomores. It was his first game, and considering the environment, McKay wanted to play it close to the vest. Look at the highlights of that game. Offtackle, *boom*—breaking tackles, running *over guys*. Sam just made an outstanding contribution on his own.

Plus, Sam was from Santa Barbara. I grew up in that area, too. It's a very low-key area. He didn't have any idea, really, about what was happening in places like Selma. He was still a kid, barely away from home for the first time when that game was played.

We already had an All-America running back in 1970, Clarence Davis, and he'd grown up in Alabama before moving to L.A. Davis was a typical example of our advantage at that time. Today he would've finished school in Alabama and been up for grabs, probably in the SEC. His family left that environment, and we just got him to succeed O.J. Simpson.

52

Bear Bryant had talked up the game. It was his baby, and if Bear was for it, the state of Alabama was willing to accept change. After Sam's game, Alabama was able to use [recent recruit] Wilbur Jackson.

Eventually, the Southeastern and Southwestern Conferences were desegregated. Earl Campbell at Texas, Billy Sims at Oklahoma—although Bud Wilkinson had integrated OU earlier—the whole region changed dramatically over night. It was great, even though we found recruiting to be harder after that.

Marv Goux played at USC and was captain in his senior year. He is one of only two Trojans to win the prestigious Davis-Teschke Award twice (Ken Antle, 1957–1958, is the other). His pro aspirations dashed by an injury at South Bend, he became perhaps the most legendary assistant coach in history, under Don Clark, John McKay, and John Robinson from 1957 to 1982. Marv is a member of the Rose Bowl and USC Halls of Fame. This interview comes from a 2000 article in *StreetZebra* called "The Eternal Trojan." Goux passed away in 2002. At his memorial service, his granddaughter, Kara Kamen, urged the Trojans to, "Win one for the Goux!"

JON ARNETT
LEFT HALFBACK
1954–1956

I GREW UP IN LOS ANGELES and attended Manual Arts High School. Manual Arts had a lot of famous people go to school there, including the World War I fighter ace Jimmie Doolittle. In those days, there were only two or three high schools in the valley. My mom went to Manual Arts before me, and when she went there, there were only about three high schools in the city.

A lot of great athletes grew up in Los Angeles, in my neighborhood, around the time I was growing up. Sparky Anderson and Billy Consolo attended Dorsey High School. All these guys played on an American Legion team that was incredible. Consolo became one of the first "bonus babies," after a pitcher named Paul Pettit. He got around $80,000 to sign with the Detroit Tigers. He'd been a track man like me, as well. I think they gave his dad the barber shop lease at the Hilton downtown as part of his signing.

There's a story I cannot confirm that Sparky Anderson's bedroom was located where home plate at Dedeaux Field is today. I can confirm that he was the Trojan batboy for Rod Dedeaux's teams. Gene Mauch and Dick Williams went to Fremont. There are those who say that Fremont has produced more major league baseball players than any high school in the nation. But if I had to bet, I'd put my money on Dorsey, what with Anderson, Consolo, and the Lachemann brothers, who were Dodger batboys, playing for Dedeaux at USC, and becoming big-league players and managers. Marcel was the pitching coach at USC for a while. There were at least four or five from Dorsey that I knew of from my era who played in the big leagues.

Jess Hill—Mr. Trojan—recruited me to play football for him. I think he was first a track man and the first white man to long-jump 25 feet. He played baseball for the New York Yankees, but he was not much of a football player that I know of. The story goes that he ran track for Dean Cromwell and planned to become a teacher and coach. He figured he'd be asked to coach football, and if he played it he'd have better experience and could get the job more easily, so he played football for Howard Jones. Later he was the track coach at USC and won two NCAA titles. But when Jeff Cravath was fired, USC—who only hires alums—chose Jess Hill as the football coach. Later he was the athletic director, so if anybody was Mr. Trojan, it was he.

Freshmen could not play varsity ball when I got to USC. We scrimmaged versus the varsity, plus we played about three games against UCLA, Stanford, and a couple of military teams. We'd play a junior college team from Santa Barbara and a Naval team in San Diego that featured the pro player Billy Wade, who was in the in Navy at the time. Maybe we played four games.

I played varsity ball in 1954, 1955, and 1956. I played two years with Marv Goux. He played the same way he coached. He was not big enough to play the position he played, but he was on Notre Dame's all-opponents team for some 30-odd years. In the huddle, he just wouldn't let you lose. Marv played center at 180 pounds. I weighed more than he did.

C.R. Roberts was also my teammate for two years, but he only played five games because of probation and penalties in my last one and a half years. He was very talented as far as running backs go at that time. He was a very big running back—he weighed around 215 or 220 pounds at the time—and was very fast, one of the fastest guys on the team. He was a good athlete. It surprised me he did not do better in pro football. I think he originally signed with the 49ers but didn't make it there. Then he played in the Canadian Football League. He was with San Francisco [1959–1962]. He was part of the "all-initial" backfield, all guys with initials like his—C.R., Y.A. Tittle.

In 1956 I was at Texas when we played the famous game he had. I was the team captain, and I always tell the story of the first integrated team to play down there. It caused problems because we refused to play unless they let our black guys stay at our hotel. The tradition was for black players to stay at the private homes of black doctors and prominent local people, but we insisted they be allowed to eat the pregame meal with us. When the UT band played "The Eyes of Texas Are Upon You," C.R.'s eyes were as big as the moon. He had quite a game. The referee, as a matter of fact, came up and said to me, "That black man can sure run."

He had over 250 yards in that game. I made 150 or 160 yards, but it paled in comparison to him. He only carried the ball a few times but made 80-yard runs. I think his yards were all in a few carries. It was a good game. I've seen a lot of great games, and it was as good as any I've ever seen. We went down there and just killed Texas.

The irony of it was I made All-America in 1955, so my senior year [1956] I was on the cover of the magazines and was supposed to be the Heisman Trophy winner. I made more yards the five games I played that season than in the entire previous year when I was an All-American, but it was not enough to be voted the Heisman. I finished fourth or fifth in the voting behind Notre Dame's Paul Hornung, whose team was 2–8 or something like that. It was 50-50 that I'd play in Canada instead of come back for my senior year at USC. I almost didn't play; I almost played in Canada because of the NCAA penalties that reduced my season.

Only God knows who would have won the Heisman over Hornung had I played the whole season. I do know anybody with a pretty good year would have beat him since his team was poor, but instead of my becoming USC's first Heisman winner, he became Notre Dame's fifth. Today we're tied with seven, so if I'd won, USC would have eight and they'd only have six!

I was made ineligible for half the season. I was 19 or 20 years old, and we were made ineligible. It still doesn't make sense; it was questionable, and I was *not* breaking NCAA rules, where you could have room, books, and tuition. But in the PCC you only could have tuition. We had a sponsor help us with books and room expenses, and USC got caught. UCLA, Stanford, and Washington voted against us. I will tell you as a fact that Stanford offered me more than anybody else. They offered a car, those hypocrites. That bothered me more than anything. I had to make a decision: play just five games or go to Canada, then go to the NFL. I was offered $100,000, which in 1956 was a lot of money, but I opted to stay at 'SC. I talked to some alumni, and they said I'd never regret staying, and they were dead right. Going to 'SC was the best decision in my whole life. I made so many friends there; it's true, you're a Trojan for life. It's affected me my whole life. That's all I can say.

55

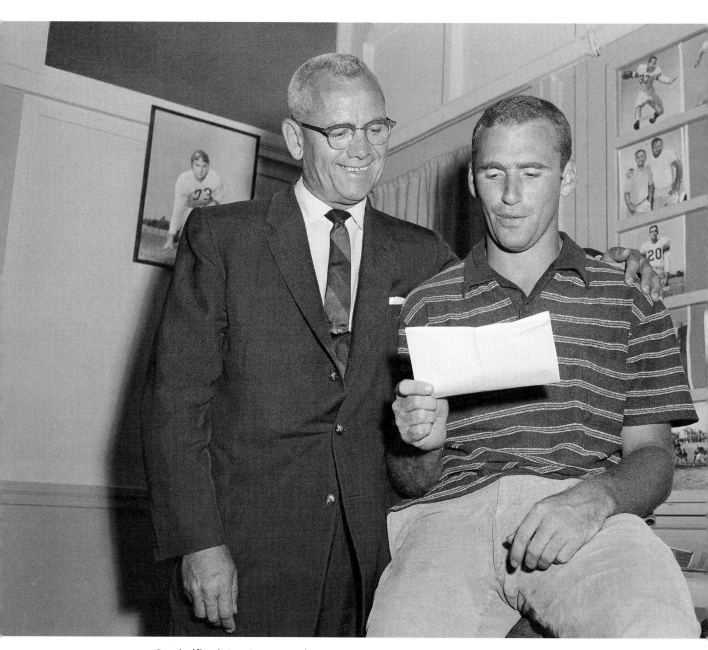

Star halfback Jon Arnett reads a statement at a Los Angeles press conference in August 1956 announcing he would stay at USC and turn down offers from nearly every team in the Canadian Football League because he believed his education came first. Standing beside Arnett is coach Jess Hill.

I heard Stanford ratted the others out after the NCAA discovered they had committed the worst penalties, so they cut a deal to save themselves by turning evidence on the other teams. Ultimately I believe Cal, UCLA, and USC were penalized. This was the 1950s, and there was a real estate boom on the West Coast. Rents in Berkeley and Westwood were beyond the ability of college students to pay, which was the main reason that the "sponsor" program was instituted, but I was only paid for tuition costs.

The scandal hurt the prestige of the Pacific Coast Conference, once the class of college football. But after World War II, the PCC went down. The Big Ten and Notre Dame dominated. UCLA had won the 1954 national championship and USC was on the verge of restoring ourselves to a preeminent status, but the penalties set everything back until John McKay restored things a few years later.

I ran track for Jess Mortensen, who was also the freshman football coach. USC won the NCAA track championship almost every single year from the 1920s to the 1970s. We were perennial champs. My sophomore year at USC I took second in the NCAA long jump with a 25-foot jump. One of the things I enjoyed the most was that medal for second place, because it was not expected. That year I also broke Jackie Robinson's PCC record for the long jump. In track, my best year was my sophomore year. I had a chronic hamstring pull, and I kept pulling it. It kept it me out of the championships, but our team won the NCAA every year I was there, if I'm not mistaken. Until restrictions on scholarships, USC dominated track like no college sport, men's or women's, ever. Now they're limited as a private school to 12 track scholarships, which is not enough depth to win with any more. You need to have a lot of second- and third-place finishes. We get people who can finish first, but you need more second and third places to win NCAA titles.

I was a center fielder on the baseball team my sophomore year before I concentrated on track and football. I gave up baseball, but I knew Coach Rod Dedeaux very well. I went to his 90th birthday party, and he said, "Man, you'd have been my center fielder." You just loved him. He never called me Jon, everybody was "Tiger." He was a great guy. He loved going to Santa Anita Race Track. He was one of a kind, he inspired players and knew the game as well as anybody. Rod was a great recruiter, a great man, a great Trojan.

The social scene at USC was quite different then. I don't know what it is now, but it segued from the rest of society. It was the sort of school that you knew a lot of people on campus. Just walking around you'd know a lot of people. Now it's like a city, but then we knew everybody. My life was centered around the fraternity and sorority parties. On weekends you'd just want to know where those parties were, and that's where you would go. It was an intimate environment, a small school.

As for life in Los Angeles, probably the best thing to say about it back then was you could drive on the freeways and get there in time. I live in Oregon now, but I go to Southern California once a month. I look at it and say, "I can't believe I lived here." There's 13 million people in L.A. now. I'm not sure of the population back then, but you could get from the campus to Manhattan Beach in 30 minutes. Now it takes two hours. You could find parking at the beach. There's no parking at the beach anymore. L.A. is a zoo now. This carries over to campus life. It was intimate, but now it's a city in itself.

Los Angeles is different now, but it was a wonderful place to grow up—a great climate, but it's not intimate anymore. I go to USC games less than I did before. I don't like the big crowds at the Coliseum. I prefer to watch on TV. When I lived there, I went to every game. I lived in Manhattan Beach or Palos Verdes Estates, and I'd go to the first part of the game. I enjoyed the tailgating, seeing all the people I knew. Then just before halftime, I'd drive home. I'd miss a few plays at the beginning of the third quarter, but I could see the second half on TV. I think Pete Carroll is an absolutely great guy. I can't say anything other than he is a super coach. I hope he stays at USC. I don't know if he can. I hope he stays 10 years.

I almost went to UCLA. Red Sanders was a nice guy and a heck of a coach. He recruited me when I was 17 years old. We went to Truman's restaurant, off campus in Westwood, for dinner. Suddenly his head went into his food. He was quite drunk, lost his balance, and his head went down into his salad. I didn't say much. The other coaches laughed to try and make up for it, but it made an impression on me and was one of the reasons I didn't go there. I just thought that I couldn't play for a man like that. But besides, I'd felt like a Trojan my whole life. At Manual Arts, I'd go to the Coliseum, I sold programs. I grew up with USC.

The Coliseum held huge crowds. I played in front of 100,000 fans many times—against UCLA and Notre Dame. With the Rams I played in front of 100,000 people many times. Notre Dame was a big rival, but to me all the teams are rivals. I relished competition and didn't care whether it was Notre Dame or anybody else; they were all the same. Once we kicked it off, it was the same as when you played in the front yard with your buddies. I was into the competition.

Playing for my hometown team, the Rams, was great. I love the Coliseum, it was home. In those days with the Rams, Sid Gillman was a super coach, but the Rams had a theory of always trading somebody for "next year." It was our downfall. We traded 11 guys for Ollie Matson. The "genius" who put that together was Pete Rozelle. We went from being half a game from first place to 2–10. Pete was going to be fired, but Bert Bell died. They voted 20 times for NFL commissioner and couldn't resolve a regional fight. Dan Reeves put Pete's name in nomination, and he became the commissioner. He'd made trades over Gillman's objections. He loved Matson because he'd been the PR guy at USF when Ollie played there, but it was ridiculous. I played 10 years in the NFL, seven with the Rams and three in Chicago. I joined the Bears in 1964, one year after they won the NFL championship. I played for George Halas with Dick Butkus, Mike Ditka, Doug Atkins, and Gale Sayers.

What does it mean to be a Trojan? As I say, it's meant a lot to me. 'SC is as close to me as anything. It's like my family. A lot of people say that. I went to school and got a great education. Back then, you had to go to school. I was a finance major and had some awfully good professors. Professor John Martin became the assistant secretary of the Treasury. USC had a great faculty. I enjoyed the school, the whole experience. There are people I met who to this day I know. I go to reunions, and there's just great support.

People have more loyalty to their college than the pro team they played on. The NFL is a business. There's no comparison. There's no loyalty in pro football. Teams once belonged to the city, but now players are like chattel— they're traded every year, they play out their contracts. It's a different money game with no loyalty. There's more loyalty with the fans than the players and owners.

When Dan Reeves was there, he was one of the great owners, along with Dan Rooney, the Mara family with the Giants. Those people were football people and they built the league. There wasn't a nicer man than Dan Reeves. Today it's a different league of owners. They do it for different reasons. It's a different kind of person. But in my day, the owners loved the club and the game.

I can't fault them because it's a business, and they all have their reasons for getting into it. At one time it was almost a hobby. For George Halas, it was

59

his life. With Halas, it was his biggest economic asset. The Reeves family had New York money. They owned a chain of grocery stores and sold them to Safeway. Dan put a good portion of that into a young company called IBM. I sat with him once, and he said he had a lot of shares and split them many times since.

Jon Arnett was an All-American in 1955. He was All–Pacific Coast Conference (1955–1956), a two-time recipient of the Voit Trophy (awarded to the outstanding player on the Pacific Coast), and winner of the Glenn "Pop" Warner Award for being the most valuable senior on the coast. Elected team captain in 1956, Jon played in the Hula Bowl, the East-West Shrine Game, and the College All-Star Game after his senior season. Arnett is a member of the National Football Foundation College Hall of Fame. The second overall pick of the 1957 NFL Draft, he had a long, successful career as a running back with the Los Angeles Rams and Chicago Bears.

C.R. ROBERTS

FULLBACK

1955–1956

I AM FROM OCEANSIDE, near San Diego, and considered going to West Point. That was my goal, a military career. I was going to go to West Point and make a military career, but as things progressed, I found I was not as good in math as I should have been. USC offered me tutorial help, but West Point did not, so I basically went to USC for that reason. USC also had a great ROTC unit drill team. It was said to be the best ROTC drill team in America, so I figured I could stay close to home, get a good education with tutorial help in math, play football, and still pursue a military career after graduation. Plus USC offered lots of help in the private sector. Finally, I liked warm weather. I was not enthused about going back to New York where West Point is.

Marv Goux was a teammate of mine, and I knew him really well. When I first went to USC, I was a mystery. People wondered about me, there were questions about who I was. I always did my best, and one time I was with a couple guys on the field, and we almost got in a fight. I'd not realized I had tangled with two of the toughest guys on the team, Marv Goux and George Galli. Goux was quite a guy. After we found out about each other, we were both good players, and the minute we got off the field, these things were for-gotten. That was real professional of him. He was one of the guys I could get along with, and basically we formed a friendship that lasted our whole lives.

All the guys didn't hang out together like they do now. When Goux played ball, he didn't do a lot of talking, no trash talk like now. Most of the time, he was in a situation where he would try and tackle me, and I'd get away, and he'd let me know it was a good run but he'd get me next time. So he was a good player, and it was good fellowship. I was an underclassman, and he was a team leader, so it was helpful that we had men like Goux. You strive to get players who have a professional demeanor.

Jon Arnett was a year ahead of me. I didn't know about any of the guys until I got to school. I'd never even seen a coach until we started to practice and didn't know any of my teammates. I wanted to play tailback, but at USC *he* was the tailback. The coaches said, "We'll put you at fullback," and I was disappointed.

What is this? I thought. Then at spring practice, I saw Jon play, and then I thought, *Hey, this guy deserves to play tailback.* He was a good player. I had no idea before that how good he was. He probably would have been up for the Heisman had the probation not interrupted our careers.

The game that defined my football career was the 1956 game at Texas. I was the first black player to play there, and this game has been mythologized and spoken about in legendary terms. Fourteen years later, Sam "Bam" Cunningham and the Trojans traveled to Birmingham and had a similar game against Alabama, though the results then were different. But that game and my game have been compared, and I became pretty close with Sam and most of USC's black players over the years. I became the "old man," a father figure to a lot of black players.

Regarding the Texas game, I have an opinion on the question as to why it did not result in the social changes, integration, that the 1970 'Bama game did. Sam said it had to do with the unique nature of the state of Texas itself, in that those people have their own way of doing things.

Because I was black, I had a close understanding with the race problem, like most guys my age. When we played at the University of Texas, it was sort of like a pride situation. My coach, Jess Hill, told me that Texas called and asked if we had two colored boys on our team. We actually had three, but they didn't know it, and they explained to Jess that this posed "problems." Jess was not sure how to deal with this, but he was an unusual man, a real God-fearing Christian, on the contrary to most hard-nosed coaches, and he had a feel for the culture and my situation. Consequently, his first inquiry was that he asked me how I felt about the trip. I just wanted to play football, so I told him, "I'll play wherever and whenever you want me to. I'll go to Haiti to play if need be."

C.R. Roberts (42) plows ahead for six yards against the University of California in Berkeley on October 22, 1955.

So Jess mentioned to the team that we might have to adjust our hotel accommodations. He mentioned that we might have to leave our black players at home. But I said, "No, I have other schools I could transfer to if you don't let me play." Basically, Jess negotiated the situation, where the team said that I go or we don't go.

Then he had to deal with the question of where I'd stay. At first they had a place outside of town, at the YMCA, but I refused. I said I'd stay with the team or nothing. In the city, there were colored people who said I could stay with them, but I was adamant about staying with the team. The team agreed and felt that if I didn't stay with the team, then they wouldn't play.

The coaches wanted that game. Texas had a "million dollar QB," whatever they called him. They had a good team, especially their quarterback, and the two coaches consequently figured they could get the game going somehow. Everybody knew that whichever team won, it would be a big thing.

It would turn out to be the best road trip I ever had, and when it started out, it was highlighted when I got on the bus at USC. It was an excellent day. The sun was shining, and for the first time on the bus, a black radio station was playing my favorite songs. I'm thinking, *Oh, man this is good.* I wanted to go then.

I'm sure integration was an issue. As I learned later, the coaches decided to have the game after they considered moving it someplace else. There were laws in place making this illegal, and many options were considered, but ultimately it was played as scheduled at Memorial Stadium in Austin, right on their campus. But the night before the game, the whole team had to leave the hotel because of me.

Well, there's nobody in the world more precise and orderly than a football coach, who plans everything right down to the minute and hates any disruption of his plans and routine. But we had to scramble and find another hotel, the whole team, the night before the game. Now this obviously was a major hassle, but it also coalesced the team.

The coaches or the schools worked it out, but Texas law did not allow integrated hotels. Coach Hill was a good man, and he moved the team to a different hotel. I always had weird ideas about how we did that, because we moved to a hotel that also did not allow integration, but there must have been some USC sympathizers in Austin, maybe somebody who owned the hotel, because somehow it was worked out and we were accepted.

When we got to Texas, all the hotel workers were black. Consequently, they were afraid for us. At first they came by and saw that we had some black players, and they said blacks can't stay in hotels there. But we were young and said, "We're with USC, nothing can happen to us." That night, black hotel workers from all over the city came and visited us. They'd take off their smocks and give them to others, so they could come visit us. All night we had visitors. The people at the hotel did not realize that all these black people were not their workers. They weren't allowed in, but they wore those smocks as a disguise. It was really nice, and we met dozens of black people, all of whom encouraged and supported us.

Well, all of these activities of course had me ready to play ball. It could have had the effect of making some of us not ready, but some of the things that occurred probably jelled our team. In those days, we didn't socialize with the team, but consequently, when the team said they'd not play if I didn't play, that made me feel good, and we came together. Basically my position was, I wanted to go out there and take care of their quarterback. I was supposed to play linebacker, so that was my focus, making sure their quarterback did not win the game for them. Before the game, that was my focus.

A lot of those workers who were happy we could stay in the hotel came to see us, and we found out that blacks could come to the game at the University of Texas for the first time, along with some Mexicans. They all sat in the end zone and cheered for us. I guess I had a lot of enthusiasm for the game. I usually tried to play a halfway decent game. I'd been upset about not playing tailback, so when I started the game, I was at linebacker and was going real good. I tackled their ball carrier, and the crowd got ugly. I learned later that Coach Hill was really worried about the effect of my tackling their players. He said, "Next time they have the ball, you don't have to go in." So I could concentrate on offense. I thought that was neat. Basically, I just wanted to play a good game. I'd not been privy to all the information. I mostly had no idea why we left the hotel. I don't think I really knew everything that was happening, so I could concentrate on the game.

I got the ball on offense, and as they say, there is such a thing as a "zone," and I found it. I ran about 12 times for 251 yards. I think I had one gain of 80 yards. There's no way to explain it, really. I was focused, the team was fired up, and the events surrounding the game worked in our favor instead of the other way. But Texas was good—there's no real explanation of how I could get the ball and run for so many yards, break holes every play. I did it all in the first half. We blew them out, and the game was over by then, so Coach Hill removed me to avoid ugliness. I've seen a tape of that game a few times. It's not very good, but I just ran, and nobody was able to bring me down.

The reaction of the Texas players and fans explains a lot about why this game didn't have the same effect as Sam's game at Alabama in 1970. It is accurate that the Texas players respected my performance. After I made a couple tackles, a couple of their guys were upset and let me know it. And on offense, after I made a couple good runs, when I got up, they would give me a bad time. But later, as I kept making gains, one of them extended his hand to help me up. Eventually, the Texas players themselves came around, so by the time Coach Hill took me out, I felt these guys were okay.

Their fans, on the other hand, never let up, even when we destroyed their team and walked off the field, having won 44–20. At Alabama, the players themselves never had a problem with USC's black athletes, and afterwards their fans were stunned into silence. This manifested itself into a belief that Bear Bryant needed black players, which was his plan in scheduling the game, to help conditions for Wilbur Jackson, who came in at that time. But my game did not have the effect of convincing Texas or southern *fans* to integrate, although the players seemed to reach this understanding.

Three or four of their guys talked to me a couple years ago, when USC played Texas in the Rose Bowl. I tried to thank them for letting me play, because there was pressure not to play us, as it was illegal. These guys played good ball, it was a fair game, and there was a respect for each other. This group of guys never even were recognized, but they took a chance so the system could be changed, and they deserve credit for it.

66

What does it mean to be a Trojan? I think being a Trojan is more special than being a part of any other group; even Notre Dame models its alumni set-up after us. Being a Trojan is something special. We play ball, but we do a lot of other things. I was on the board of governors many years, I was involved in the school's mentoring program, and when there is a need, USC comes through in an extra special way. We're human beings, but we're very feeling and very excellent people who do a lot of things the best, in football and in life. Nobody could stop us. We proved it when we beat a team that went to the Rose Bowl.

Had I played my senior year, and Jon Arnett been allowed to play more than the last five games of his senior year, I think we'd have been one of the best teams ever to play at USC. The probation scandal of the mid-1950s set USC and the conference back just as we were about to become the dominant team in the country after a down period. It was not until John McKay that 'SC gained that stature again, but the teams I played on with Arnett and Marv Goux were potential powerhouses. The Texas game demonstrated that, too.

USC and football put me on a different path than the one I'd planned on had I gone to West Point. I've thought a lot about that. Perhaps Colin Powell got the job I might have had. I'd wanted to be a fighter pilot but had an astigmatism in my eye, so I was the leader of a crack drill team in the USC ROTC. The military was my life. They actually had to change the rules for me to run the drill team, because the captain had to be an upperclassman, but I was the commander as an underclassman. It broke my heart when in spring practice I made the football team and got ready for drill competition, but it was the same day as the last day of spring practice. I thought since I'd made the team that it was all right to miss football practice for drill competition. But I didn't understand the public relations aspects of college football—the press was out there, and I was told I had to be at football practice.

My executive officer and I still talk about that. He still thinks I was the best drill commander in the world, but they told me in no uncertain terms that I *will be* in spring practice. It was the day before the drill competition, and the commander came down and said, "You're here to play football. Let us fight the wars." So I was out of ROTC. I'd always missed events like the North-South All-Star Game. I didn't play in that because I went to Fort Ord for drill competitions, which I felt was more important. But football ended my military career. I played in Canada and with the San Francisco 49ers, then had a long career in the teaching profession, which I loved, but my first love was the military.

C.R. Roberts may have been the greatest Trojan you never heard of. Moved from tailback to fullback because of Jon Arnett's star presence, his career at USC was cut short by the mid-1950s probation scandal, but his performance against Texas in 1956 must rank among the greatest single-day games in college football history. Roberts was a first-team All-PCC running back in 1956. Drafted by the New York Giants, he played professional football for the 49ers and in Canada before becoming a teacher.

MONTE CLARK

RIGHT TACKLE

1956–1958

Ⅰ CAME OUT OF KINGSBURG, CALIFORNIA. It's a tiny California farm town in the San Joaquin Valley, so small that Bakersfield is considered a big city, so to speak. Our rivals were towns like Chowchilla. However, two of the greatest athletes of all time came from Kingsburg. Rafer Johnson was ahead of me. He won the 1960 decathlon at the Rome Olympics. His younger brother, Jimmy (who was two years younger) played on the same teams with me. He became an All-Pro defensive back with the 49ers.

Al Davis was an assistant coach at Southern California when I was there. He was 26 years old and was billing himself as "the smartest young coach in the nation," but he wasn't. You have to respect what he's accomplished, though. He *was* a smart guy, and I never had problems with him. It is pretty remarkable what he's accomplished.

Willie Wood was our quarterback and later team captain in 1959. He had leadership skills. He's not doing well, and a teammate named Bob Schmidt is helping him. He was extremely talented, from Washington, D.C. He's a Pro Football Hall of Fame player, so you can't say much beyond that. I don't know that he could have played quarterback in the NFL, but I wouldn't have put anything beyond him. He starred for Vince Lombardi's Packers and won numerous world championships in Green Bay.

I formed a basketball team in school. We had all these "sanctions guys" who could only play five games. They were called "five-game seniors," and we formed a basketball team and called them "no-game seniors." We won the university championship hands down. Willie was on our team and was the best basketball player in school, including the basketball team. I think he played with Elgin Baylor in high school.

Ken Flower was a good friend and a good man. He was a great basketball player at USC. I know a guy named Clyde Connor of UOP. He was raving about what a great player Flower was. Kenny went into the radio business in his native San Francisco and was for many years the media chief for the 49ers.

The McKeever twins were teammates of mine. They were excellent players and had good size. They could run like heck and were good players. Mike died tragically in an auto accident, but I can't believe Marlin is dead. He was doing fine and then suddenly passed away.

Lon Simmons used to be with the Fresno Giants. I knew him well. He was the announcer for the San Francisco Giants and the 49ers, and is in the Hall of Fame. He lived in Glendale at one time and was a good pitcher, who I think was recruited to play baseball at USC by Rod Dedeaux, though I don't think he ever did.

Don Buford was a star in football and baseball when I was at USC. I looked at the highlight tape of that season during "Salute to Troy," and I have to say he was one of our best players, a very productive performer. That tape reminded me that he made interceptions on defense and some long runs. He was a heck of an athlete. I got to spend time with him in Miami when he played for the Baltimore Orioles. They had spring training there, and we'd get together all the time. He taught my oldest son how to throw. My son Bryan turned out to make it as an NFL quarterback.

Rod Dedeaux was a great coach. I watched as many games as I could. I loved baseball and knew all the players, and he impressed me with the unique job that he did. I was a big fan of his. Bruce Gardner lived in the same dormitory I did. I didn't really know him well, but I watched him play all the time. He had "major leagues" written all over him until he got hurt. Ron Fairly was an All-America baseball star for Rod Dedeaux. Catcher John Werhas became a Christian minister. That was quite a departure. I didn't think he'd be a minister. He was also a starting basketball player.

I played more than a decade in the National Football League. I'm not in the College or Pro Football Hall of Fame, but I still feel I was a valuable player. I was a defensive tackle for the 49ers. I played a little bit of offense when somebody would get injured. After three years, I injured my neck. I

Monte Clark was a hard-nosed, old-school football player in college and the NFL, and later as a coach.

ruptured a disc, and I didn't think I could play. I figured I'd be in the hospital if I hit somebody, so they didn't let me hit anyone. I was traded to Dallas. Tom Landry told me I'd be the offensive right tackle. I studied every night and started the game on Sunday. I told him I knew the plays, and he said, "You're going in there."

I made it through a year thinking, *The next shot I hit somebody, I'll be back in the hospital.* Then I was traded to the Cleveland Browns. Jim Ray Smith was an All-Pro guard from Dallas, and he was getting into real estate in his hometown. He told the Browns he'd retire if he wasn't traded to Dallas, so they made the deal. Dallas gave them me.

I played seven seasons for the Browns. We won the world championship in 1964, defeating Johnny Unitas and Baltimore in the NFL championship game. My teammate was the great running back Jim Brown. It was one of the best teams in pro football history. The next year we lost in the playoffs to Vince Lombardi, Willie Wood, and the Green Bay Packers. That was the first of three consecutive pro football championships for the Pack.

I became an assistant coach after my 11th season as a player. I retired and joined the Miami Dolphins' staff as an offensive line coach in Don Shula's first year. Shula didn't really know me, but he got a recommendation on me from Blanton Collier. Collier had succeeded Paul Brown as head coach at Cleveland and coached me there. He was one of the players who played with Shula when they were with the Browns. Shula had faith in Collier's opinion and hired me on the phone.

When I was in Miami, we beat O.J. Simpson 16 times in a row. The 1972 Dolphins were a great team. Whether they're the best team in NFL history is subjective, but what remains a fact is that nobody else has done what they have done, which is run the whole season, playoffs, and Super Bowl unbeaten, and we're pleased to retain it.

My youngest son, Boomer, became very friendly with a player I coached in San Francisco, a great big defensive lineman from Hawaii, Levi Stanley. He'd sleep in his room, and they were really good friends. There were a lot of good moments in football.

What it means to be a Trojan is that I was always very proud for 11 years to be introduced as "Monte Clark from the University of Southern California."

71

Monte Clark was the team captain in 1958 before embarking on a long professional career with the San Francisco 49ers (1959–1961), Dallas Cowboys (1962), and Cleveland Browns (1963–1969). He started every year in college and pro football, except when he was injured. Monte played for some of the greatest coaching legends in NFL history, including Red Hickey of the 49ers, Tom Landry of the Cowboys, and Blanton Collier of the Browns. In 1964 he was a teammate of Jim Brown's when Cleveland captured the NFL championship. Another teammate in Cleveland was Bill Nelsen, who helped quarterback USC to the 1962 national title. Clark became an assistant coach under Don Shula in Miami and was on the staff when the Dolphins went unbeaten en route to the 1972 Super Bowl victory, and later was head coach of the 49ers and Lions.

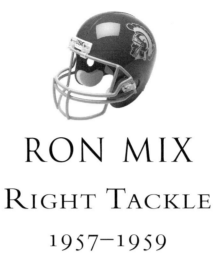

RON MIX

RIGHT TACKLE

1957–1959

I WAS AT HAWTHORNE HIGH SCHOOL before Brian Wilson, the Loves, and all the Beach Boys were there. I met them later in life, but Mike Gillespie was two years behind me. He is a longtime friend who grew up in the same neighborhood, and we probably played sports with each other. He was on USC's 1961 College World Series champion team and became the USC baseball coach from 1987 to 2006, winning the 1998 national championship.

I was recruited to USC in 1956. It would have been by Bill Fisk Sr. and Mel Hein. Hein's in the Pro Football Hall of Fame with me. Al Davis was on the staff until my sophomore year at USC. He's in the Pro Football Hall of Fame, too. My teammate, Willie Wood, is also in the Pro Football Hall of Fame. I can't say, but I'd bet there's no other program with so many Hall of Famers from the same era, except, of course, if you're talking about USC in other eras. How about the 1979–1980 Trojans? Anthony Munoz, Ronnie Lott, Bruce Matthews?

Al came in with Don Clark. He was one of his assistants. The first time I met him I was in the locker room. I was doing leg exercises. He was standing on a bench looking me up and down. Al asked me, "Do you lift weights?" I said I did, and he said, "Yeah, not many coaches approve of lifting weights, but I think it's important."

I thought he was another player at the time. Later that day he was introduced as the ends coach. I was an end at the time, so he was my "personal"

Pro Football Hall of Fame inductees (from left) Dick Butkus, Yale Lary, Ron Mix, and Johnny Unitas pose with their busts after the enshrinement ceremony in Canton, Ohio, in August 1979.

coach. I owe a great deal to him, in my development as a football player. He took a great interest in the players and worked with me after practice.

Much has been written over the years about Davis' philosophy, and whether his experience at USC and in the city of Los Angeles formed his view of the pro game, and where the best players are trained. It's been said that USC ran more pro sets, that the Coliseum better duplicated a pro atmosphere, and that L.A. was a big city in which the popularity of USC was marketed more in line with a pro style than a college town.

I don't think Davis limited his vision to the USC model. I think he just recognized that if a player went to a big-time football school such as USC, there was a greater chance that player would develop into an outstanding pro. That said, he was also signing players from little-known black colleges, and many of those players flourished in Oakland, too.

In 1960 the Baltimore Colts and the Boston Patriots drafted me. Al left USC when John McKay got the head job, joining Sid Gillman's staff with the Los Angeles Chargers. There was maneuvering, and I left Boston to sign with Gillman, Davis, and my new hometown team, the Chargers. We played at the Coliseum, then the franchise moved to San Diego. In 1963 Al left San Diego to become the Raiders' head coach.

I'd been with the Chargers for 10 years when Al obtained me for the Oakland Raiders in 1971. He brought me out of retirement. I'd taken the bar exam after going to the University of San Diego Law School and had been out of football for a year. I'd passed the bar and was technically an attorney when, to my surprise, I got a call from him, saying he'd traded David Grayson and some defensive backs for me. He asked if I was interested in returning to pro football. I could make $18,000 as an attorney or join his team for two years at $45,000. So it seemed like a wise decision, but things didn't turn out the way I'd hoped.

I played at 270 pounds, but I'd stopped stuffing myself, so I was down to my natural 225. It took a two-month period to gain the weight back, but I'd lost my quickness. I was not the same player. I'm sorry about that. I'm fond of Al Davis. I was on the taxi squad in 1972 and the last game ever played while I was still a Raider was the "immaculate reception" game at Pittsburgh.

Two of my teammates at Southern Cal were the "Twin Holy Terrors of Mt. Carmel," Mike and Marlin McKeever. Marlin, Mike, and I were probably the only three serious weightlifters on the team. We trained at Redpath Gym in Inglewood. All coaches in all sports discouraged us from lifting. The mantra was that we'd lose fluidity, but that didn't seem logical to us.

Marlin, Mike, and I all got stronger than anybody else. I don't want to sound immodest, but we were better-conditioned than anybody else. We were incredibly strong college players with a huge advantage that we had over the players we played against. I was immense at the time. In my senior year, we each weighed 225 pounds at a time when most linemen went both ways between 210 and 230, but Marlin, Mike, and I attained incredible strength. We could military press 300 pounds each, and you can imagine your confidence going into games, lifting up a player. It wasn't just the strength, it was the way it made you feel, the way you saw your body change, the results you achieved through effort.

It was just a tremendous advantage we had over opponents. My senior year [1959] was the first season I started, and it was amazing I made All-America with no publicity, but it was because of the strength increase I made. The preseason publications paid all their attention to Marlin and Mike, but my play reached such a high level that suddenly all the coaches began to tout me for All-America. It was astounding that this could occur, to make All-America without any attention from the publicity staff.

I remember the "Steve Bates incident" at Berkeley. It was Mike who tackled him. Bates was either a running back or a wide receiver, and Mike broke his jaw. There was no penalty called, but because of the severity of his injury, the California team and their alumni, from that point to the present day, feel it was an illegal hit by Mike.

It was interesting in that of the two twins, Mike was the "good" one. Marlin was the "evil" twin, but it was Mike who was the one who got publicly hammered for that play. I don't have an opinion and don't remember if the film was definitive enough to determine whether it was a late hit. Common sense tells me if it was late or excessive, the referees would have called a penalty, but they didn't.

Sports Illustrated ran a big cover story on the incident, calling into question the safety of college football and the nature of "dirty play." I do not recall that Berkeley sued USC over the incident, but I'm told they did and that the film exonerated Mike, but that never fit the template Berkeley created for USC, which is essentially jealousy because we win all the time, and they went from greatness to mediocrity.

John McKay was an assistant defensive backs coach when I was there. You could just tell even then he had a unique personality, a little bit of an impish personality, which was unusual on that staff. Every other member except Hein and Ray George were intense Marv Goux types, but he had an impish way. I actually thought it was out of place, that it was not what we were.

Football was a primeval sport at that time. The truth is the USC practices were so demanding, so tough, that I felt the games were easy. I played an unskilled position, tackle, the last two years. It was so tough and left me so exhausted that I told myself I'd play two years of pro football, and that would be enough to buy a house and a car, and I'd never see this game again. We went both ways and special teams with no TV timeouts.

Our practices were two and a half hours of pure hitting and running. I was completely exhausted, and candidly I'm surprised any of us graduated, because it left so little energy to devote to schoolwork or to pay attention to grades. Then, when I went into pro football and went one way as an offensive tackle, it was so easy that I would have liked to play longer, except your body wears out.

Don Clark was a good coach who came in under a real handicap. Before he came in, the university was penalized for a whole bunch of abuses, funneling money to athletes, and as a result the university was placed under three years' sanction with no participation in the Rose Bowl. There were a number of other sanctions, such as all the seniors being suspended and forced to choose whether they'd play the first half or the second half of the season. I don't recall, but I'm told the 1959 USC baseball team, which at the time was called the best college team ever, was denied a chance to compete in the College World Series because of football penalties. That team included Bruce Gardner, a great left-handed pitcher and a tragic figure who later committed suicide.

It was very detrimental and had an effect on recruiting, as you might imagine. It took a while to rebuild the team, but Clark did an extraordinary job. We had an outstanding team by his third year, which is an unusually short amount of time to turn a program around. He had excellent recruits, such as Willie Wood, and the McKeevers were still their usual dominant selves. However, in that third year, Clark committed the ultimate sin. We started out 8–0, then lost to UCLA and Notre Dame.

I went to the University of San Diego Law School and was the Chargers' team attorney when Mike Garrett was playing here, but I was not involved in Mike's decision to go to law school, which helped prepare him to become USC's athletic director.

Now I specialize in representing retired pro athletes, working for their workers' compensation benefits. I'm involved in trying to help retired football players as a group. The Hall of Fame and the NFL Players Association asked if I'd help a guy in need, and one thing led to another. We did a good job, and I'm proud to do it.

Half the members get very little. The wife of a member gets less than $45,000. I help them get a supplement to bring them up to that amount. Al Davis is one of the lone voices in ownership wanting to see benefits improve for retired players. You have to wrest it from them.

Ron Mix, like many of his fellow Trojans, was one of the greatest football players in history. Through hard work, he made himself team captain, All-Coast and All-America in his senior year (1959). In 1960 the Baltimore Colts of the NFL made him their first-round draft pick. But Mix went to the fledgling AFL and ended up with one of his college coaches, Al Davis of the Los Angeles (later San Diego) Chargers. A perennial American Football League All-Star, Mix was reunited with Davis in Oakland (1971–1972) and elected to the Pro Football Hall of Fame (1979) and USC Athletic Hall of Fame (1997). After retirement, he became an attorney specializing in sports labor law.

The SIXTIES

HAL BEDSOLE
LEFT END
1961–1963

IWAS RECRUITED TO USC BY JIM SEARS, a Trojan great in his own right, and later by Don Coryell. He later went to San Diego State when John McKay took the head coaching job at USC. I was brought in as a quarterback at first. I was the L.A. City Player of the Year as a quarterback at Reseda High School in the valley. We lost to Craig Fertig and Huntington Park in the city championship game. I played a year at Pierce J.C. in Woodland Hills. McKay recruited athletes—this is the reputation he had, a coach who did not recruit by position but rather sought the best athletes and then found a position for them—but it didn't come about by McKay's choosing. Pete Beathard, for instance, was not the L.A. City Player of the Year, but the fact that McKay moved me to receiver and kept him at quarterback proved that he knew what he was doing.

USC was playing the 1960–1961 regular conference schedule like any other football team, and then the NCAA mandated a two-way program. They instituted many new rules about substitutes, how many substitutions per quarter. They mandated that the 11 players on the field had to play both ways except for a "walk-on."

There had been platoon teams modeled after the "Chinese bandits," which was LSU's nickname for their defense, mostly specialists. They were No. 1 in the country in 1958. McKay didn't fashion his scheme based on the "Chinese bandits," though. He was an innovator in his own right and learned he had to play 11 guys. For years, a lot of teams played both ways. On occasion a quarterback or wide receiver didn't play both ways, but in 1961 there were changes; a one-time substitute per quarter, except for a walk-on. McKay figured out which particular guys could not play this or that position, so he would take the best athlete by each position and find a solution to his dilemma, which was that a tight end might be made into a tackle; a quarterback was made into another position. He found the best 11 athletes on the team. In high school, the best athlete was invariably the quarterback, just as the best baseball player was a pitcher, the best athlete on the basketball team a point guard. Still to this day, people would be shocked at how McKay had this epiphany and turned the whole program around, by utilizing a system whereby he found his best athletes and then distributed them to available positions, so the best 11 on the team were all on the field out there at the same time. He adapted to NCAA rules changes, and it suited his style and the program.

You looked at Pete Beathard, who was a great defensive player, and you're not going to take him out of the game. So a Hal Bedsole they'd keep in there as a wide receiver. Ron Butcher was a high school tight end you'd move to left tackle. Skill position players were moved to non-skill positions. I was not the best pass receiver, but I was the best athlete for playing defensive end and wide receiver.

79

You needed to get Damon Bame in the game as a linebacker at 185 pounds. He couldn't play offense, so he was a walk-on. It was good thinking, because in 1961 McKay was developing his coaching style, his innovations, his ideas. He was instituting the I formation, which was revolutionary. Iowa was the No. 1 team in the nation, and we played them early in the season. They had Paul Krause, Wally Hilgenberg, some great players like that, and they were leading 35–14 when McKay put some others in the game, experimenting with his personnel. I got the chance to play and caught a 78-yard touchdown pass, and a 40-yard touchdown, then a two-point conversion. We rallied to within a point and had a chance to tie, but McKay always went for the win. So he went for two, but we didn't get it. In 1961 we lost two games by one point and one game by three. We lost to Iowa 35–34, to Pittsburgh 10–9, and to UCLA 10–7—so that's three defeats by five points, which is similar to Pete Carroll's first year in 2001. Eight points would have meant three more wins.

It was the 1960 win over UCLA that helped McKay keep his job. Bill Nelsen beat Billy Kilmer 17–6, and that made Dr. Norman Topping believe

McKay could succeed. Had he lost, he was gone. We were 4–5–1 in 1961 and lost in the rain to Notre Dame, but McKay said, "I know we're gonna be good."

The whole 1961 season, there was a lot of experimentation. We went to the I formation, single-platoon, and McKay told Topping he had confidence, but we lost to UCLA by three. By this point, though, he'd figured out who could play in the new substitution system and who could play his way.

In 1962 it took several games to get anybody's attention, but most teams didn't score on us. We gave up 55 points in a 10-game regular season, and Illinois had 16 of those. We never thought we were the best team in the country, we only had one blowout game, a 25–0 win over Notre Dame. They had an All-America wide receiver named Jim Kelly, who held quite a few Notre Dame records, but we held him down. Hugh Devore was their coach, and it was not a great team. He was an unheralded coach. Notre Dame was the only team we really dominated. We beat Washington 14–0, but they literally could not move the ball. We stopped Roger Staubach and Navy 13–6. We didn't feel like a team that rolled up 40 or 50 points a game like later Trojan teams, like the 1972 national champions. We beat UCLA in a close game, 14–3.

80

When we played Wisconsin in the Rose Bowl is when we felt we really were champions, but there was no predicting that game. No Big Ten team had ever come out to Pasadena and threw the ball the way they did that day. Their quarterback, Ron Vander Kelen, was the Big Ten Player of Year, but he was not as good as Pete Beathard. Pat Richter was another good player, an All-America receiver for them. Lou Holland was a nice little running back, but in comparing the two teams position-by-position, the way they do in sports, none of their guys were guys we'd take, not in my mind. But Wisconsin was favored because the Big Ten had long dominated the Rose Bowl, and the dominance of McKay and USC, and the Pacific-8 Conference later, was not yet established. But we were convinced we could smoke Wisconsin, and considering that we led 42–14 late in the game, it's clear we could and should have.

I scored a 57-yard touchdown and later a 23-yarder, and we never passed again. Wisconsin coach Milt Bruhn was a guy McKay liked, and he didn't want to run it up on him. "He's a nice guy, let's just run the clock out and get out of Dodge City," said McKay. Then all kinds of freak things happened; a fumble, a snap over the kicker's head, and Vander Kelen went to the air 29 straight times.

Hal Bedsole hauls in a pass from quarterback Pete Beathard in the Rose Bowl against Wisconsin in January 1963.

McKay, I think, admitted later that you've got to smoke 'em, then say you're sorry afterward. I can't speak for John Robinson, who had games like that, where he had a big early lead and let opponents catch up and almost lost some big games because of it. But I can speak for McKay because he told me personally. He'd come up to you during the game and say, "Tell Pete this or that," and his comment, "Just run it out and get out of Dodge City" back-fired then. If we had been up 49–14, Milt Bruhn calls it a day and turns off the machine, but we gave them just enough daylight.

Plus, remember, we played both ways then, and we got tired. They were running up and down the field on us, and we couldn't run the clock out. Plus we had players at odd positions because two offensive tackles were out early. Gary Kirner sliced his hand, and Marv Marinovich got thrown out in the first quarter for slugging a player. We had non-lettermen playing in the Rose Bowl. [USC held on to win 42–37.]

USC's never really acknowledged or appreciated the significance of what we did, from a historical point of view, but we hadn't won the national title in 30 years, even though we'd had great players like Frank Gifford, Ron Mix, and the McKeever twins. USC had been on probation, and people wondered, *Would USC ever be like those 1930s Thundering Herd teams, dominant teams?* The 1962 national championship team came in, and McKay figured out something special and started a run. It was "showtime." From 1962 to 1981 was a big-time run. You had Alabama under Bear Bryant paralleling that same time period, but those two decades between John McKay and John Robinson were probably the most dominant 20-year period any college program has ever enjoyed.

This was the beginning of a real golden age at USC, in California, in all sports. The Giants and Dodgers came to the state, and it was a period of great excitement. There was a population boom after World War II, the schools were expanding, and the talent base was incredible. Forty-nine of our 50 players on the 1962 team were from California.

"Why should I go outside the state?" McKay would ask, rhetorically. Today Pete Carroll would laugh at that, but then we could do it. You still need to dominate your base in the L.A. area.

The 1960s were the peak of the rivalry and success of both USC and UCLA. And a lot of what John Wooden did with UCLA basketball, and John McKay with USC football, is built on a big advantage we had in the West. That was the full-scale recruitment of black athletes, which the South was not doing, and much of the country was not doing it the way McKay did it.

McKay was not prejudiced in any way. He only wanted football players, and USC had a history of playing blacks that went back to Brice Taylor in the 1920s. In the 1930s the USC-UCLA game was an integrated game, with Jackie Robinson playing at UCLA, and this had a big social effect. USC had blacks in the 1940s and 1950s when almost nobody else did. We had guys like Willie Wood and C.R. Roberts. USC never had a problem in this area. What happened for McKay is that he was the guy who had guys attain superstardom. Prior to McKay, there were no black consensus All-Americans or first-round draft picks at USC. But under McKay, he got the elite recruits, the kind of star players who were role models. This meant that USC was a program that other black kids wanted to play in. The level of quality athletes, white and black, got higher, and elite-level guys got into 'SC, guys like O.J. Simpson and Marcus Allen.

In the 1990s, which was arguably the worst decade in the history of USC football, we still had the most pro football players, but most were linemen or linebackers. But in order to have a high caliber team like Pete Carroll has, you need skill guys. Another thing I'd have to say about McKay is that he was not afraid to play a black quarterback. The reality was that it was difficult in 1970–1971 when there was a dispute over whether Jimmy Jones (black) or Mike Rae (white) should start, but he said if you're the best player, you were going to play. Give McKay credit, because there were a lot of teams that didn't play black quarterbacks for a long time. USC did it first with Willie Wood in 1957, and McKay stuck to his guns despite great pressure and criticism with Jones over Rae.

What does it mean to be a Trojan? Well, when I played, USC was not the phenomenon that it is today. It was not quite there. It had been a famous school, but we'd been on probation, and we had yet to attain that phenomenon, which grew with McKay. My interest was the fact that there was a lot of history there—it was a private university and had a prestigious "family" of USC players and alumni who, in the real world, could help you in your life and career. There was a saying at school, whether you were an athlete or not, that, "USC takes care of its own." When I got out, it was a fact. I had a short career in the NFL and went right back to USC and asked, *Who can help me in the real world?* I was living proof it was a family, that they reach out.

Over the years, USC sent many people to talk to me about the broadcasting industry. Bob Wood, the former president of CBS and past president of the USC Trojan Club, was a member of the board of trustees. I once met him in the locker room as a player. I called him in New York, and his secretary asked me if he was expecting my call. I said no, and she said he probably wouldn't speak to me. I just said, "Hey, this is Hal Bedsole," and he got right on the phone and asked what he could do for me. He gave me the leads I needed, and I went into the broadcast business. Later they'd send me players and non-players who graduated from USC, and I was always a contact for them. I was flattered to be asked. Then I was a guest lecturer in the USC graduate school, and I also taught in the UCLA adult education program.

I don't go a month in my life without the phenomenon of being a Trojan happening to me in some way. I was the first person in my family to graduate from college. USC broadened my horizons. The fact is I was a player and a participant in a real-world atmosphere in which I got benefits from being an athlete, as well as from being a USC student and graduate. You meet all kinds of people, people who go on to fame and sometimes infamy in different fields, people from different countries. It's all part of the USC experience. A lot of judges, attorneys, and media professionals came out of USC, and a lot of people went into public life, into politics.

USC over the years maintained a sense of tradition, a decorum. When there were campus protests, and as colleges especially west of the Mississippi became staging grounds for protest, USC remained patriotic. The biggest change over the years is the level of academic excellence. The school was always great fun; it had fine facilities and super athletics, but some people questioned the education. They were just envious of our network, but what's happened is Dr. Steven Sample has turned it into a major university with great graduate schools. He highly elevated the prestige of our academics, while none of the other things changed.

Many of the alumni, I for one, felt there was a time the emphasis on academics, while fine, meant a choice had been made: we were now a great academic institution, but that could never coexist with being a sports power, at least not in football. Dr. Sample and some others made tough decisions about entrance requirements, accelerated SAT scores, and made academics a first priority. It took a while for all of this to take place, and we figured out a way to get great people in there, the right kind of athletes in line with the academics, athletes who could uphold our tradition. There was a lot of attention paid to this, but we knew there were schools where this tradition was upheld, at Penn State and Michigan. Mike Garrett and Pete Carroll get the credit. You need coaches who say, "We don't get every kid we want, but we can compete for and get the elite kid who is a great student–athlete." This is what USC has become.

I'm proud to be a Trojan. I did graduate, which shocked some people, but I'm part of the school in all ways. I applaud what they have done. There were grumblings, some felt Dr. Sample would ruin our athletic heritage. But lo and behold, they changed, and now they have elevated every aspect of the University of Southern California to compete not just as a great sports school but a great school with terrific students.

Hal Bedsole was an All-America wide receiver for the 1962 national champions, catching two touchdown passes in the 42–37 Rose Bowl win over Wisconsin. He was twice all-conference; was selected a *Playboy* Preseason All-American (1963); played in the 1964 Coaches All-America Game, College All-Star Game, and Hula Bowl; and is a member of the USC Athletic Hall of Fame. Drafted by the Vikings (NFL) and Chiefs (AFL), he played three years for Minnesota before embarking on a long career in the broadcasting business.

WILLIE BROWN

RIGHT HALFBACK

1961–1963

I was born in Tuscaloosa, Alabama. My family moved to Long Beach, California, when I was 18 months old. I graduated from Long Beach Poly High School, played for Coach McKay from 1960 to 1963, and graduated in 1964. I was a member of the 1962 national champions and made a key interception of a pass by Wisconsin's Ron Vander Kelen at the end of the '63 Rose Bowl to preserve the win, 42–37.

One of my early influences was Dave Levy. Coach Levy had gone to UCLA and coached at Poly High School. John McKay hired him, and Coach Levy is one of the reasons USC caught up to, and maybe even surpassed UCLA when it came to social progress and opportunities for black athletes.

USC always had a good record in this area. Brice Taylor had been our first All-American in the 1920s. C.R. Roberts was a superstar in a game at Texas, but UCLA seemed to be the school that attracted black athletes in Southern California. Jackie Robinson had gone there, and they seemed to get the really super black stars. John Wooden's basketball program was built on integration.

Maybe USC was seen as a conservative school, a private university, and not as open as UCLA, but Coach Levy and Coach McKay turned that around. I was part of it. When I came to USC, guys like Mike Garrett started to think about USC. I would tell them what a great coach McKay was, and that helped, but it was Coach Levy who really mentored us.

Willie Brown was an all-conference halfback on the 1962 national championship team. He played three seasons in the NFL, but returned to USC to become the school's first African American assistant coach.

Once Garrett complained to Coach Levy that he could not rent an apartment in Pasadena because of race quotas. He was really mad, but Coach Levy gathered a number of the black athletes together and spoke to us like a "Dutch uncle." He said we needed to make the most of our opportunities at USC—athletically, scholastically, and socially—and use that to further ourselves and therefore pave the way for those to follow. Coach Levy said we can't force whites to change their opinions, but it happens through positive examples, and we have to let it happen. It was the kind of thing an older, wiser man can pass on to young people.

The Los Angeles Rams made me their third-round draft pick. The Chargers of the American Football League made me their sixth-round pick, as this was prior to the merger. I signed with the Rams and played with them for two years, then with the Philadelphia Eagles for one year. When Coach McKay hired his first black coach, he did not wait until there was a demand for it. He hired me, and it was a great opportunity. By the time O.J. Simpson came to school, we had the reputation of being the school where black players wanted to go. McKay and Bear Bryant set up the 1970 Alabama game, and it did volumes for race relations. Prior to the game, though, there were a lot of concerns on the part of our black players, going in to the South. Politically, there was a lot going on. Racially, there were incidents happening all throughout the country.

I talked to Charlie [Weaver] the other day. I heard that [he and Tody Smith] had guns, and I'm not surprised if they did. A lot was riding on it. We received hate letters sent to McKay and some of the players, so going back to the Deep South, our guys were not used to that, and now they're exposed to that situation. I heard about that gun story, but I didn't see it. But I'm not surprised.

But there were problems in our ranks. There was a quarterback controversy involving Jimmy Jones and Mike Rae, and the white players would go to Craig Fertig, the black players would air concerns to me. It was divisive, but Coach McKay had hired me in part to handle this kind of thing. McKay never said, "Tell them to shut up," or anything. He was conservative and authoritarian, but extraordinarily attentive to their needs, and he knew I was a sounding board.

Bear Bryant and McKay were close friends. Bear offered me a job to go back to Tuscaloosa. I would have been one of the first black coaches, but I didn't want to go back to the South. My father had grown up there. My father recalls going to 'Bama games and sitting in the section for blacks, high in the stands. He went to Spelman College. The University of Alabama would give them hand-me-down equipment. As much prejudice as there was, though, the black community thought the Crimson Tide was their team. When we played in that 1970 game, I had relatives pulling for me, but who still wanted 'Bama to win!

I remember black people outside the stands, cheering for USC, plus people in the stadium, blacks jumping up and down cheering. They recognized the bus and cheered us after the game. They surrounded the bus, there were blacks everywhere, and they were very happy. They were rooting for us; they'd come down and were cheering for us. Our black players just took it all in, and did it with wonder. As I sat in the bus, I did recall they held candles and Bibles; people were crying; it was very emotional. This was *not* a regular game. It was just monumental. The players, who normally would be rowdy after a win, were quiet. They'd played well but knew something important was going down.

Sam Cunningham played a big part in what Paul Bryant was trying to do. It was Bryant and McKay, trying to set up something. He did come into our locker room and all. I think Sam met some of their players, plus the press was all around Sam.

It served a wonderful purpose, a wonderful purpose. Man, I really believe sports can transform a lot of things. It just helped relationships; it pushed it along.

Willie Brown starred on both sides of the ball for John McKay's 1962 national champions and was named All–Athletic Association of Western Universities (AAWU, changed to the Pacific-8, 1968) in 1962 and 1963. He earned the Davis-Teschke Award (1962), was team captain, and winner of the Roy Baker Award for back of the year (1963). He was chosen for the Hula Bowl, East-West Shrine Game, College All-Star Game, and the Coaches All-America Game after his senior season. Drafted by the Rams (NFL) and Chargers (AFL), he played for Los Angeles (1964–1965) and Philadelphia (1966) before being tapped as USC's first black assistant coach. He was on the staff of the 1970 team that ventured to Birmingham, Alabama, and helped end segregation. Today he works in the university's athletic department.

CRAIG FERTIG

QUARTERBACK
1962–1964

I CAME OUT OF HUNTINGTON PARK HIGH SCHOOL, and John McKay recruited me in his first year, but USC was after me before he was hired. Guess who came out to look at me first? Al Davis, that's who. Al was trying to get the job that McKay got. It dawned on McKay early on that Davis was after that job, so he didn't retain him on the staff after Don Clark left, because he knew Davis would be maneuvering behind his back the whole time. It worked out for both guys.

My father was Henry Fertig, the chief of the Huntington Park Police Department. They called him "Chief." He also owned the same little beach house down in Balboa Bay that I live in now. My dad was "Mr. 'SC." He went to USC the same time I did. When I was a senior, he took classes there, too, and we ended up in the same class together. I asked if he was checking up on me. Heck, he was more into partying than I was. Once he urged me to miss class or blow off studying or something; he said, "Let's go to the 901 Club and get a beer." I said, "I need to study, Dad." He just laughed and said, "The professor's the chief of police down in Hermosa Beach, a pal of mine. I take care of all his parking tickets, so we're in." And we were. If you ever had parking problems, just call the Chief!

Chief was the "chief of security" for Trojan celebs and the like. At Austin, Texas, he was with John Wayne, pouring whiskey into the Duke's plastic cup while driving him around Memorial Stadium, and Duke's giving them the "hook 'em, horns" sign. The Longhorn fans are all cheering Duke, see, because they know he's this cowboy guy and figure he's rooting for Texas. They don't know he played at USC, and the whole time Duke's telling Chief what the Texas fans can do with his middle finger.

Coming out of high school, Notre Dame recruited me. I'd never been on a plane. I also visited Stanford, Washington, and Wisconsin. I read all the letters schools sent me, but I just wanted to travel. Dad was set on 'SC, and I wanted to go there. Dad had taken me to my first USC game in 1948. We tied Notre Dame 14–14 to deny them the national championship, and I just said, "I wanna be part of this."

I played in the California Shrine high school game at the Coliseum. Craig Morton also played in that game, and Steve Thurlow, who went to Stanford. Baseball might have been my best sport in high school, but it was not like it is today, where kids concentrate on just one sport. I was not fast enough for track. Remember what McKay said about me? "He's awfully skinny, but he makes up for it by being slow."

Pete Beathard was ahead of me. We're lifelong friends; we were recruited together. Assistant coach Dave Levy said, "If we could have Beathard's body and Fertig's brain, we'd have the most unique quarterback in the nation." Beathard was a great athlete.

So Pete and I played baseball for Rod Dedeaux when we got to USC, but one day McKay's secretary, the lovely Bonnie, strolled on out to the field and told Rod, "Coach McKay wants to see Beathard and Fertig." Well, Rod knew where his bread was buttered. He had a great program, but it was all paid for by football, so he said, "Take 'em." I looked at Pete, and he looked at me. We were trying to figure out what we did wrong. Beathard said, "I'm your roommate, I haven't left your side." We walked in, and McKay was sitting there reading the sports section, so all we saw was smoke drifting up from his cigar. He just said, "You guys aren't very good at either sport. Make a decision." We said, "Well, we'll play football." And he just said, "That's being smart, boys."

In 1962 we were the national champs, and I was the third-string quarterback, but Coach stole something from LSU, called the "Chinese bandits." The first-team offense and defense would play seven minutes in the first quarter, and then he'd send in these "specialists," mostly sophomores, and we'd play the rest of the first quarter, the last four minutes or so. We'd do this almost every quarter. Thirty-three guys all knew they would play, and that

Quarterback Craig Fertig discusses a play with head coach John McKay during the 1964 season.

was just great for morale. I never started, but I did play. I ran deeper than the deepest wide receiver. I mean, the only way I could go deeper was if I was running to Julie's Trojan Barrel. I'd run to the track and then up the peristyles. I was never a threat to catch the ball, but I took a defender off somebody else way downfield, and we were a ball-control offense, rushing and short passing.

That unbeaten season saved McKay's job. They were gonna fire his behind. Dr. Norman Topping verified this—we all knew it. When we beat Notre Dame 25–0, that just solidified the national title. I scored the last touchdown in that game, it was a bootleg run for the last six points.

In 1963 Beathard was the first draft choice by the AFL and the NFL—the Kansas City Chiefs and Detroit Lions. I suggested to him that he sign with Henry Ford and Detroit, but Al Davis and Sid Gillman were making the AFL an exciting league, so he went with Don Klosterman and the new league.

The 1963 season was a disappointment, but a lot of guys were hurt, and we went 7–3. Washington won the conference. I'd had to block Dick Butkus of Illinois the year before, and I said, "This isn't in my contract." Thankfully, they made me the quarterback after that.

In 1964 we were not really sure what we would have. We were supposed to win the conference, but we lost to Washington 14–13 and didn't play Oregon State, so it went to a vote. They told us if we beat Notre Dame, we'd go to the Rose Bowl. After the Notre Dame win, we had a party. One of our guys had just been drafted, and we went to a steakhouse, it was a big celebration. The TV was on, but nobody was really listening. Then Fred Hessler, the voice of the Bruins, came on TV, and we all saw he was talking about the Rose Bowl selection. We turned on the sound and heard him say, "This is a crime," and we knew right away we'd been robbed. He said Oregon State, which had beaten Idaho 10–7, God bless 'em, were going to the Rose Bowl, and we were done.

Now, this is what it means to be a Trojan. After the euphoria of victory over Notre Dame, followed by the biggest letdown you ever saw, learning the Rose Bowl had been denied us, there were two attorneys in the restaurant. They were USC guys, and they just opened up their wallets, and the next thing we saw were two dollies with four cases of champagne, and they said, "We don't beat Notre Dame every day." And we just turned it into a party.

That game against the Fighting Irish featured a couple of Notre Dame guys from Southern California. John Huarte had played at Mater Dei High School in Santa Ana, and his favorite receiver, Jack Snow, had gone to St. Anthony's in Long Beach. Huarte and Snow were lifeguards or something, but they spent the summer right outside my door on the beaches in Orange County, running routes and practicing, Huarte passing to Snow. I don't know how they concentrated. If you ever spend time on those beaches in the summer, there's so many beautiful girls to distract you, I don't see how you can get any work done. But that's their story, and they stuck to it.

Anyway, we were moving the ball in the first half, and here is the key: on Thursday we had a chalkboard on the field, and Coach took the chalk and said Notre Dame's defense had thrown their opponents' quarterbacks for 79 yards in losses. So we brought the flanker back in to block for me, and I liked that, it was a damn good idea. Fred Hill was our split end, and Notre Dame, stubbornly or arrogantly, insisted on playing him man-to-man. We moved and threw the ball, and Mike Garrett ran well, but he got tired. Rod Sherman shifted and coughed up the ball twice. We were on his ass after that. We'd been driving, and he'd cough it up, and Huarte would eat up the clock. They went up 17–0, but then they fumbled on our 5-yard line.

That was the key. Otherwise, it was going to be an uphill battle if we had been down 24–0. But Coach said at the half, "We'll take their opening kick, and if we just do what we can do, we will score." And we did. Garrett took it in, and then we held. I hit Fred Hill in "Sam Dickerson's corner" of the end zone, and we held again. Now it was all about time, because Huarte took so much off the clock. I hit Hill on a post pattern, which was the big play on the drive, and then we were going to go back to Sherman, who'd fumbled the ball before this.

We were on their 15 with 1:50 left in the game. It was fourth and eight, and we were trailing 17–13, so a field goal was not an option. McKay called for "84 Z delay," which was designed not just for a first down but aimed for the end zone. Garrett went in motion, and Notre Dame—stubborn or arrogant or however you put it—sent their strong safety with him, and I let them get enough past Sherman. I knew if I could just hit that seam, he would have a clear shot at the end zone. If you look at the photo, obviously I didn't see it because they knocked me right on my behind, but I heard that big Coliseum crowd roar and knew something good had happened. There was 1:33 left.

Huarte was a ball-control, play-action quarterback and not the kind of guy to take a team down the field in a two-minute drill. Notre Dame threw it with loft, and our safety picked it off. Huarte has a place in Pacific Palisades and a tile business. He's successful, a member of the Jonathan Club with J.K. McKay, and we've been friends over the years. "The Game Is On" is a banquet we started in the back room of Julie's, three Notre Dame guys and three Trojans. Tommy Hawkins and I exchange lettermen's sweaters. One year Regis Philbin was there, and we did a comedy routine with him. We're different from any other rivalry. It's about mutual respect.

Both USC and Notre Dame are about class. We can tell they're a class program and they don't cause problems. The key word is *tradition*, both schools have it—they're steeped in it, and so are we. As a player, you want the guys who preceded you to be proud that you are carrying on what they created, perpetuating what the other guys did. We have plenty of respect for UCLA, too. I'm good friends with a lot of ex-Bruins, and most of us are that way. We usually root for them unless it's for the Rose Bowl.

93

I got drafted by the Pittsburgh Steelers in 1965, but that was short-lived, and Coach McKay brought me in as a coach. I have as many great memories as a coach as I have as a player. One memory that isn't so great was the 51–0 loss to Notre Dame in 1966. But, in a lot of ways, that game tells you what it means to be a Trojan. Ara Parseghian ran up the score, trying to impress the pollsters so he could win the national championship over Michigan State and Alabama. But one of the reasons we got blown out was because McKay never stopped trying to win. We've faced other coaches, Parseghian among them, who would just run the ball into the line when they were out of it late, hoping to avoid turnovers and keep the score respectable, but not McKay. He kept putting the ball in the air, and they kept getting it back and scoring off a short field. But we held our heads high.

A month later, we refused to settle for a tie and went for the win, a two-point conversion against Purdue in the Rose Bowl, and we lost. But you had to respect McKay for trying that instead of playing it safe, going for a tie like a lot of coaches did.

McKay had seen California guys like Huarte and Snow playing for Notre Dame, so he hired Mater Dei's coach, Dick Coury. He brought in six players. Toby Page, who quarterbacked our 1967 national champions, was one of those guys. Bruce Rollinson, the coach at Mater Dei now, played at USC. We just said, "Mater Dei's *our* Catholic school." Page called that audible against UCLA in 1967 that resulted in O.J. Simpson's 64-yard, game-winning touchdown run. Half the guys on the field never heard him call it, the crowd was so loud. Toby always gave me credit for calling that audible, but I never remembered giving those instructions.

Coach Coury saw a seam in UCLA's line when they set up for kicks and brought in tall Bill Hayhoe to block Zenon Andrusyshyn, and that was the difference in a 21–20 win that gave us the national championship in 1967.

Then in 1970 I was part of Coach McKay's staff when we went back to Alabama to play in that memorable game that is considered a pivotal moment in civil rights history. Coach McKay asked me to drive him to the Los Angeles Airport, but I never knew what was up. He was meeting Paul "Bear" Bryant. Coach Bryant invited the Trojans to come down to Birmingham to open the 1970 season. He knew we had a highly integrated team, which was a big testament to John McKay, who probably opened more opportunities for black athletes in the 1960s than any coach anywhere. Bryant wanted a classy Trojan team to demonstrate that an integrated program can work in college. He knew his fans and alumni would respect McKay because Bryant respected him. I sat in on history when these men planned that game, but I didn't know it at the time. The idea of it was to pave the way for Wilbur Jackson and John Mitchell to integrate 'Bama football in 1971. Sam "Bam" Cunningham had a huge game for us, and after that recruiting black players in the South was just smooth, at least compared to the way it had been with Jackie Robinson and other milestones.

The next year, John Mitchell ran past McKay and me on the sideline on the first kick in the rematch at the Coliseum, and McKay wryly looked at me and said, "Well, that's what you get." We lost that game, and while McKay and all of us wanted the South to integrate, it hurt us in a way. We'd had the pick of the great black athletes in the South, but now they'd go to places like 'Bama and Tennessee, and the SEC built itself into the powerhouse it is today on the strength of this. But it's all worked for the best.

I understand a movie's going to be made about that 1970 game. J.K. McKay wants Kevin Costner to play his old man. Jon Voight can play Bear Bryant. Colin Farrell can play me!

We did not know the ramifications of that game at first. We were just scared to death of a real good team and didn't realize what we accomplished by winning and helping them. Afterward, Bear thanked Coach McKay at midfield. It was just amazing to me that he looked at a loss as something that helped his program, but it did. There was a consensus at 'Bama, but Pat Dye, who was a good friend and an assistant under Bear, knew it was politically incorrect to come out and say they needed to get black players.

McKay wanted that rematch at the Coliseum because it was a big payday. And he knew Bryant could tell his group that they could come out and attend parties with Hollywood starlets in 1971. Notre Dame was the only other team Bryant could ask to come down to Birmingham at that time that would have had the same national impact we had. He needed a big name, and he thought he could beat us. Little did he know.

In 1971 we didn't know what they had. 'Bama didn't send us a whole lot of film the next year, but what they did send showed Scott Hunter passing the ball out of the "Green Bay offense." But they practiced the wishbone in secret, and we were unprepared for it. It was 14–0 right away before we adjusted, and then they just kept the ball away from us and played great defense. They beat us 17–10.

The 1972 Trojans were the greatest college football team of all time. The 1971 Nebraska Cornhuskers were bigger but slower. We moved the ball better with the pass. The 1995 Nebraska team gets a lot of mention, and for me it's hard to compare eras because players got bigger and faster, but I can't think of a team that could beat the '72 Trojans.

95

Craig Fertig passed away in October 2008. This was his last interview. He was a member of USC's 1962 national champions, but became a certified Trojan legend in 1964 when, down 17–0 at the half, he engineered a comeback to beat Notre Dame 20–17 at the Coliseum. The team captain and recipient of the Davis-Teschke Award for most inspirational player his senior year, Craig was an assistant coach under John McKay from 1965 to 1973, and 1975. Craig entered the USC Athletic Hall of Fame in 2001. He was drafted by the Pittsburgh Steelers, was the head coach at Oregon State in the late 1970s, and was

Tom Kelly's longtime sidekick on Fox Sports TV's football telecasts. He always joked, "Back to you, Tom," a phrase he repeated for years at speaking engagements. In later years he gave tours of the USC campus. His father, Henry "Chief" Fertig, attended USC and was considered one of the school's all-time boosters. His brother-in-law, Marv Marinovich, was captain of USC's 1962 national champions. His nephew, Todd Marinovich, led Troy to victory in the 1990 Rose Bowl. His son, Marc Fertig, lettered four years (1989–1992) on the 'SC baseball team.

BILL FISK JR.

RIGHT GUARD

1962–1964

I WAS AN ALL-AMERICAN IN 1964 and had always wanted to be a Trojan; I was born to be a Trojan. I came out of San Gabriel High School, which was very competitive. In those days, you had to win your league title in order to get into the CIF–Southern Section playoffs. My dad had played against Jackie Robinson, who went to a rival high school, Muir, in Pasadena. In Jackie's day, he played in the L.A. City Section, even though Pasadena is not part of the city of Los Angeles.

My dad was a huge influence on me, having played at USC and coached there. Bill Fisk Sr. played at USC and was an assistant under Jeff Cravath and Jess Hill from 1949 to 1956. We picked up a lot of stuff, my mom kept a scrapbook. My dad played with the Lions and the 49ers. I asked him what he remembered most, and he said a College All-Star Game he played in, and the band or the public address played "Fight On!"

We went both ways in my day. I was an offensive guard and a linebacker. I was 6′ tall and weighed in at 210 pounds, but by the time I got to be a senior I was 225 or 230. The rules were different. We went both ways, and for this reason we did not bulk up the way they do today. When we played Washington, I never went off the field.

It was a crazy time in 1962 with some crazy rules instituted about substituting, and John McKay set up the red, gold, and green teams. So many guys played that morale was great. You had to substitute the whole team. They had changed substitution rules, so we went two ways. Pete Beathard had to play defensive back. Craig Fertig didn't do much in 1962. He didn't play much until his senior year. He backed up Bill Nelsen and Beathard.

We had a small weight room, and I was one of the guys who lived in that weight room. I got a key and let myself in. Gary Kirner and a few other guys lifted weights, but the coaches didn't like us lifting weights. The thinking back then was completely different from today—the fallacy being that weights tied you up, slowed you down. Once I was lifting by myself, bench-pressing 430 pounds, but I couldn't lift it and had to let the weights crash to the floor. Everybody came running in to find out what the commotion had been. We had a special group who were into weights despite the coaches admonishing us not to. I got up to 450 pounds on the bench. Assistant coach Mike Giddings said I'd bench myself right out of the league. Everybody wanted speed and agility and said you couldn't use weights because it would slow you down.

Mike Garrett was a little guy who realized the value of weights. He was also a good baseball player, and he advised his teammate, Tom Seaver, to start lifting weights. Seaver became one of the first baseball players to really benefit from weight training. I was doing my graduate work at that time, and they were doing that, but I'd done it since my senior year in high school.

Craig Fertig was always a fun guy on trips. Talk to Craig about a game against Ohio State at the Coliseum. He came in, and we were on our own 20. Craig took his first snap from center and dropped the ball. I was supposed to be pulling out of the line and went to my left. I tried to grab it and kicked the ball 20 feet in the air. So to this day he always asks me if I was trying a drop kick.

McKay was an old school coach who did not believe in a lot of water on the field. He'd always say to watch how much you drank, that it would slow you down. I thought, *Man, that's ridiculous*. McKay was aloof. I had one teammate who'd see Coach McKay and would want to hide behind a tree. McKay would call people "Billy" or "Tommy" or "Johnny." He'd refer to you like that, but you'd see him coming and go the other way. He did the jokes with writers, but not with players. At practice he'd be up on the tower with a megaphone, and you'd hear him and just stop. Coach Marv Goux would grab your face mask and kick your face. That was how it was then.

In 1962 we were an integrated team that traveled to Dallas, Texas, to play segregated Southern Methodist. I knew about the C.R. Roberts game at Texas in 1956, and I know about the 1970 Sam Cunningham game at Birmingham in 1970. Our game fell in between those, but there were no problems in Dallas in '62. It neither caused the problems of C.R. Roberts' game in 1956 or the changes of the Sam Cunningham game in 1970. We won the game. What I do remember is that it was hot and the bugs were huge. We should have run over them, but the score was closer than it should have been.

My dad was on Howard Jones' 1939 national championship team, and in 1962 we won the first national title since that '39 team. They called us a "Cinderella team" because we were not rated to do anything. In 1961 we didn't have a good record, but we surprised everybody the next season. Now it's all PR. The times are different. There weren't all the ratings systems like we have today.

I faced some great players. I played against Dick Butkus at Illinois. In 1962 we went to Champaign and defeated the Illini 28–16. It didn't matter to Butkus, it could be an exhibition or an all-star game, if he was opposite you, he'd try and kill you. I played against Alan Page of Notre Dame, both at offensive guard and on defense, where I played nose guard or tackle. He moved, he slanted quick.

Pete Beathard was so good, he could run or throw out of the I, and he was a great athlete. The other side of that was he'd be nervous in the huddle. It would take him a while to calm down. I was not surprised that he enjoyed success with the Houston Oilers. Our other quarterback, Bill Nelsen, was tough as nails. That was the difference in the two quarterbacks. Beathard was a great athlete, but Nelsen was really tough. He was like a drill sergeant, then Pete would come in and he was quiet. If Nelsen dislocated a finger, he'd just pop it back in. Nelsen once led USC to a win over Billy Kilmer and UCLA, when I was on the freshman team. My first varsity year was in 1962. Kilmer had a reputation for toughness, too, but Nelsen was tougher than Kilmer, who was more of a partier. Later, Nelsen led the Cleveland Browns into the playoffs, and you'd see him on TV, playing in freezing cold weather on a muddy field, and his knees by then were like glass, but he was always tough.

In 1964 we had high expectations even though we no longer had Nelsen or Beathard. McKay called me into his office and asked Craig and me to give

99

more senior leadership. We had a good team, but the season was a disappointment, since we beat Notre Dame after being promised the Rose Bowl, only to see Oregon State go for barely beating Idaho.

Notre Dame was unbeaten and one win from Ara Parseghian's first national championship, with Heisman winner John Huarte at quarterback. I was in there the last series at guard, and of course Craig Fertig hit Rod Sherman for the winning touchdown, bringing us from a 17–0 deficit to a 20–17 victory. Everybody went wild like I've never seen. They were just super excited. When the gun went off, people were on the field, and you could not get off the field. The tradition is for seniors to go over to the student section and say good-bye after their last home game, but I couldn't get to those stands for the introductions. I was hyperventilating.

I've been asked if I see Notre Dame players very much, and what they tell me about being on the other side of that, but I really haven't seen a lot of those guys over the years. Craig sees those Notre Dame guys a lot.

What it means to be a Trojan is to connect with being a USC guy, not being a so-called "big man on campus." I was brought up to be a Trojan because of Dad. My dad coached there. I was five, my brother was seven, and we had full 'SC uniforms. He'd bring home blocking bags, and as a kid I sat on the equipment bench. I was always in the locker room. I remember Marv Goux when he was a player. For me, I realized my dream of playing there. UCLA offered me the first scholarship, and at first I said, "Well, I guess I'm going to UCLA," which upset everybody until USC gave me a scholarship. Ask everybody, and they'll tell you, it's a Trojan family. It's the Trojan huddle, it's the former players.

100

I coached for 40 years at Mt. San Antonio College. I was the head coach for 18 years, so I couldn't go to many Trojan games since we played on Saturdays. But then I retired and started to take my kids to the games. My son paints his face cardinal and gold, and the last couple years two of my coaches, Rocky Seto and Demetrice Martin, have been on Pete Carroll's staff, so I get to say hi to them and hang out around the team.

Carroll is tremendous, his enthusiasm, the way he relates to players. McKay was not there for you like that, you were afraid of him. But Carroll throws balls to guys, he laughs. It's not all Xs and Os, it's how you treat people. I love his practice schedule, how they compete every Tuesday. He's changed the way football is coached.

The question is whether his way is unique to college, or whether it works in the pros. That's hard to say. Pro football is a business involving a lot of money, so there's a difference from the enthusiasm and fun with college players. There's not as much in the pros, it's a different environment, especially from when I coached at the community college level.

When I was at Mt. SAC, one of our big rivals was Pasadena City College. Harvey Hyde coached them. He and I worked out together at the Pasadena gym. I've enjoyed hearing his radio reports with Chuck Hayes on *Trojan Talk*.

I've come a long way from the old days when I was just a little guy sitting on the bench when my dad was an assistant. The *L.A. Times* used to do a series of articles about great past events, and once they ran a photo of Aramis Dandoy returning a kick 100 yards versus UCLA. I looked at the picture, and there was a kid on the sideline running downfield with him. That was me. J.K. McKay was a little kid who'd run around the sideline when I was playing, too. When USC played in the Rose Bowl, he'd watch the game from a particular place next to the end zone, and he said he'd always envision catching a touchdown pass in that corner of the end zone. In the 1975 Rose Bowl, he caught the winning touchdown from Pat Haden in that very end zone.

Playing football at USC was so special, like the fact that a lot of USC players were in the movies. Once we all took a bus to see a showing of *Spartacus*, and when Marv Goux came on screen, we all yelled for him. People in the theater were wondering, *Why are they cheering?* Craig Fertig to this day brags about killing a Roman soldier in that movie.

Bill Fisk Jr. was a member of John McKay's 1962 national champions and the 1964 team that beat Notre Dame. In that season, he was All-America, all-conference, and team cocaptain. He was selected for the East-West Shrine Game and the Hula Bowl. Bill was the head football coach at Mt. San Antonio Junior College in Walnut, California. Fisk's father, Bill Sr., played in two winning Rose Bowls and was a member of the 1939 national title team.

TIM ROSSOVICH
DEFENSIVE END
1965–1967

THE WAY A KID FROM ST. FRANCIS High School in the San Francisco Bay Area becomes a Trojan is that I was friends with Gary Beban, who starred for a nearby high school in Redwood City, and we went on recruiting trips together. I was recruited by Stanford. I was born at Stanford University Hospital in nearby Palo Alto and grew up almost next to the campus, in the Los Altos area. By my senior year, I was fortunate enough to attract 125 scholarship offers. My mother's first choice was Stanford. Coach John Ralston was a wonderful man, but he had bad football teams. Coming from a Catholic high school, Notre Dame was next on the list, but it was all boys then, and that was *not* to my liking. Gary Beban and I were co–Peninsula Players of the Year, and we took a lot of trips together, including to Los Angeles. He liked UCLA the best, and I liked USC the best. Stanford was too close to home, and they weren't good. I didn't want to play for a bad team, and I didn't want to play for a southern or eastern team.

The decision-maker for me was when Coach John McKay showed me his 1962 national championship ring, and he said what he says to everybody: "Do you want one of these?" or something like that. He had an office overlooking Tommy Trojan. They'd have somebody take you around campus, and he'd just say, "I'll see you on Sunday before you go home." The next thing you know, Ron Schwerdle, who's now a big movie producer and was the team

Tim Rossovich of the Eagles brings down Larry Brown of the Redskins in this December 1970 game at RFK Stadium in Washington.

manager at the time, picked me up downstairs in a limo and took me to a beach party. I spent the weekend barbecuing and having fun playing at the beach. We came back, and I took a quick tour of the campus, and then we went to Coach McKay's office. He said, "What do you think?" I just said, "Where do I sign?" *After playing on a patch of grass at my high school, I can play at the Coliseum?* It was a wonderful experience and an easy choice, and I was still in California.

Of all my teammates, Mike Battle was one of the most memorable. He was a little guy, but nobody had a bigger heart than he did. He always had something to prove. Whatever he wanted to prove, he was going to prove that he was the baddest, toughest dude and nobody was going to be his master. Marv Goux loved him. He was a Marv Goux–type of player all the way. Marv recruited me and talked my parents into believing that this is where I should be. He drank tea with honey, and I never forgot that.

O.J. Simpson was the only person I saw who was more talented—because of his size—than Mike Garrett. O.J. was God-gifted with size and speed. Garrett was a senior when I was a sophomore, and he could outrun people. At Cal, when he was returning a kick or a punt, he caught the ball, and all of a sudden eight or 10 Cal players hit him at the same time, and they all went down in a pile. Garrett squeezed out like a seed from a grapefruit and ran for a score. Not to take anything away from O.J., who was far and above anybody in his time, but Garrett was awesome.

St. Francis was good and they've remained good to this day. We never played O.J. in high school. He played in the San Francisco Academic Athletic Association, and I played in the West Catholic Athletic League against St. Ignatius, Riordan, Serra, Bellarmine, Mitty, those schools. When I started at St. Francis, there were 300 students, and the coach built the football team into the top power in the Central Coast Section.

The 1967 UCLA game was wonderful. They came in No. 1, and I think we were No. 2, and it was not just for the Rose Bowl or bragging rights for L.A. It was for the whole ball of wax—the national title, the Rose Bowl, the Heisman Trophy—it all came down to that. It was close, 21–20 on a blocked extra point.

People think that in a game of that magnitude it's different, the intensity level is higher, and once or twice the on-field intensity is amped up. But it's a big question and hard to answer except for the fact that it's your job, it's what you're there for. You're responsible, and if you have any integrity and care about your reputation, if you care about what you do, you want to be respected by your opponents. You want them to have to look over their shoulder at you. It comes down to what they do best, and what we do best. And, after you dump somebody on their back, you lift them up and slap on them on the back and say, "Nice play." The next time they're going to be looking for you and saying, "Where is he?"

The 1967 Trojans were one of the best teams ever, and we set the record for most first-round draft picks from any school in a single year. Ron Yary was the first pick by Minnesota. There was myself (Eagles), Earl McCullough (Lions), Mike Taylor (Steelers), and Mike Hull (Bears), plus Adrian Young was drafted by the Eagles like me. He was my best friend and cocaptain, but he was pissed off that I was chosen in the first round and he was not. I was 6'5" or 6'6", 220 or 225 pounds, but Adrian didn't have that kind of size.

I never lifted weights. We had a little weight room down in the bowels of the old gym. Bill Fisk was in there all the time. There was some Russian shot-putter who lifted weights there. All there was were a few barbells, a couple of dumbbells. Now they have million-dollar equipment.

We had great baseball teams at USC when I was there. Garrett played baseball with Bill "Spaceman" Lee and Tom Seaver. I didn't really know Spaceman all that well, but Seaver was my fraternity brother. He was one of the Sigma Chi crazy guys. God, he had such talent. He proved that in his pro career. Seaver was intelligent and had a good personality. He was fun to be around, and we were there to be the best we could be as athletes and as people. With the Mets, he had a reputation for his intellect, and he returned to USC every year for years until he finally graduated.

105

We beat Indiana in the 1968 Rose Bowl 14–3 to clinch the national title. It was as much a game of redemption as it was a game of glory because we'd lost to Purdue the year before, and of course I totally blame that on myself. The score was 14–13, and I'd missed a 47-yard field goal a little wide to the right. But those were the days of straight-on kickers, so it was a pretty good shot. We trailed 14–6 and scored in the last minute, and McKay went for two and the win instead of kicking for the tie. But we failed and lost to Bob Griese. McKay took my kicking shoe off my senior year.

Finishing No. 1 in 1967 was a double blessing. It had been a wonderful season until we went to Oregon State and played in the mud. Bill Enyart ran through us, and it poured rain. We lost 3–0. He was about a 260-pound fullback. O.J. was not a "mudder." He could not run in the mud. Somehow, some way, Enyart pounded close enough for a field goal, and we lost 3–0. Well, my God, we were fortunate because the other teams in the top 10 went down too, so it came down to UCLA and that memorable game. It was something for all of us to remember, for everything. It was so close.

Beban passed for 301 yards. I was right in his face but he still completed passes. He was a wonderful athlete. He didn't have the size or the arm for the NFL, but at the college level he was amazing.

Indiana played us in the Rose Bowl. They were coached by John Pont, and we handled them, 14–3. The Big Ten was going through a period in between the dominance of the 1940s and 1950s, and before the great rivalry of Woody Hayes at Ohio State and Bo Schembechler at Michigan. Our conference was better, and we demonstrated it. That game was a long time ago, but I know against Indiana we played good defense and pounded it out. That was our way, the way our guys did it. We only gave up 87 points all season. O.J. didn't need to do *all* that much. It was pretty much a defensive struggle. When you give up less than a touchdown a game, you're going to win most of them. Our only loss was 3–0. You'd think a national title team could muster more than that.

106

They call the years I was at the University of Southern California the "golden age" of USC, and also of Hollywood, of the city of Los Angeles. The Dodgers, Angels, and Lakers were all established by then. Movies transitioned from the old studio system, and some of the people most responsible for that were at USC then. Among them were George Lucas and John Milius, two brilliant filmmakers.

Over at UCLA, Francis Ford Coppola was in their film school with Jim Morrison and Ray Manzarek of The Doors. Steven Spielberg was hanging around with all these guys.

I knew Rod Dedeaux and his son, Justin, very well. Justin was a student and played on the baseball team. The Pittsburgh Pirates wanted to sign me out of high school, and every year Rod wanted me to come play baseball. I wanted to go to the beach and party, so I never did, but baseball was my favorite sport. I was better in baseball, but I knew if I went to the Pirates I'd be stuck in their farm system for years. I figured I'd be a "smart guy" and take a scholarship to college. It worked out; a national championship and 10 years in the National Football League.

I'm always asked about "setting myself on fire," which I did on the cover of *Sports Illustrated*. I had a cast on at the time. I'd hurt my knee and got the okay to use the Philadelphia Eagles' team jersey. NFL Films and Steve Sabol filmed me doing it, wearing the green jersey. I had a full wet cast.

To be honest, Sabol, who was living with me in an apartment complex, was a master manipulator. We just came up with this "Where are they now?" segment. He had me on his show, and I told him a story about being on fire. Gary Pettigrew, a defensive tackle, was with me, and I told the story about when I was at 'SC and they said we couldn't park in the parking lot. That upset me, so I turned over one car. The gas cap came off, and gas leaked out. Someone had been smoking a cigarette. Sabol was in the room and saw the fire. They had all these hoses out. I was naked, and I jumped through the flames, slipped, and fell. So I was in the fire and got burned a little bit, but I was fortunate I had no serious burns. They turned the hoses on me. I learned from that that I could burn a certain period of time before sustaining serious injury. The legend got around, and *Sports Illustrated* came around. They asked me if I'd light myself on fire. They said, "We'll put you on the cover." So I said okay.

I played for the Eagles and then San Diego, where I was a teammate of Mike Garrett, who had come back to pro football after taking time off to play professional baseball. Johnny Unitas and Dan Fouts were on the team with me.

107

The Trojans today I think are doing pretty well. My wife follows football much more than I do. Being a Trojan means, "Once a Trojan, always a Trojan." If they need me, I'm there for them. That's the feeling of respect John McKay and Marv Goux instilled in all their players. It's a family forever. It's about respect, and the experience to have gone there is one I cherish forever. After football, I had a 25-year acting career, and I did stunt work. Those were special years.

Tim Rossovich is one of the greatest college linemen of all time. A 1967 consensus All-America and All-AAWU selection, he was the cocaptain of the national championship team that defeated Indiana in the Rose Bowl. He played in the 1968 Coaches All-America Game and College All-Star Game. A recent inductee into the USC Athletic Hall of Fame, Tim was a first-round selection of the Philadelphia Eagles, playing in the NFL until 1976, before launching a long career as a Hollywood actor and stuntman.

RON YARY

OFFENSIVE/DEFENSIVE TACKLE
1965–1967

I PLAYED ONE SEMESTER AT Cerritos J.C. What attracted me to USC was that my coaches instructed me to go there. My high school coaches from Bell-flower directed me to go there. I didn't know USC from Johns Hopkins, but my coaches explained the tradition of USC.

Once there, incredible people surrounded me. Tim Rossovich's attitude was that he brought intensity and leadership. He was very intense, but off the field he knew how to have a lot of fun. He made you laugh.

Mike Battle was the same way—extremely intense and reckless on the field. *Off* the field, he was also very reckless and knew how to have fun. He played with reckless abandon.

Adrian Young was reckless on the field, too. You have to be completely reckless. I mean this completely. Let me put it to you this way: the only place I ever felt completely safe, where I knew I was safe, was being in the middle of the football field at game time. I was more at home there than sitting on my couch watching TV. I've never been anywhere or done anything else where I felt as centered as in the game of football. You have to be reckless, careless, and unconcerned of the consequences of what you do. You have to feel immortal, or you don't play up to your maximum ability.

Young was smart. He had decent size and good strength, but his smarts and field vision were assets. We were all smart, all of us were. One guard, Steve Lehmer, got a master's degree; another, Fred Khasigian, became an

Ron Yary (left) talks with coach John McKay and Nate Shaw during a December 13, 1966, practice before the Rose Bowl game against Purdue. Both players received second-team All-America honors by the AP.

orthopedic surgeon. Chuck Arrobio, our tackle, became a dentist. We had smart guys on our team plus some average students who were lucky to play at a great university. Mike Scarpace was a great lineman, too.

The 1967 team was special. Mike Battle was not a stupid guy, but some football players get trapped in childhood for life. It's a kid's game, and some don't mature and become fully adult for some time. You don't study, you're not mature, and you form bad personal habits off the field. Mike just took longer to adjust to life, that's all. He needed everything he had on the field to be great.

Blocking for O.J. Simpson was something you didn't appreciate until you played *against* him. I didn't get a chance to watch him run when I was blocking. You didn't keep your eyes on him, and of course my job was pretty much, in that era, making the holes for him to run through. We lived and died in a seven-hole system, not like runners today, where the hole develops as the line explodes. The running back runs to daylight. When we played the one-hole to the right of the center, 10 people were in there, and you had to dig them out. In the new era, if a guy's in the center, he'll be slanted; the guard stays with him.

The direction of the line was designed for O.J. Simpson. But he was restricted in his day by the holes in the blocking scheme. He was a runner with great athletic ability, but he didn't gain as many yards as he could have in a more wide-open modern offense. But he was an incredible running back, and once he was in the secondary, you knew he was going to get more than the average running back. It would take the defensive backs to chase him down.

In the 1977 Super Bowl, there were seven Trojans playing for the Oakland Raiders. Steve Riley and I were with Minnesota. The 1967 and 1972 Trojan national champions were almost the junior varsity squad for the 1976 world champion Raiders and NFC champion Vikings.

That said, I had no time to reminisce or look back at my college days. I was captured by that moment. I'd already lost three Super Bowls. In 1970 we'd lost to my teammate, Mike Garrett and Kansas City, and damned if we're going to lose another one. It was the hardest game I ever lost in my life. Losing to the Raiders really bothered me. It never stuck with me to lose most of the time because I played up to my ability. But that day, I was bothered because I was a four-time time Super Bowl loser [1970, Chiefs; 1974, Dolphins; 1975, Steelers; 1977, Raiders]. I didn't have time to look and reminisce, it was too intense a game. But in retrospect I became proud that so many USC players were Super Bowl champions.

110

Ron Yary is one of the greatest football players in American history. A two-time consensus All-American (1966–1967), he became Troy's (and the West Coast's) only recipient of the Outland Trophy in 1967, the year USC won John McKay's second national championship. He was a Playboy Preseason All-American in 1967 and a three-time all-conference first-teamer. He is a member of both the National Football Foundation College Hall of Fame and the USC Athletic Hall of Fame. In 1968 Yary was the number-one pick in the entire NFL draft, selected by Minnesota. USC's five first-rounders set the record for most first-round selections from one school in a single draft. He played for the Vikings (1968–1981) and the Rams (1982), participating in Super Bowls IV, VIII, IX, and XI. A perennial All-Pro tackle in Minnesota, Yary is a member of the Pro Football Hall of Fame in Canton, Ohio. His brother, Wayne, played football at USC from 1969 to 1970.

ADRIAN YOUNG

LINEBACKER

1965–1967

I WAS BORN IN DUBLIN, IRELAND. My parents are both full Irish. My father was a soccer fan. He worked for a paper mill in Ireland, where all the factories had mill teams. I rode a bike in Ireland and was 10 years old when I came to America.

My father came to America in 1953 and moved to Baltimore, where he lived with relatives and saved money. Then he sent money for my mom, my brother, and I. We came on a boat to New York, not unlike my countrymen who came to Ellis Island around the turn of the century. We stayed in Baltimore with relatives, but my father recognized that there was opportunity in California. The defense industry was booming, and there were many small machine shops that serviced the industry.

My father opened a machine business in the Norwalk area, but then we moved to La Puente, where I entered Bishop Amat High School. My freshman year, they moved back to the Norwalk area, to La Mirada, but I stayed at Bishop Amat as they had a great football program and excellent academics. Every day, I hitchhiked from La Mirada to La Puente. I'd hitchhike at Highway 39 and Whittier Boulevard, then hitchhike back. The whole time I played sports. My freshman year, I played basketball and ran track as well as football. I had an academic scholarship. So, even though it was very difficult, I was determined to stay at Bishop Amat.

I fell in love with football and decided after my first year that it was my main interest. Oh, boy, was I happy when I was finally old enough to get a car to drive to school and back. I graduated from Bishop Amat in 1964. My coach was Phil Cantwell. Later Marv Marinovich's brother, Gary, became the coach there, and he coached J.K. McKay, Pat Haden, and Paul McDonald.

Even though I was Irish, my family had never really heard of Notre Dame. I had no frame of reference on the difference between Notre Dame and USC, and I didn't even know what football was at first. But I became well acquainted with the game at Bishop Amat, plus I had good grades and could go anywhere I wanted.

I understood discipline. Catholic schools would pit ethnics against each other, like Italians versus Irish. At St. Canisius in Dublin, where I'd gone before coming to America, the priests wore a leather belt as part of their wardrobes, and they'd take that belt out and whack you with it for talking. They were tough guys, and you grew up a tough guy in that environment.

Our uniforms at Bishop Amat were based on the Notre Dame style, and Coach Cantwell had played for Frank Leahy at Notre Dame. It's been asked of me many times, why would I pick USC despite so many things in my life pushing me to Notre Dame? It wasn't really the sunny climate that I had gotten used to in Southern California. Rather, I just remember going to the Coliseum, and the horse was circling the field. My brother at the time was at UCLA, and I'd been there, but I was attracted to 'SC's style, the projection of their image.

112

As a kid from a poor background, you learned so much at USC. Across the hall from you might be the son of a famous Hollywood entrepreneur, but we were all in it together, we all belonged. It was USC. Sometimes, only people who have been through it can relate to it.

At USC, you are comfortable around wealth, and you are in an arena where expectations are tremendous. People you live with expect big things from you. You have peers who went through this experience with you, and they all have high expectations. So, during that time, when many are grasping for what they will be in life, at a place like USC you gain a sense of confidence in yourself. It was a nice setting. People have always said it's a bad neighborhood, but living in a gritty urban setting, and it was more so then than today, this was part of the overall education experience. It made for a more well-rounded life experience than if you attended college in a rural farm setting.

The football team had really impressed me. They had guys like Damon Bame, Pete Beathard, Hal Bedsole, Ben Wilson; those guys were incredible. Your dream is some day to participate at that level. USC had won the national championship in 1962, so there was an expectation coming in that we would do something like that. But we met with some disappointment, and when my senior year [1967] rolled round, it was the last chance for a lot of us.

O.J. Simpson had transferred in from City College of San Francisco, and when the season started, it was immediately obvious that we were a definite contender for the title. When we traveled to Notre Dame in October, the game had every possible ramification attached to it.

This is the game that everybody associates me with, on many levels, not the least of which was my Irish ancestry, and I've been asked many times what we did on defense that week. I was a linebacker. That week, Tim Rossovich and Jimmy Gunn, who were defensive ends, brought additional pressure from outside, similar to what the modern New England Patriots do with their 3-4 defense. So we ended up having an outside linebacker become a stand-up linebacker, and this placed more pressure on their quarterback, Terry Hanratty.

He was obviously confused. We dropped one weak end, Gunn, so my drop went to the center of the field. When they tried to hit crossing patterns, I had quick feet and could really run backward. I was like a rover. This was a hybrid between a linebacker and safety, and it was only then becoming common in football. You saw it with George Webster at Michigan State, and a guy like Rossovich, despite being 6'5", 235 pounds, was fast and agile enough to cross over and handle some of those hybrid responsibilities. We did this, it wreaked havoc on offenses and had Hanratty utterly confused.

We had big guys as strong safeties and defensive ends who became rover backs. The athleticism of the game was changing. My great strength was speed and good hands. I was a student of the game and took a liking to the chess aspect of football.

Coach McKay gave me lot of latitude, so I could audible, I could call blitzes if we went to the strong side but they went to the sideline, and I could go the opposite way. Instead of the weak side, we could go to the opposite side of the field if the opponent went from one side to the strong side. That was the joy of football for me.

If you look at that game, Hanratty was constantly coming off the field, shaking his head, waving his hands at Coach Ara Parseghian, asking for help because he did not know how to handle our defense.

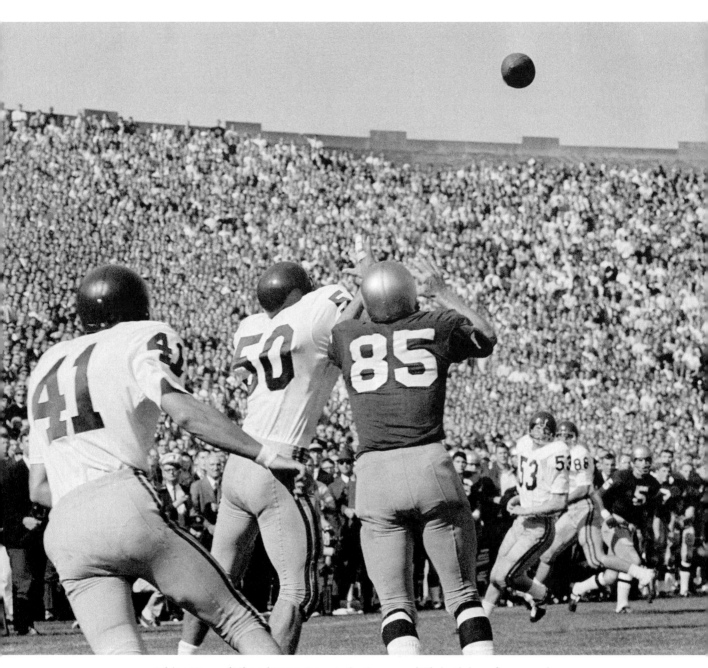

Adrian Young (50) and Notre Dame's Jim Seymour (85), both leap for a pass by Fighting Irish quarterback Terry Hanratty (5), in the second quarter of the October 1967 game in South Bend. Young intercepted the pass on the 6-yard line.

In 1967 we really kind of put USC on the path to what they became, what they are now. We brought in some great assistant coaches around that time. Mike Giddings left to go to Utah or Utah State, then Dick Coury came in from Mater Dei, and with him started that Mater Dei connection. We already had a Bishop Amat connection. It was important for McKay to get the best players from Catholic programs in Southern California, to deny Notre Dame this talent pipeline.

Coach Coury had a sharp eye and noticed that UCLA's Zenon Andrusyshyn was a soccer-style place-kicker. Coury put Bill Hayhoe in front of him, and Zenon's kicks kept getting blocked, and that was the difference in a 21–20 win for us.

That Bruin game of 1967, the backdrop was that it was a great opportunity for us, because we had lost at Corvallis [Oregon State], in the rain and mud, the previous week, 3–0. We had landed in Corvallis on a Thursday or Friday and went straight to the field. It was raining cats and dogs, and you could tell McKay knew we were in trouble. Our strength was our ground game. O.J. was incredible, but they responded with a fullback named Bill Enyart who pounded away at us all day long. They kicked a field goal and beat us 3–0. To this day, I dispute that field goal. It was raining hard and not easy to see, and that referee put his hands up early. The NBC announcers all had angles questioning it, but it counted.

115

I don't think we lost to Oregon State because we were looking ahead to UCLA. They were just a good team that beat us on a muddy day. O.J. had a good day, but we just could not score. But I said after that game that we get to play UCLA, we get to play a team that's ranked No. 1, and if we win, we could be No. 1. It was almost a relief to have our destiny still in our hands. Plus so much else was riding on that game: the conference title, the Rose Bowl, the Heisman Trophy between O.J. and Gary Beban, and the usual bragging rights in Los Angeles.

This is one of those games, like the 1966 "Game of the Century" between Notre Dame and Michigan State, or the 1969 Texas-Arkansas game that redefined college football. Color television was becoming pretty regular, and this made the games a brilliant kaleidoscope, a pageant. Old-school announcers like Bud Wilkinson were fading out and being replaced by guys who would become synonymous as the "voices" of college football, guys like Chris Schenkel, who'd say, "And here come the Trojans," or Keith Jackson.

The country got a full dose of California sunshine, and the USC–UCLA game had the added attraction of both teams wearing home colors, which made it brighter. And that was the first year we had song girls because a wealthy donor, who'd refused to give to the school if we had females on the field other than in the marching band, died that year.

I think that game was pretty even. Some have said UCLA outplayed us, but we benefited from Beban's not being 100 percent. He had sore ribs and had to leave after I tackled him. He came off the field, and after O.J.'s touchdown put us ahead, he was not at 100 percent to lead a comeback drive.

To this day, I'm a hated guy over in Westwood because I tackled Beban and he got hurt. Once I was introduced to a woman, and when she heard my name, she just turned away from me and called me a dirty SOB. But like the tackle made by one of the McKeever twins against Mike Bates of Cal back in 1959—McKeever was exonerated when Cal *sued*, if you can believe it, and the tape showed it was legit—mine was a clean hit, it was just part of the game, and that's the truth.

We won, and that was what propelled us to the national title, but Beban was voted the Heisman. At the time, I thought it was wrong. Politics plays a part in what happens. Frankly, I was an All-American, but others were as good. But I was on the right team with good PR. My focus was always on the enjoyment of the game, playing the game for the thrill of it.

What does it mean to be a Trojan? Well, Marv Goux is as good an example of what this means as anybody. I don't recall all the specifics, but after the final practice of the week, we'd gather in the old physical education building. This place would have an echo—the ceiling was no more than eight feet high—and the band would be crowded down there, and it was an electric feeling in the old "dungeon." Marv would give his pep talk, and he'd say that we'll rape, pillage, take no prisoners, steal their confidence, don't let them in our territory.

Yet Marv was a sweetheart, the real deal, and very emotional. There were these racquetball courts, and I recall that I tried to play for my footwork. Marv would play, I can't recall against whom. If you were one of Marv's guys, he'd invite you in. Marv had this rubber suit, but after playing him, I knew it was not to sweat in but rather to withstand the power of the balls these guys would drive against each other. He was friendly, but when business was at hand and the battle was to be won, there was no messing around with Marv Goux. But away from that, he was a real nice guy.

The period I was at USC, the mid-1960s, was considered a golden era in so many ways. First, it was the middle of the greatest period of athletic dominance, under two athletic directors—Jess Hill and later John McKay—in the history of college sports. The football team was the best in the nation. The Trojans dominated everything: baseball, tennis, track, swimming, you name it. This was the era of the Bruins-Trojans basketball rivalry when Lew Alcindor was at UCLA. UCLA was at its peak in football, so the rivalry between the two schools has never been more intense. It was a time when USC and UCLA represented social progress when much of America was still segregated.

The 1960s saw the rise of California as an electoral juggernaut, the rise of Richard Nixon and Ronald Reagan. A lot of USC guys were with Nixon, and many of them later went down with Watergate. There was a huge military-industrial complex in Los Angeles and a population explosion that made L.A. bigger than Chicago. It was the '60s, the politics of the era, the "Summer of Love," rock music, and a big decade for Hollywood. USC's film school got hot, and I was there with George Lucas, John Milius, and Tom Selleck, among many others.

Tom Seaver was a baseball player at USC at the time. He was a Sigma Chi, and I spent a lot time over there. I knew him socially. He was friendly, a little cocky, plus he was a baseball player who was as tough as a football player. He had great big legs and the body of a running back or tight end, and he liked to project himself as a tough guy. There were a lot of baseball/football guys, like Mike Garrett, who was good friends with Seaver. They'd hang out together, and with Justin Dedeaux. His dad, Rod Dedeaux, was the baseball coach, and I thought he was a motivator. While I knew him, I knew his daughter better, she married my agent, who was also my business law proctor, which tells you a lot about how the agent's profession has changed. Dedeaux had a winning persona. He and McKay were drinking buddies.

McKay was a wit but kept his distance. He had his reasons. He hired Goux to get involved with guys. He was like the CEO of a corporation, looking at the macro, not the micro. My nickname was "Ado," and McKay called me that. It's hard to explain, but when we played Notre Dame, he had a way of gauging our intensity and preparation. McKay picked captains. The players voted on captains, but each week McKay picked captains for that week, and he chose me before the Notre Dame game. During pregame warm-ups, he was watching us closely. Back in the locker room, he quietly approached me

117

and said, "Ado, we're beaten already." I was the quasi-leader already, and he said, "I want the two captains, you and other guy, to speak to the team because this locker room is dead."

It's a challenging environment in South Bend. We had not beaten them there since 1939, plus we'd lost 51–0 in 1966. I gave a talk. I sensed that McKay wanted something extra from me, that this was a game he really and truly wanted above all others. He stood back, and I spoke. We had played there two years before in 1965, and they beat us. Toward the end, their fans waved handkerchiefs at us, mocking us as we left the field in defeat. I said this time it would be different. I had to wipe tears out of my eyes—it was emotional and apparently set just the right tone for that team. But it was McKay's intuitive ability to sense when something like that was needed that made him a special coach, because he did not usually call for that sort of thing.

What I liked about McKay was that he did not just think hard work all week would get us in, but he was sensitive to the team's emotions. What I remember about that 51–0 game was McKay went for it on fourth down even with the game gone. McKay created an environment where winning was the only option. We lost 51–0 because he never stopped trying to win. You never killed him. He never admitted he'd lost. It was like *Braveheart*, like some Gaelic fighter, noble in a lost cause, fighting like Trojans, and this was what it means to be a Trojan. After we lost 14–13 to Purdue, after missing a two-point conversion in the 1967 Rose Bowl, he was asked if he was upset about going for two. He said that we came to win. When we beat Indiana 14–3 a year later in the Rose Bowl to capture the national championship, he said, "The point of the game's to win, isn't it?"

The losses to Notre Dame and Purdue sowed the seeds for the greatness of 1967. I distinctly recall McKay never played for ratings. Ara Parseghian was running draws in the fourth quarter to kill the clock and protect his ratings, but not McKay.

O.J. Simpson had the most incredible ability to change gears, and his work ethic was excellent, on par with Garrett's. Garrett was a hard worker at practice, he was inspirational. I was a freshman, and Garrett was the running back on the varsity, and every time he took handoffs, he would run 45 yards extra, and this became a tradition. You said, "Do that, no excuses." And O.J. followed that.

O.J. was strong, with strong hips and legs more so than a really big upper body. He could turn and go any direction and knock over a defender, or glance off them like Jim Brown, whose ability he had. The '67 team had swagger all around because we worked every practice as hard as we could. When I was a sophomore, that team was as good but lacked the work ethic of my senior year. That team worked as hard as Coach Goux would push them, and it was most inspiring.

That 1967 team was inspired. An example was Pat Cashman. At the end of the year, he was hurt and told not to run sprints, but he said, "I want to run." He then intercepted an important pass against Beban. That spirit was why that team excelled. We had the proper chemistry, and the whole team had respect for each other.

Over the years, being a Trojan put an indelible mark on me, to have been willing to take on the challenge of going to USC. Being first-rate enough to differentiate myself in some respect gives me confidence that it if I put myself in the right place with the right people, I will have success.

Finally, having come here from Ireland, I have a special understanding of what it means to be an American. I came here with my folks when I was in the fifth or sixth grade. My brother has a PhD now, I became an All-American and an entrepreneur, and I wore shorts when I got here. The opportunities in the United States are great for those willing to take on the challenge to be great. I owe so much to this country and to my alma mater.

119

Adrian Young was a consensus All-American, all-conference linebacker, and member of the 1967 national champion Trojans. His four interceptions in the 24–7 victory over Notre Dame made him a bona fide legend and spurred Troy to its first victory in South Bend since 1939. He was team captain and voted the Davis-Teschke Award for most inspirational player as a senior, playing in the 1968 Coaches All-America Game, College All-Star Game, and Hula Bowl. Drafted by the Eagles, Young played for Philadelphia, Detroit, and Chicago in the NFL from 1968 to 1973.

MIKE BATTLE

DEFENSIVE HALFBACK

1966–1968

My Uncle Art played for the Trojans. He was from Huntington Park, where Craig Fertig's dad was chief of police. I grew up in El Segundo, where the Obradoviches and the Bretts—Ken and George—lived, then moved to Lawndale where I was pals with Fred Dryer. He graduated the year I came in, but I played against him in junior college when I was at Long Beach City and he was at El Camino. He's a crazy guy, too. Once in New York, we both got in a mess of trouble that can't be retold. He hung out at the Playboy Mansion with Hugh Hefner and that Hollywood crowd.

Back then, Lawndale was thought of as near the beach, the South Bay. It was next to Hawthorne where the Beach Boys grew up. Mike Gillespie, later the baseball coach at USC, went to Hawthorne High with those guys.

I played in 1966, 1967, and 1968. O.J. Simpson was my teammate for the last two years. His athletic talents were unreal. He was the first back who was that big and fast, and moved with power and speed. He could run 9.7 in tennis shoes, plus he possessed the wisdom of the game when he was a player.

Tim Rossovich and I roomed together. We had a house off frat row, 32nd Street or some place. We'd go to the beach or to the Colorado River all the time. We'd go with these groups, and these people owned places at Tahoe. I'd go up there. These kids all came from wealthy families. Tim's family had a little money. I didn't have a pot to piss in, but I'd go along for the ride.

Safety Mike Battle (17) hauls down fullback Ron Dushney (38) of Notre Dame with a textbook tackle late in the game on November 30, 1968, in Los Angeles, which ended in a 21–21 tie. The Trojans stopped the Irish from penetrating deep enough for a field-goal attempt to break the tie.

It's hard to talk about John McKay. He was really funny when he did interviews, but he was deadly serious when he talked to you. He hardly said a word to me in three years. He wanted to know if you were hurt or not. I was only out a couple plays in three years. I had a bad bruise on my thigh, and when it happened, I came out and he asked me when I could come back in. I only missed two plays and was back in. That was the only time I missed in three years.

Marv Goux was something else, man. We played in all the Rose Bowl games, and his birthday was always that week. He'd do one-arm push-ups for every year of his life on his birthday. When we played for the national title for the second-straight time in 1969, he did one for each of his 36 years.

Goux was a tough guy—I wouldn't be scared to fight him, but he had the respect. Some guys didn't like his kind of BS. There's the story of Greg Slough, who'd been in the Special Forces in 'Nam before 'SC, and he just looked at Goux like, *I killed V.C., don't touch me.* Things have changed. Now, if you bruise your pinkie, you're out two weeks.

Toby Page was a good quarterback, but like everybody he was always getting hurt. We had to switch around all the time, and nobody got too much time. It was Steve Sogge and Page, but neither established full control.

122

Mike Holmgren was a sophomore and a great guy coming up. He knew what he was doing, and you knew he'd do something with football. At scrimmages or team meetings, he'd be the other team's first-team QB, so the defense would go against him. He always had a clipboard in his right hand and was writing things down, studying the game. Mike was a great guy, but he didn't want to be hit too much. He was perfectly suited for coaching and won a Super Bowl at Green Bay.

Coach Rod Dedeaux called me "Tiger." He wanted me to play center field. It was no big deal to me. I'd played some baseball in high school, but I loved football too much.

We lost 3–0 in the mud at Oregon State in 1967. Oregon State slowed it down, but I didn't think their field goal was good. But "Earthquake Bill" Enyart had a good game. The grass was six inches tall, and we slipped and slid and lost, but we beat UCLA 21–20 to propel us to the national championship. They were *really good!* That George Farmer kid got behind me for six. I couldn't believe he could run that fast. Gary Beban was great. We were lucky to get out of there alive.

If O.J. had not had a bad game, we'd have won a second-straight national title in 1968. But he lost three fumbles in the loss to Ohio State at the Rose Bowl. The 1968 team had a lot of people talking dynasty and "all-time this" and "best ever" that, at least until the Rose Bowl defeat. But I think the '67 team was better. I was on the defense, and we only allowed 87 points all season.

The social scene at USC was great. I had the best time of my life going to parties, hanging out at the beach. It was during a time when everybody was part of this revolution. We didn't have any hippies on our team, but we did a lot of beach stuff, partied, and had a great time. It was the most fun I ever had. I'd rather play 30 years of college than one year of pro football.

I played with Joe Willie Namath and the New York Jets. He was a good guy and the smartest quarterback I've ever been around. He studied and knew defenses and could read the second, third, and fourth man as well as any quarterback I've ever seen. The man was good, and his legend off the field is real. I hung out with him at Bachelor's III in Manhattan, and it was a wild scene, man.

Tom Seaver was a Trojan who was a big New York icon, too, but he wasn't part of that Big Apple party scene. I played golf with his dad once at La Costa. He was a great guy and a world-class golfer. Frank Gifford was a man about town in New York, as well.

Craig Fertig's a great guy, and he tells all these stories, but I would not want them printed. Hid dad, the chief of police, got me out of jail one time.

The appropriately named Mike Battle may be the epitome of the Marv Goux–type of hard-nosed Trojan football player. At 6'1", 175 pounds, he attacked football and life with ferocity. Battle set numerous records for interceptions and punt returns, made All-AAWU, and earned 1968 All-America honors. He was a member of the 1967 national champions and played in three straight Rose Bowls before spending two seasons with the New York Jets. His uncle, Art Battle, lettered in 1946 and from 1948 to 1949.

STEVE SOGGE

QUARTERBACK

1967–1968

I CAME TO USC FROM GARDENA HIGH SCHOOL. Toby Page and I played together. When he was a senior, I was a junior. I started most of 1967. Toby got hurt in the first game of the year. It was unfortunate for him, but fortunate for me that I had a chance to play.

O.J. Simpson was our star tailback both years. At times I thought they should charge me admission just for the pleasure of having him in the backfield to hand off to, or pitch or throw to him. He was a phenomenal athlete and the hardest-working player I ever played with. He certainly made my job easier than it would have been without him.

We played Ohio State in the 1969 Rose Bowl with a chance to get back-to-back national championships. It was one of the most ballyhooed games in college football history and is still shown regularly on the classic college football station. It's one of the all-time most famous games ever.

They were outstanding, and we were not overconfident. Most of our games were not outright blowouts. We went down to the wire in most of them. Anybody who played for John McKay played their hardest all the time. It was not a letdown. One team has the edge, then the other team adjusts and counters the initial advantages, and realistically at the end of the game, the best team usually wins. They had a great team and played better than we did, winning 27–16 to finish No. 1.

Steve Sogge quarterbacked the Trojans to the No. 1 ranking among the nation's college football teams on November 6, 1968. He called a key fourth-down play—a pass instead of an expected run up the middle—that carried USC to a last minute 20–13 victory over Oregon a week earlier.

125

I never watched Woody Hayes on their sideline. I didn't know him at all. My only memory of him was at the kickoff dinner, where he spoke. I'd describe him as a unique personality and quite a history buff, a real World War II guy who coached football like George Patton directed military tactics. He had interesting stories and would have been an interesting guy to play for. McKay was a great football coach who got the best out of his players. He was extremely disciplined and knew what he wanted. He expected everybody to do their best at all times.

McKay and Woody were similarly conservative, although McKay was a little less rigid in terms of off-field behavior—haircuts, opinions, and the like. Woody used the regional dissimilarities between Ohio and California as a motivational tool. He built California, and us, I guess, as a symbol of New Age laxness, antiwar unpatriotism, "softness," and such. But in truth USC was not a hotbed of protest over Vietnam, and we were every bit as tough in football.

I had a good baseball career at Southern Cal and played with fantastic players. In 1968 we won the College World Series. We had lost the College World Series semifinal in 1966 to Ohio State 1–0. Tom Seaver signed with the Mets and was not with us, so that might have made a difference.

I caught Bill "Spaceman" Lee. What can I say about Spaceman? In summary, there wasn't anything he'd do that would surprise anybody. At one point I think he disappeared a couple days and showed back up. He was a unique individual with great confidence in his pitching ability. He had absolute faith that any pitch he'd throw on any given count, any given pitch to any given hitter, would be a strike and would get the batter out.

People talk of Spaceman as this crazy character, but he was very disciplined and knew what pitches he wanted to throw. Nothing I recall ever bothered him because of his confidence, his belief in his ability to pitch no matter how tight the situation.

He had the ability not to be too tense. He was never overstressed on the mound, which is a true advantage. He had the stuff to get anybody out at any given time. He'd throw a three-two curveball and not worry about it being a ball. He'd throw it for a strike.

He once said, "The three best teams I've ever seen were the 1975 Cincinnati Reds, the 1968 USC Trojans, and any Taiwan little league team." This was a testament to Rod Dedeaux, because our teams had talent, but we had the discipline of those Taiwan teams. That's how we played the game.

We were always in the College World Series finals with great teams. It led off with Rod, of course. He was probably the best psychological manager or coach I ever had the opportunity to play for. His ability to convince you no one would ever beat you was such that all we had to do was go out and play the game. Until the final pitch was thrown, we believed we'd win any game. There'd be two outs in the bottom of the ninth, and he'd say, "We're still in this thing." He was the leader of our team and had all of us convinced that nobody could beat us. We had some really good athletes, but I wouldn't say we were so much better athletically than everybody. We had a stronger belief that we'd find a way, somehow, to win the game.

126

Tom Seaver was my teammate but not for a full season. I was a freshman in 1965 when he was a sophomore. He was 10–2 with a 2.47 earned-run average and established himself as one of the best prospects in the nation. I caught him with the Alaska Goldpanners, where he had the reputation of being an elite pitcher.

When I was a sophomore, I caught him in the early part of the season. It was the first or second year of the winter draft, and the rules were different. Atlanta drafted him, and he decided to sign in January or February, and forego the college season. But it violated NCAA rules, and the signing was disallowed. He was no longer considered an amateur and was unable to come back and play for us, so he ended up going to the Mets, and the rest is history. But had he been with us, it might have made the difference since we lost the semifinal game by one run.

Tom was different than Lee, who was more a finesse pitcher. Seaver was more overpowering, with great stuff. He threw what we call a "heavy ball" that had great movement on his fastball with control. But it beat my hand to death. He had phenomenal stuff. I was almost glad he'd signed because it was so hard to catch him.

After USC, I signed with the Los Angeles Dodgers and was in the minor leagues with that group of guys Tommy Lasorda nurtured from Ogden to Spokane to L.A. I was with Lasorda in Spokane. There's only so much I can say on the record about Tommy. I played with Steve Garvey, Ron Cey, Bill Russell, Davey Lopes, Steve Yeager, Joe Ferguson, Bobby Valentine, and Bill Buckner; all those guys were similar. Some of the farm clubs Tommy managed with that group are among the best teams in the history of minor league baseball and formed the core of Dodgers teams that won four National League pennants and a World Series.

Rod was close friends with Tommy. They hung out together a lot. Tommy had a great personality, he was funny, and he knew the game. He'd keep you loose in the dugout as well. Practicing, he'd say, "You guys make good money but not much of it, but it's all good."

I can't overstate the role of USC in my life. That experience in school, opportunities I had, winning two national championships, in baseball and football—I was on a team and have lifelong memories that I will carry with me for all time. I learned a work ethic, I learned confidence, and my confidence grew. I grew up in an athletic environment where you learn that, just because it's tough, it doesn't mean you won't win. It's not just the memories, it's my self-worth, my ethics, my confidence, and belief in myself. These are the intangibles of a college education. It's great, but in true-life scenarios, there are plusses you pick up from the experience.

I was fortunate to play for two outstanding coaches, Rod Dedeaux and John McKay. I learned different things from both of them, and these are life-long lessons.

Quarterback Steve Sogge played for the 1967 national champions and was the team captain in his senior year (1968). He was all-conference, won the Trojan Club Award (for most improved player), the Davis-Teschke Award (for most inspirational), the Howard Jones/Football Alumni Club award (for the senior player with the highest grade-point average), and was a two-time Academic All-American. He was also selected to the Hula Bowl. A star for coach Rod Dedeaux's baseball team, Sogge caught two future big leaguers, Tom Seaver and Bill "Spaceman" Lee, and was a member of the 1968 College World Series winners. Sogge played in the Los Angeles Dodgers organization.

JOHN McKAY

HEAD COACH

1960–1975

COACHES ARE DIFFERENT TODAY than in my day. You don't see as many Bobby Knight types today. I like Bobby personally. I know him through [former USC basketball coach] Bob Boyd, and we're friends. When USC hires a football coach, his record the first two years is favorably compared to my losing record in 1960–1961, yet they never live up to what I accomplished after that.

What people forget is that we had a losing record for most of the six seasons before I got there, plus we were on probation my first two years, so it's hard to get guys steamed up. We just didn't have enough speed. USC had been penalized by the NCAA in the wake of a conference-wide recruiting scandal dating back to Jon Arnett's career in the mid-1950s. Even USC's national-best 1959 baseball team was banned from postseason play.

My strategy was to recruit great athletes, regardless of position. I respect high school coaches, who know that the best athlete on the team is usually the quarterback. It's similar to youth league baseball, where the best athlete is usually the pitcher. Bobby Chandler was a quarterback in high school. Hal Bedsole was a junior college quarterback. Lynn Swann and Anthony Davis were high school quarterbacks.

Applying this philosophy to linemen, who because of their size don't play skill positions, we looked for guys who could run, cover kicks, and had the ambition to do those things. Linemen were not as big then. Now I see some fat guys playing. Ron Yary would be just as good today, given training techniques. Weight training was not the thing to do. Billy Fisk was an All-American lineman who played at 245 pounds, but most linemen were 235. Tom Seaver was a baseball Trojan who was one of the first to lift weights, back in the 1960s.

We won the national championship in 1962 alternating quarterbacks. In general I don't favor the practice, but we had three "teams." Pete Beathard went both ways. Bill Nelsen ran the "gold" team, and Craig Fertig was on the third team. That was a special season; we beat Notre Dame 25–0.

We beat Wisconsin in a wild Rose Bowl. We were up 42–14, but Marv Marinovich got kicked out for punching a guy and Gary Kirner wasn't suited up. We lost all our tackles, had guards playing tackle, so we couldn't rush the passer, and Ron Vander Kelen just sat back there and passed. Willie Brown saved us with an interception at the end. He never got the publicity he should get. Vander Kelen was the MVP and set the Rose Bowl passing yardage record, but never did much past that game. Brown played for the Rams and the Eagles.

Some players and others have said that, given almost unlimited scholarships, USC could recruit so many great players that our bench guys were better than most teams they played, and that you would recruit a player for the sole purpose of keeping him off a rival's roster. I've said it a million times, that's baloney. The budget was for 100 scholarships, and I never used more than 72. I allocated the rest for baseball and track. I recruited Mike Holmgren, who sat on the bench for four years, but it was never my intent to do that. No kid will come to school just to ride the bench, the excitement is to play. Jim Fassel, who coached with the New York Giants, sat on the bench before transferring to Long Beach State.

One of the things we did was nullify Notre Dame's recruiting advantage with Catholic schools in California. After John Huarte and Jack Snow came out of Mater Dei in Santa Ana and St. Anthony's of Long Beach, I hired Dick Coury from Mater Dei. He brought in a lot of players, including Toby Page. After that we brought in guys from Bishop Amat in La Puente and Serra High in the Bay Area.

Bishop Amat High School was the best program in the state in the 1960s. Adrian Young, Pat Haden, and John Sciarra played there. My son, J.K. McKay, played there, and later Paul McDonald was their quarterback. Bishop Amat was great, they had very good teams, and some of the best high school

John McKay took over as coach in 1960 and orchestrated a 20-year era of Trojan dominance.

passing teams ever. Phil Cantwell and later Marv Marinovich's brother, Gary, coached them.

There was a charisma at USC. Rod Dedeaux was my buddy. We both got along with the kids and liked to have a good time. He had a gregarious personality, a sense of humor, and I got along well with him. We both got along well with the press.

When we lost to Notre Dame 51–0 in 1966, I told the team to take their showers, that "a billion Chinese don't care if we win or lose." The next day I got two wires from China asking for the score. I guess Chairman Mao was taking a break from the cultural revolution, which started that year, 1966.

Pat Haden was the best prep quarterback in America. His father was transferred to San Francisco, but he wanted to keep throwing to my son his senior year at Bishop Amat. He moved into my home, which made it hard on recruiters from Stanford and Notre Dame. I thought we had a good advantage. We were close with the Hadens, and later my son, Richie, was going to stay with the Hadens instead of transferring when we moved to Florida. Haden was a great player in college and an accurate passer in the pros. He's a very intelligent guy.

At 5′11″ he was considered too short to be a successful pro quarterback, but that's a bunch of baloney. Doug Flutie proved that wrong, too. Fran Tarkenton's not 6′ tall. You throw passes through the creases, not over linemen. The same is said of wide receivers, yet Lynn Swann never had a problem at 5′11″.

We had some players who had a reputation for being kind of crazy. Fred Dryer once said he heard Mike Battle was institutionalized. Tim Rossovich was once featured in *Sports Illustrated* eating glass and setting himself on fire.

Well, Fred has a sense of humor. I heard Battle was married, but I don't know. I don't really know what was up with Rossovich. Once I was called to his dorm because he had mooned some girl, but then I found out the girl mooned him first. Neither one was ever arrested, and they were both fine players.

It broke my heart when the O.J. Simpson case hit the news. I still don't know what happened with O.J. I do know this: the guy I knew, and the other players knew, never would have done anything like that. It was just terrible; he was one of the most admired guys in America.

The 1974 USC–Notre Dame game might have been the greatest, most exciting sporting event in L.A. history. Fifty-five points in 17 minutes against Notre Dame. I've been asked to what extent do I feel that the hand of God just controlled my team's destiny, and to what extent did I think I controlled the outcome of that game. All I can say is, if I was in control, we'd have scored more than six points in the first half. I have no idea what happened, it was the damnedest thing I ever saw. I did tell the team at halftime that A.D. [Anthony Davis] would return the second half kick for a touchdown, and we were going to win that game.

Ara Parseghian must wake up in a cold sweat thinking about it. Ara never coached again. I hear from Ara every once in a while, but I try to be kind about reminding him. I'd made a vow after the 1966 Notre Dame debacle. I told the press we'd never lose 51–0 again, but over time it was changed to "We'll never lose to Notre Dame again." We almost never did.

Regarding college football dynasties, you have Knute Rockne, Notre Dame, 1920s. Howard Jones, USC's Thundering Herd in the '30s. Bud Wilkinson, Oklahoma, 1950s. In recent years, Miami dominated the 1980s, and now we are seeing the Bobby Bowden era at Florida State. Still, many believe that Trojan football from 1962 to 1982, which encompasses my tenure and John Robinson's, and includes four Heisman Trophy winners ending with Marcus Allen, is the greatest era of dominance in history. Well, I guess that's true or close to being true. At least we never had a player go to jail. We did have very good players.

I want to say something about the academic accomplishments of our players. Jealousy caused our detractors to say we did not have student-athletes, but that's baloney. Let me talk more about Pat Haden, a Rhodes Scholar; Bill Bradley, another Rhodes Scholar, and a future politician. Pat Haden's a wonderful young man whom I never had to worry about. In all honesty, Bill

Nelsen, Craig Fertig, Mike Rae, Vince Evans, et cetera, we never had anybody who was trouble. They were all smart guys. Haden went to law school,
but he was never really a political person. Bradley, too, he's a quiet guy. You
have to wave your arms around and pound the table to be heard in politics.

My son, J.K., went into law and practiced at a big L.A. firm, as did Haden.
J.K. went to Stetson Law School and practiced a few years. Now he's in Beverly Hills, and he works with Ed Roski's company. He was involved trying
to get a professional football team in Los Angeles. It's a tragedy that they don't
have one. J.K. played for me with the Tampa Bay Buccaneers.

I'm often asked, "What is the greatest college football team, for a single
season, of all time?" The answer to that is easy: the 1972 USC Trojans.

Jim Murray is the greatest writer of all time. I had good relations with
journalists. One of the greatest writers in the Los Angeles press corps was
Bud Furillo. Bud and I were friends. He was around a long time, with the
Herald and all over. Furillo may be, now that Murray has passed on, the man
who has seen it all longer than anybody else in L.A. Mal Florence was a Trojan and a good writer, a friend with great knowledge. John Hall of the *L.A.
Times* was another great guy. I never knew Bob Oates that well because he
covered pro football. Jim Perry was USC's former sports information director. He and I wrote a book together, *McKay: A Coach's Story*.

In 1976 I left 'SC and took the Tampa Bay job. Before free agency, it was
harder to build an expansion team quickly in those days. The team started off
with 26 consecutive losses. Do I have regrets? Yes. When I assembled the
team and got my first look at them, I knew I'd made a mistake. I said something like, "We stunk and then it got worse." Somebody asked me what I
thought of my team's execution, and I replied, "That's a good idea." However, we were the fastest expansion team to make the playoffs in 1979, and
we made it three times.

I consider myself a Trojan for life. I still follow them on TV. The best part
of my life was being a Trojan. We would walk through campus to go to
lunch, and you could just feel the great atmosphere, everybody was electric.
That's something I'll always miss.

In 2000 USC was named College of the Year by the *Princeton Review*, and
our school is really involved in a positive way in the surrounding community
near campus. What people don't realize is that, with all those riots that have
occurred all around that neighborhood, nobody ever touched the university,
because people there know what the university means to the area. I stayed in

touch with athletic director and former Heisman Trophy winner Mike Garrett. I heard from Garrett recently about a reunion of the 1974 team.

I was close with Paul Bryant. I want to touch on the role that the 1970 USC-Alabama game played in civil rights progress. I heard Reggie Jackson tell a story about how he knew the South would integrate. He played for the Athletics' Birmingham farm club in 1967, and Charlie O. Finley brought Paul into the clubhouse. Paul met Jackson, who had played football at Arizona State, and told him he was the kind of player he could use. Fast-forward three years. Sam "Bam" Cunningham scored four touchdowns in our 42–21 victory at Birmingham.

Cunningham was black. Alabama was still all-white. Paul Bryant came into our locker room and asked if he could borrow Cunningham. I said sure. He took him into the Alabama locker room and had him shake hands with each player, and he introduced him by saying, "Fellas, this is what a football player looks like." Bryant always said Cunningham did more to integrate the South than any speech.

USC, and UCLA with Jackie Robinson and Kenny Washington, has a long history of providing opportunity for black athletes. 'SC's first All-American in the 1920s, Brice Taylor, was black. Back then, you never heard of civil rights. Nobody was let in because of their color, they had to qualify like everybody else. Like Simpson, he had to go to a junior college before he could get in.

My other son, Rich, is having success as general manager of the Buccaneers. Well, he played football in high school and at Princeton. He's a smart kid, and he's doing very well in his current job.

134

He was an Irish Catholic from West Virginia, with a gift for wit and humor. For 16 years at the University of Southern California, John McKay was one of the greatest football coaches of all time. His teams won four national championships (1962, 1967, 1972, 1974), five Rose Bowls (1963, 1968, 1970, 1973, 1975), two Heisman Trophies (Mike Garrett, 1965; O.J. Simpson, 1968), and were unbeaten three times (1962, 1969, 1972). McKay was named AFCA Coach of the Year and also the Football Writers Association of America Coach of the Year in 1962 and 1972. His 1972 Trojans are considered by many to be the best team in college history, and the 20-year run (1962–1982) that he started and was completed by his successor, John Robinson, is the most dominant two decades any program has ever had. He was elected to the USC, Rose Bowl, and College Football Halls of Fame. He cowrote *McKay: A Coach's Story* with Jim Perry. McKay left USC in 1976 to take over the Tampa Bay Buccaneers, leading them to the 1979 NFC Championship Game. His son, J.K., is a Trojan legend, and his other son, Rich, is one of the most successful general managers in pro football. This interview, one of the last he ever conducted prior to his passing, occurred in 2000 and appeared in a *StreetZebra* magazine article titled, "He Was a Legend of the Old School Variety."

The SEVENTIES

JOHN VELLA
OFFENSIVE TACKLE
1969–1971

I GRADUATED FROM NOTRE DAME HIGH SCHOOL in Sherman Oaks. My sophomore year I played offensive tackle. That was 1969, and we were the Rose Bowl champions. We had an unbeaten season. Bob Chandler was my teammate. He was just a great guy and a great player who had a great career with the Bills and the Raiders.

However, we had one tie, and it cost us the national championship. We tied Notre Dame 14–14 but beat them my junior and senior years. The reason they tied us in 1969 was we had Chandler as an upback blocking back—we would put him to the left or right of center, two feet back. Notre Dame saw that and put Mike McCoy in that gap, between the center and the guard. McCoy was one of the biggest, strongest men in the nation, and Chandler is 175. McCoy ran over him and blocked a punt, which led to a score.

The first game of that season was at Nebraska, a capacity crowd, plus they started sophomore Johnny Rodgers. We won 31–21. Talk about being excited, afterward I was completely drained. In the first quarter, I needed a "second wind." That was one of the top five places to play: there's a sea of red, with great, enthusiastic fans. They have a big home-field advantage, but we had a good day. One thing I remember about that game was my teammate, Fred Khasigian, who was a bright, great player and leader. He went on to become a dentist. Many times I would come to the line, and I was too fired up, I wasn't thinking straight. He'd remind me what I was supposed to

John Vella sits in the
locker room following
the Raiders' 1976 AFC
divisional playoff game
win against the New
England Patriots at
Oakland-Alameda
County Coliseum on
December 18, 1976.
*Photo courtesy of Getty
Images*

do on this play and that play. He straightened me out, and this happened at Nebraska. I was blanking out, but Fred knew what to do. He'd give me a short description and set me straight on what the play was, and I'd not screw up, and he helped me a handful of times in that Nebraska game. It's like a good baseball catcher or manager coming out to the mound to settle down a pitcher. I was drawing a blank, I didn't know, what's the snap count?

Another great game in 1969 was a night game at the Coliseum versus Stanford and Jim Plunkett. What I remember is the last drive: Gerry Mullins caught a pass for a first down and got out of bounds. He probably didn't catch 10 balls all season, but he made a key play or two before. He seemed awful good that season. Ron Ayala was one of the best field-goal kickers we ever had, and there's no more clutch kick than to drive it through for the game-winner with zeros on the clock. That was for the Rose Bowl, and in those days, it was the Rose Bowl or no bowl.

A couple years before that, UCLA had been the Gary Beban–O.J. Simpson game. All those games were big games, and that continued into 1969. This was John McKay versus Tommy Prothro. UCLA was at the height of their football and athletic history. John Wooden was winning basketball championships every year, and their football team had never been stronger. It was a period of huge growth in California, so West Coast sports was at a dominant peak.

If I remember, our quarterback, Jimmy Jones, was 0-for-12 or something for 59 minutes, then finally he completed some passes on that final drive. Mike Rae was a freshman and ineligible. I think we had Jim Fassel and Mike Holmgren backing him up, and we weren't going to go to either of those guys. Well, Jones threw an incomplete pass on fourth down and the game was over, but they called pass interference on UCLA and gave us life. Jones then hit Sam Dickerson deep in a shadowy corner of the end zone to win 14–12 and send us to the Rose Bowl. Pete Carroll was a teenager sitting in the stands that night.

140

People remember me as an offensive tackle at USC and with the Oakland Raiders, but for one year—my junior year of 1970—I played defense. I got a call from John McKay's secretary in the summer, that he wanted a meeting. I thought, *What is this?* He told me he wanted to know what I thought about going to defense in my junior year. Prior to the 1970 season, Tody Smith was getting hurt all the time, some of the older veterans were not coming back. So I played both offense and defense in summer practices. McKay didn't make up his mind until after one week of practice in 1970. I went to the defense, but the funny thing was, I was on the preseason All-America team as an offensive tackle, so the switch was confusing. Sid Smith had gone in the first round to the Kansas City Chiefs, so I filled in and found myself up against Alabama's John Hannah in the 1970 season opener. Our defense would switch, and he'd face Tody Smith. So, when he's asked about it, he has memory problems, but I was up against him. Later with the Raiders, he remembers me on offense.

The opener in 1970 was at Birmingham, and some of our black players brought guns. It wasn't until we got to Alabama that these kinds of things came up, and it caught me by surprise. Tody Smith, my roommate, had brought a gun. I questioned Tody at the airport, or maybe on the plane. He had a briefcase, I think, which was not like him. I just thought it was odd, so I asked him, "What is that? What have you got?"

He just played it off, but in the room at the hotel, I asked him again. The briefcase was on the bed, so he finally admitted that he'd brought a gun, which really took me aback. I asked him to show it to me. I just asked him, "What do you need that for?"

I guess at the hotel there'd been some words exchanged. Tody had heard it and just felt really defensive. Now I became more aware of the catcalls after seeing Tody with that gun in his room. I became aware of the interaction between the black players. Everything just became clear; it opened my eyes.

Regarding the whole issue of whites and blacks, as I said, at USC it just wasn't an issue. We'd all pretty much played integrated football all through high school in California. I think Marv Goux might have been dealing with our black players in anticipation of the Alabama trip, but the whole thing kind of caught me by surprise because, from my angle, we were so far from any of that. I'd been recruited with and played against black players; I'd been with and next to black players. It was accepted, so I have a hard time really remembering any racial incidents on our team. We were about competition, and if you were good enough, you were accepted.

I do remember the crowd at Legion Field. Crowds in the South can make a decisive difference. They had a national reputation, the place was all red, there were 70,000-plus, and the place was packed. You knew you were the visitor. What I also remember was that it was a one-sided, easy victory. Sam Cunningham was playing his first game, and he rambled for more than 100 yards and two touchdowns, but lots of our best players dominated.

We won that game 42–21, but we had a disappointing season at 6–4–1.

So my junior year I played defense, and in my senior year I moved back to offense. I speak to groups and always joke that the only touchdown I ever scored was against Notre Dame and Joe Theismann, when he got trapped in the end zone and I recovered and scored. They were unbeaten and ranked No. 1 when they came to the Coliseum. We were just trying to salvage our season. It was pouring rain, but it was an offensive shootout. We won 38–28 and intercepted Theismann about five times. It cost the Irish the national championship, and Theismann lost the Heisman Trophy to Jim Plunkett.

We started 2–4 my senior year. I look back, and we had no Clarence Davis or O.J. or Reggie Bush. We had Lou Harris and a guy nicknamed "Sugar Bear." Those guys fumbled a lot. For some reason, we didn't give it to Cunningham like we should have. But give credit to that team, because we went into South Bend and beat Notre Dame 28–14.

What does it mean to be a Trojan? We had coaches and leaders like me, John Papadakis, and John Grant, leaders who weren't intimidated despite being 2–4, and the Fighting Irish were unbeaten and vying for the national title, but we played like Trojans and won in their stadium. Papadakis was brilliant. John knew the press would come to us, and he said, when the reporters ask me, "How did you beat Notre Dame?" to answer, "With the glory of Greece, the grandeur that was Rome, and the undying pride of the Trojans!"

As for me, it was that game. It didn't matter the record, and it was no surprise to us that I could block Walt Patulski. We could run, and we had a few plays for Edesel Garrison, and he outran them. We practiced it, and it worked. Garrison had a good week at practice. He'd had a lot of drops, but that week he was featured, we got the ball deep to him, and he caught it. And, sure enough, we ran the ball and won the game. So to me, that's what it means to be a Trojan.

That was when the whole Jimmy Jones–Mike Rae question came to a head, and it had a racial edge to it; Jones being black and Rae being white, but we overcame it like Trojans.

John McKay and Pete Carroll are no comparison in personality. Carroll's more outgoing. McKay was the head coach. Assistant coaches were hired to communicate with the players, and for the most part, that's how he communicated. Both were able to recruit good players, and both won. Shoot, USC football was the power I. We were bigger and stronger. McKay made us believe that, and so it was like, *Let's go now, we're gonna run the I back at 'em, let 'em know it's coming, they can't stop us.* They taught us that, then we'd a mix in a pass, and that's what it means to be a Trojan.

John Vella played for the unbeaten 1969 Trojans, who beat Michigan 10–3 in the Rose Bowl, and played in the 1970 game at Birmingham, Alabama. He was an All-American and All–Pac-8 lineman in 1971, when he was team captain, was voted USC's best lineman, and played in the 1972 Hula Bowl. His brother, Chris, played for USC. Vella was drafted by Oakland and starred as a lineman for some of John Madden's greatest Raiders teams, including the 1976 Super Bowl champions (who beat the Vikings at Pasadena's Rose Bowl). Today Vella is a successful entrepreneur, the owner of a chain of San Francisco Bay Area sporting goods stores called Vella's Locker Room.

SAM CUNNINGHAM

FULLBACK

1970–1972

I was born in Santa Barbara and went to Santa Barbara High School. Marv Goux was born there and went to the same high school and junior high that I went to. I think Santa Barbara is the second-oldest high school in the state of California. I played football, basketball, and ran track for the Dons. I did the decathlon at USC, but I was not really on the track team.

I was recruited by many programs, and I took many trips: to Michigan State, Oregon, Cal, Arizona State. Frank Kush, the coach at ASU, was crazy. Colorado recruited me, but I did not take that trip, I was too tired. I got a letter from Alabama. I'm sure Coach Bryant would have used me if I'd decided to be the guy to come there, but it was a tough situation for black athletes in the Deep South. So, yeah, they tried for me, but I wasn't going to go there.

Marv Goux was the main recruiter for this area, but he did not have to do a whole lot of recruiting for me. He knew me, his brother knew me. Santa Barbara was not very big, maybe 60,000 people and three high schools—a small Catholic school plus a couple public schools. At that time and place, my parents knew what I did before I even got home.

I graduated from high school in 1969, and the first time I met Coach John McKay was at dinner with him. He was funny, different from my high school coach, who was a retired military man. As a high school senior, you didn't really interact the way grown-ups would. McKay struck me as a pretty decent man, and his credentials spoke for themselves. The USC freshman football team of 1969 consisted of lots of great high school athletes, most of whom had competed in high school football or track, so we knew each other. It was cool to me—I grew up competing, nobody had ever spoiled or catered to me, and it had always forced me to play and compete. So it was like that at 'SC. After you get there, the recruiting is over, and they don't tell you you're the best anymore. Maybe some others had not had to compete as much as a prep. But for me it was easy. We all bonded and hung out together at USC: Manfred Moore, Charle Young, Rod McNeill, Chris Chaney, Allan Graf.

Eventually we formed something we called the "Big Five," and it consisted of Charle Young, Rod McNeill, Manfred Moore, Edesel Garrison, and myself. Later Lynn Swann became the "plus one," but he was younger, smaller, and we made him fight his way in. He made himself a pain in the behind, so we'd mess with him. It was all in good fun—we loved each other, and it was just the right chemistry. Lynn was from Northern California; he'd gone to this preppy high school and was a real hot shot, so we had to mess with him just to keep his head from getting too big.

That freshman year, we played three games, against Stanford, Cal, and UCLA, I think. Freshmen couldn't play varsity in those days. This was an incredible group of athletes, and expectations were huge that we would form a great team. But we thought it would materialize into Rose Bowls and national championships immediately. That was the expectation at USC, where the Trojans had won or come close to several titles in the last couple years, had unbeaten teams. We went to the Rose Bowl like it was on the schedule, so I figured it would be that way for us.

The first game of the 1970 season certainly convinced us that our time was now, that what we expected would materialize immediately. That was the famed game at Alabama. Going back to 'Bama, I just kept it simple: get in and play well, and don't dwell on the political side. I did not grow up in the Deep South. I knew if I got in and didn't play well, I wouldn't get in again. If I got a chance, I had to execute. It was exciting. It was our first road trip, and if I'd known how historical it was gonna be, I'd have paid more attention. But it seemed like just another game at the time, at least for me. My priorities were: get in and play well so I can get in and play again. At USC, there were a lot of guys who were good enough to play, so if you didn't get the job done, it'd be a long time before you got in again.

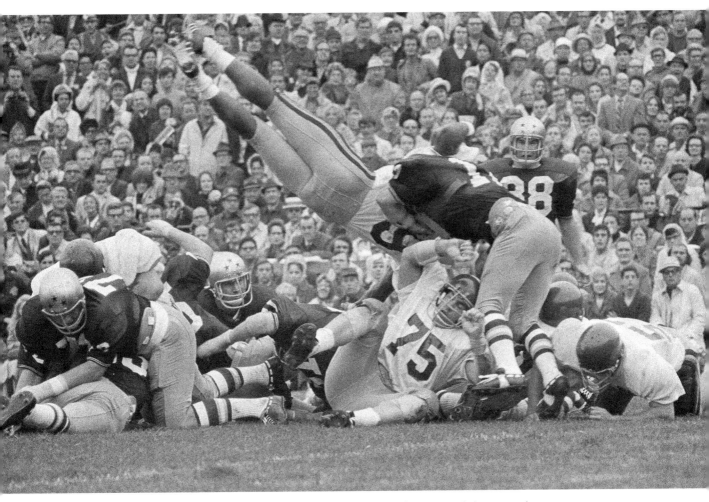

Sam Cunningham goes up and over the top for one of USC's touchdowns against Notre Dame on October 23, 1971, in South Bend.

That said, you knew this was a special game between two great football powers, and we happened to win that game. I could run to daylight or over people. That night at Alabama, they didn't have anybody who could stop me. That's just the way of it. Rod McNeill was more of a daylight runner. It didn't make any difference if somebody was in my way, I could go over him or around him. But that night I mainly just went over people.

The nighttime crowd at Legion Field was into it at first—they had every reason to feel they'd play well—but as the "Tide" turned, they were trying to figure out what was happening. There are times when I'm in the stands, and my team is being destroyed, like the first half of the 1974 USC–Notre Dame game. In the first half, the fans were not in it until that last touchdown that Anthony Davis scored before the half, so it was like that. We came out like gangbusters, they were hyped from the beginning, but we took the wind out of their sails. They were watching history. I mean, there's only one story. That's what they saw. There was no way for them to spin it. I was not paying attention to Bear Bryant. Again, my focus was always the next play: do well, and if you make plays, you get to stay in the game.

It's been written that you could hear black fans outside the stadium, but I was not acutely focused on that. I was caught up in the fact that I had a chance to play, and I never dreamt of it. I was not focused on the small group of black fans sitting behind the end zone rooting for us. We played a near-perfect game and destroyed them 42–21. Their fans were silent, every ounce of what they brought was gone.

As we showered and got to the bus, I heard the black fans who were outside the stadium. We delivered something to them—we won the football game, which was the first thing. When you win, other things happen. And when you win in so dominating a fashion, whatever had been talked of or planned or put in motion now had a full head of steam. I tell people we didn't have time to savor or enjoy, we had to get ready for Nebraska after that.

For me, there was no real weight off my back. It was a senior team; they had played two years and knew what it was to deal with the pressure of being a Trojan. I had been a baby, and now I knew I could play college ball.

Charlie Evans, a white senior fullback, was ahead of me. If I was going to get significant playing time, I'd mostly be taking his time. He started that game and even scored a touchdown, but he was expecting a glory year. You don't get a lot of chances, and he knew the consequences that come from that—that your best shot rolls around, and either you make the most of it or you don't. I was a sophomore, but that game set the tone so that I got a lot of time after that. He was a good player and played, but he did not attain the kind of glory he hoped and might have achieved had he gotten the playing time he hoped for. I never talked to Charlie about it. I'm told it grates on him to this day, and I'm sure it does. But he carried the ball before I did, scored a touchdown in that game, but not the first two TDs.

Clarence Davis had a good game and normally he would have scored the first touchdown, being the starting tailback. He was an All-American in

1969, and if there was a civil rights story that night, everybody thought it would revolve around Clarence. He was already an established star, had been born in Birmingham, and symbolized the flight of black athletes from the South. But what made it so different for the fans looking on was that we had an all-black backfield and started a black quarterback, Jimmy Jones.

This was really unusual, not just for the South. It was something you saw at USC and almost nowhere else. Willie Wood had been USC's black quarterback and captain in the late '50s, which was really groundbreaking. Minnesota had a guy named Sandy Stephens, and Michigan State had a black quarterback, Jimmy Raye, a couple years earlier. That was about it.

That game at Birmingham is considered a seminal moment, but it could have happened earlier. USC had a history of black players, going back to Brice Taylor in the 1920s, although they kind of dropped the ball for a few years after that. But in 1956 USC went to Texas with a black running back, C.R. Roberts, and he had a game comparable with mine. The Texas players shook his hand and accepted him because, when you play, you have a sense of respect for courage and talent that can't be denied. But the Texas fans kept jeering him, and change did not result. Besides, Texas is a different mentality than the rest of the U.S. They just have their own way of doing things.

147

After the Alabama game, I got a chance to speak to Bear Bryant outside the locker room. I think he also talked to Clarence Davis and a few others. You don't normally get a chance to talk to the head coach after games—that was unique. Then I got cleaned up and moved.

Tody Smith was a senior on our team that year. Tody was cool, and he had a lot of pressure, being a senior plus the younger brother of Bubba Smith. His father was a well-regarded coach in Beaumont, Texas. Tody's attitude going to Alabama was different from mine and some of the black players from California; his perspective being from Texas was not the same as mine. His brother, Bubba, was a real character.

Fred Lynn was a football player at USC when I was there, but he quit and concentrated on baseball. Later he was asked about that and said, "My football career ended courtesy of one too many hits from Sam 'Bam' Cunningham." Fred became an All-American on several College World Series champions at USC, and in 1975 he was the American League Rookie of the Year and MVP with the American League–champion Boston Red Sox.

Fred was not a "come up and stick your nose in it" kind of guy. Fred was a talented athlete and needed to play baseball. Most of this came out years later. It was not part of the conversation at the time, but it shows how much talent he had that he became a great baseball player. We had a lot of multi-sport athletes. Rod McNeill ran track; Charle Young was good in hoops; Anthony Davis was a baseball star. We had lots of great athletes, but you had to determine what you wanted to be at some point.

Charle Young was a leader. We were all young and great athletes. He and I hung out together a lot. If I needed somebody at my back, I wanted it to be him, as I hope it would be for him, too. He came from Fresno, which is different from Santa Barbara and took more adjustment to the social scene at 'SC. There were not a lot of blacks on campus then. Before it became a non-denominational university, USC was a religious university, and it was very traditional, conservative, and for the black athletes at that time we needed to be cognizant of this. It was not a discriminatory attitude, but you sensed that there were rules of conduct, and we had to live within those rules.

Marv Goux told us, "Just don't do anything to disgrace the university, the football program, your teammates, your family, or yourselves." We understood this and lived it. You have to understand, within the black community, there was not much there at 'SC. There was a cycle of movement, as many had lived through the 1965 Watts riots, and there was an increase in black recruits who were brought in to keep the football program as great as it was—and if you get an education while there, then so be it. Charle Young knew that there was a trade of sorts, education for football—opportunity for us, glory for the school.

The neighborhood around USC had undergone some major change after the Watts riots, but USC is very important to that community and has always been viewed as a friend. It was not bad for us, and the university has expanded. So slowly but surely USC has helped to keep the area relatively benign. People are sending their kids to a school that's asking them to pay a lot of money, so they want to feel it's safe for them. There's a lot of history in that whole neighborhood area, and USC has always been part of it.

John Papadakis and I never competed against each other for the fullback job, but we had competed versus each other as shot-putters in high school. He's really emotional and takes it personally, but he made me a better player because I had to stand up and fight when we had physical confrontations. We developed a great friendship because of what we went through. John had been a running back, but they turned him into a linebacker. I could have played linebacker. My philosophy about the game was that I just wanted to play. I was not worried about statistics or even my position. I wanted to play and I wanted to win.

I was never so vain that I needed to be the center of attention, the star. I was not raised to worry about how many times I touched the ball. It was a team sport. I just wanted to be part of it and win.

It all comes down to what people think about you 30 years later. If you can make yourself think of that, you will act differently. Either you're humble or not. If people throw all this money at you, you have to stay the same. We did the same as the original cats who played football, only we made more money in the NFL than our predecessors. I've seen so many amazing athletes—and I might say I did the same thing that some guy does today, and he makes millions, but I don't make a big deal of it.

I got the ball a lot my junior year. There was no dedicated tailback. I made All-America in 1972 because the team was so good. Charle Young only averaged about two catches a game, but he'd make 20 or 30 yards when he did catch it. John McKay made comments that he did not use me to run the ball as much as he'd like, and my yards were not all that high, but Charle and I were All-Americans in part because there was a recognition that we'd sacrificed for the team. We had so much talent spread out that no one guy was going to have sparkling stats. I don't know how you become an All-American. There's a lot that goes into it, the right team and publicity, but I never worried about it and just let things happen.

149

The reason some people thought the 2005 Trojan team was better than our 1972 team was we were "vanilla" in what we did. We could've run what Pete Carroll's team runs today and been even more untouchable. The only problem with the 2005 team was they lost leadership on the defensive side of the ball. They got caught up in the hype, and we never got caught in the hype. We had cats who grew up together from '69 on and had no great success or bowl games for two years prior, so we were really hungry. You come to USC and the expectations are the Rose Bowl, but we didn't have anybody in '72 who'd been to one.

Now they have so many guys drafted, they're not as hungry as we were in '72. Back then, you would come in, and the Rose Bowl was the only game. If you didn't make it there, you didn't go anywhere, so the motivation was to try and get there. To get to the Rose Bowl, we felt we had to go undefeated. Coach McKay said it was one of the easiest teams he ever coached. He said, "I just had to make sure we got off the bus." I just looked at my teammates, and I could see their mindset. We'd say, "We got this." It was the most fun I ever had playing, hanging out, that journey, the outside bonding. We partied together, ate together, were broke together, visited families in our home-towns—we were all we had. There was no discrimination against the black players at USC, but it was a social scene on campus that took getting used to, so we bonded with teammates because that was our comfort zone.

We were bound by the people we were there with to make this work, and we did. Football is hard work. It's a test of your heart and emotion, your sin-cerity. It's assumed you will be in shape, but beyond that, you have to want it bad—and we wanted it bad.

Mike Rae was our quarterback, and we were so run-heavy that the quar-terback just had to hand off, but he could throw any pass he needed. He had been great at Lakewood High School. It always amazed me when any passer came to 'SC. Guys could go to Stanford where they'd throw, they could go anywhere and play. Mike really had to wait his turn, but he had a chance at the pros, and it worked out in the long run. There were just a lot of great athletes.

Edesel Garrison was ahead of us. He'd come in on a track scholarship, then decided to concentrate on football, but he'd been a state champion sprinter at Compton High School. Anthony Davis was a sophomore in 1972 who got lucky because he was third-string and we had some injuries. Rod McNeill was injured, so A.D. got to play. Allen Carter also got hurt, and he was great, the fastest of all the running backs we had. But A.D. was special. He was A.D. He had a great sophomore year on a great team, but any one of those run-ning backs could have done well. McNeill had a bad injury, but he gutted it out and got his share of playing time.

The real key to that team was the defense. In 1970–1971 we ran an even-front defense and did not move well out of it. Nebraska, Alabama, and Okla-homa ran wishbone lateral offenses, and against them, we were always behind. McKay changed in 1972. He ran an odd-front defense and brought in Richard "Batman" Wood, who was by far the pearl of that defense. This guy came from New Jersey, across the river from New York City, and was an unreal player and a unique character.

I introduced myself to Wood, and he introduced himself as "Batman" from Gotham City. I asked, "What do you play?" and he said, "Linebacker." I said, "You don't have big legs," and he just kind of looked at me like I was crazy, like, *When you see me play linebacker, you will not question my ability to play that position.* He was not as imposing-looking as a Ted Hendricks, but he was a great athlete. Then there was safety Artimus Parker and Charles Phillips, who was a rover—linebacker and safety—he was 6′3″ and incredibly athletic, later a great pro with Oakland.

That 1972 team could have beaten some lower-echelon teams in pro football. Washington State coach Jim Sweeney was asked if we were the best team in the country, and he answered, "No, the Miami Dolphins are."

John Hannah was my teammate all those years in New England. He was an All-Pro, a Hall of Famer, a great blocker to run behind. He'd been on that 1970 Alabama team we beat, but we did not really talk about 1970. Why would he want to talk about a game they didn't win? I wasn't going to grind him about it. John was from Alabama, and he had to get adjusted to the fact that probably 40 percent of the NFL was black in 1974. But he was a gentleman and friend, a good teammate. Before integration really took, you had a lot of players coming out of the black colleges, but they weren't as fundamentally sound as guys who played at big schools.

A large part of the effect of the 1970 game is that it forced a change in those small schools. Plus the AFL had an effect, as well. The AFL had created additional pro football jobs, and that meant more black players, a lot of whom had been at black colleges. Al Davis got out ahead on this. He scouted lesser-known black colleges and found guys like Willie Brown and Gene Upshaw. Vince Lombardi built the Packers with a fair number of these guys, as well.

151

Sam "Bam" Cunningham was the hero of USC's legendary 1970 win at Alabama that is credited as a turning point in ending segregation. He was an All-American and captain of the 1972 Trojans, generally considered the greatest college football team ever. In USC's 42–17 thumping of Ohio State in the 1973 Rose Bowl, he scored four times to earn Player of the Game and eventually Rose Bowl Hall of Fame honors. After playing in the Hula Bowl, College All-Star Game, and Coaches All-America Game, Sam was made the first-round draft pick of the New England Patriots, where he played until 1982. He is a member of the USC Athletic Hall of Fame. His brother, Randall, was a star quarterback with the Philadelphia Eagles and Minnesota Vikings.

ALLAN GRAF
OFFENSIVE GUARD
1970–1972

I GREW UP IN SYLMAR. I had an older brother who graduated from San Fernando High, and they wanted me there also. So, after the 10th grade, I transferred to San Fernando, where I went from a predominantly white school to one of the most integrated schools in the L.A. City Section. I came in and fit right in. I had to prove myself to my new teammates, but they made me the captain of the team, so I guess I did that. San Fernando was the best program in the state in the 1970s. In the 1960s it had been Bishop Amat, and in recent years it's been De La Salle, Long Beach Poly, and Mater Dei. But in that era San Fernando was second to none.

They'd won the 1966 city title but lost to Carson the following year. Carson, Banning, and Granada Hills were great programs, but we were the best. We went undefeated and beat Westchester. In the early 1970s, they won with Anthony Davis and Manfred Moore. Later, Charlie White starred there, as did Manfred's brother, Anthony. Manfred played with me, and I was the first from San Fernando to go to USC.

In my senior year, I was the L.A. City Co-Player of the Year with a guy from Beverly Hills. I was the league player of the year, the valley player of the year, and an All-American. I played on defense at San Fernando. I was 6′2″ and 250 pounds in high school. In those years, that was pretty big, but I was the smallest guy we had. We had a guy who was 6′5″, 280, and a Samoan who went to Utah who was 6′3″ and about three bills. In that same year,

Santa Barbara had some twins who were both 400 or 500 pounds. They played with Sam Cunningham. We were a good-sized team. We had a guy who became a pro wrestler. In those days, if you were 250 and 6′2″ or higher, you were a big guy.

Meeting John McKay, who was recruiting me, meeting all his people, was a great experience. I was pretty good, and all but one of the Pacific-8 Conference schools recruited me in 1967. I had a big year. Rod Humenuik was one of the offensive line coaches. They wanted me to play defense and recruited me as a defensive tackle. I loved to tackle, was very aggressive, and had speed. That's what they liked. They lined us up and said, "Graf, now you play offensive guard." I was just stunned, but you can't tell Coach McKay, "I play defense." You have no say unless you're O.J. Simpson. I said to Humenuik, "You told me I'd play defense." He said, "With your speed, you're a great pulling guard. You have a natural tendency to pull with your hips." I guess they needed me to do that. I had 4.9 speed, which was pretty good, so that was my first inkling.

Going back to when I was being recruited, they told me to go to Julie's. McKay had his own booth. I was very nervous. I'd heard all the stories of him. I found him friendly with a dry sense of humor. He was low-key. He said he'd watched a lot of film and, "Dave Levy's seen you; he loves you. Rod's seen you; all the coaches love ya. I like you a lot." Then he asked me, "Do you wanna play with the best?"

I said, "Yes, sir."

"If you wanna play with the best," he said, "this is where you're gonna be. I promise you a Rose Bowl." He stuck his hand out, and I think he was pretty shrewd and confident. He showed me his 1967 national championship ring and said, "Do you want one of those?"

I said, "Yes, sir."

"This is where you're gonna get it," he said.

And I said, "Yes, sir. Where do I sign?"

When I first got there, it was still the "Wild Bunch" of 1968–1969. I was on the freshman team, and in those days we played three games, against UCLA, Stanford, and Cal. The rest of the time, I was on the service squad for the varsity to go against. These were some pretty big guys. They were older—21, 22, 23—and there was a big difference in the maturity level. I'd jumped into a team with a Marv Goux banging people on the helmet and kicking people. It was a culture shock, and I was thinking, *What kind of*

maniac coach is this? But he backed it up all the time: "This is how we do it, listen to me." He's a tough guy. I was a pretty good racquetball player, and he'd just kill me. He was tough for his size, and now I know how he played at his size. Coaches could hit you—there was no rules preventing that—and he scared the crap out of everybody. But he was a very intense, knowledgeable defensive coach.

They tried to get McKay to take me off the offensive line in 1971, but it didn't work. Offensive players react a lot differently than defensive players. Marv and I almost came to blows one game. He got on my case, and I said, "That's it." One redshirt freshman just walked off the field in 1968. He was a big, 300-pound kid. Goux called his mother a whore, and the guy started to sniffle. He walked off and decked Goux in the chest. Goux went down, and that guy said, "I'm done," and walked off. He wasn't around long.

That's when I thought, *I'm not in San Fernando anymore.* It was an eye-opener. Goux had so much energy, he could gong you on your helmet and it hurt. It was very intense, but afterward I was glad. Years later we became even closer friends. He respected me for what I was. I said, "You were tough." And he said, "You were a tough mother, Graf." I had the speed and agility to play on offense. Everybody hated but respected him, and he'd compliment the offensive players going against his defensive guys.

Dave Levy called it a "mild form of hate," but it became love. In 1972, fortunately for us, there was a lot of love going around. The coaches weren't as tough on us that year. He respected this team more than any other team. We were smart football players. At the 25th reunion, he and McKay said that. We had sharp guys like Charle Young, who became a Christian minister; Manfred Moore, who became an entrepreneur; Dave Brown, who became a teacher; Pat Haden and J.K. McKay, who became corporate attorneys. Haden was a Rhodes Scholar and a broadcaster. Lynn Swann became a broadcaster and was the Republican candidate for governor of Pennsylvania. John Grant was a success at what he's done. I made it in the movie industry. A lot of guys who did well in life were on the same offensive line for three years. Craig Fertig loved us. They'd put stuff in, and we'd pick up on it. I'd say to Dave Brown, "Okay," and we knew what we were doing. John Robinson came in that year, and we started passing on first down.

It was a big transition year for them. Dave Levy thought he'd be the next coach, and he didn't get it. Robinson was brought in to become the offensive coordinator, and Levy became the defensive coordinator. I think it was kind of hurtful for Dave. I'm not sure why he was never named head coach other than the fact he went to UCLA.

Are the 1972 Trojans the greatest team of all time? How can you ask me that? I'm biased. I want to say this, if you ask guys who played in the pros—Batman Woods, Charles Anthony, Sam Cunningham, any of those guys—they will tell you the best team they ever played for was the '72 Trojans. I had a lot of fun at the College All-Star Game. There were seven or eight of us versus the Dolphins, who were unbeaten that year. It was a big thrill, and McKay said he wished we could have just had his team. We could have beaten them instead of the all-stars. That tells you the high praise he had for that team. Ask J.K., he'd say his dad was very sorry to go to Tampa. But for that kind of money, I guess, you do it. Later he said he wished he'd stayed. If he had stuck around and done what John Robinson did, he might have broken Bear Bryant's record for wins. Guys spend 38 or 40 years at one school like Joe Paterno. I'm sure he had regrets despite getting a lot of money. His legacy would have been huge.

I was a free agent with the Rams and the last guy cut in 1973. I wanted them to trade me to St. Louis. They kept me behind an All-Pro, Tom Mack. I wanted a trade or to go free agent. When you're the last man cut, it's too late to get with another team because all the rosters are filled.

155

I joined the World Football League. Craig Fertig brought a lot of 'SC guys, and we were going to go up to Portland. This was 1974, 1975. They played half the season and collapsed. That was my career. Unless you're a big-name guy like Larry Csonka, your career was over. An "average Joe" lineman was penalized. I never got back in. They didn't like that I went to the WFL. McKay wanted me in Tampa, but he got pressure not to hire WFL guys. It turned out to be a break for me. I doubled for Dick Butkus in the movie *Gus*. I was the same size and looked like him. Disney produced it, and I became a stuntman.

Eventually my expertise in football movies led me to work as a second unit director in films like *Gridiron Gang*, *Necessary Roughness*, *The Program*, *The Waterboy*, *Jerry Maguire*, *Any Given Sunday*, *Friday Night Lights* (both the movie and the TV series), and *The Replacements* with Keanu Reeves. Now I'm working on *The Express*, the story of the first black Heisman Trophy winner, Ernie Davis of Syracuse, who died of leukemia. I've been an actor and in commercials. I play referees and coaches, I cast myself in football scenes I direct. I was also the right-wing NRA guy who pulls a gun in the doughnut shop scene in *Boogie Nights* where everybody gets shot and killed except for Don Cheadle.

I've written screenplays and ultimately hope to get a chance to move beyond second unit "football directing" to directing a feature-length movie. You ask anybody in the business, and they'll tell you I'm the guy when it comes to doing what I do. Being a Trojan in the film industry, years ago, was an advantage. All the producers were big USC guys. I was told, "When you leave football, come see me." Marv Goux always set up summer employment for players as extras. I was on all those TV episodes of *Emergency*, I worked in all the Universal shows and got a taste of what it was like, plus I did an episode of *Marcus Welby, MD*. I got to do a scene with Robert Young, who was the doctor of a high school team on the show, and I got to pick him up. I made $50 extra for picking him up. I thought, *This is easy work*.

I came back and got into the business. I worked for some big producer I'd known from when I was at USC, who asked me what I wanted to do. I said I wanted to be a producer or a director. I came back to him, and he thumbed through this book—as if jobs as producers and directors were just listed—and he said, "The best I can do is the mail room for eight bucks an hour." I said, "Wait a minute, all those years you sat at my table at banquets and told me you'd start me off as a producer." He said, "Sorry, that's all I got," so I became a stuntman.

There's a lot of USC people in the business. They used to help you more, but now they're younger, they're not the old guys who loved me when I first came. Russ Saunders was a production manager. The statue of Tommy Trojan is modeled after him. I worked with him and picked his brain. He later died. It was sad. He was a good guy, still working hard at 70. I met a lot of guys like that. Some producers I wish would have more loyalty, but there's still the future.

USC gave me a chance to make friends and expand. Charle Young and I came from different backgrounds. He's from Fresno and I'm from San Fernando, but I had no problem with a big mixed-bag team and whatever. Some guys from Orange County had problems, they'd never been on a team with that kind of mixture. Charle was big: 6'4", 235 pounds, a good-sized tight end. We worked together doing construction at a Beverly Hills parking structure, right in the center of town. It was my junior year. He was a good guy, very philosophical guy. A hippie-type guy. The war was heavy back then, and the draft was brought back. My number was 96, so if I didn't keep my grades up, I'd have gone. The black-white issue was tough for some. We were close, but I resented that, in the awards, they thought I'd get Lineman of the Year. I graded out No. 1, but the coaches pushed Charle as an All-American, and he was the Lineman of the Year. He was a tight end, not really a lineman, but the position was changing. They canned it after that. Tight ends weren't linemen after that.

I saw him years later after he became a minister. We had Crusade for Christ, Athletes in Action. There were a lot of good Christian guys on that 1972 team. I believe that was the difference why that team succeeded where previous teams failed.

He went into that. It was very cool growing up in that era—it was a time of change, socially and economically. The war, race issues, all that was right before us. Being athletes, the change was even more relevant. It was unusual to have a black quarterback. I don't know how much tension it put on that team in 1971. Some said Mike Rae should have started. Rae was solid in 1972, he led us to a national title. He was a natural leader, and that made a difference. He was a good pro, too. Pat Haden backed him up. Rae always felt like there was another quarterback fighting for his job, but it worked out in the long run for him. A lot of little things make that team unique.

157

Allan Graf played for the 1972 national champions, considered the greatest college team in history. He was selected for the 1973 College All-Star Game in Chicago and, after a try-out with the Los Angeles Rams, played in the World Football League. He is now the leading second unit movie director in Hollywood, famed for his work on football movies like *Necessary Roughness*, *Any Given Sunday*, and *Friday Night Lights* (film and TV versions), among many others. He has also appeared as an actor and in commercials.

ROD McNEILL

TAILBACK

1970, 1972–1973

I STARTED AT SOUTHERN CALIFORNIA in 1969, one of the all-time great classes, the one that included Sam "Bam" Cunningham. Freshmen did not play varsity then, so the freshman team played three games: against the Cal and Stanford frosh, and against the "Brubabes," UCLA. We were undefeated. Coach Craig Fertig gave us our marching orders.

Coming from the South originally, I'd seen segregation, I'd experienced it. So when we made that trip to Alabama in 1970, it was not so much that I had a fear factor, but any fear I had was related to an incident from when I was growing up in North Carolina.

My brother and I were playing tag, and my brother accidentally knocked a little white girl down. We got up and looked around, and all the white folks were staring at us. It was frightening. We always saw coming to California as coming to a dreamland—it was so much a part of the American life, what we saw on TV. Back in North Carolina, we only dealt with other black people, and suddenly we were around whites or Hispanics, but all the people were welcoming and friendly. I was student body president of my junior high school. The lesson I learned was that the South was one thing, but people don't have to be segregated in order to get along.

It's remarkable how vividly I recall key events, and now that I know the inside stories, it's clear that the point of the Alabama game was to help the country come together. Football was a common denominator—football and

Christianity. At the hotel in those days, all the blacks in the hotel were porters, they carried the bags, and they looked at us like we were deliverers. They saw young black men who were college students and great athletes, professionally dressed, carrying ourselves with pride, standing tall, equal with our white counterparts, pride and respect all around. They had never seen this before. It took me back to growing up in North Carolina. My folks had gotten involved in the civil rights movement and had participated in lunch counter arrests.

I did not realize the significance of that game until later, but there were things that stuck out: at the bus after the game, the thing I recall the most was that we were saviors. Several blacks came to me and thanked me, we had shown them we could play the game at that level. People would say it in a hushed way, like they didn't want to draw attention to themselves.

There were no negative comments from the Alabama whites. People were embarrassed, we had beaten them so badly. But I really feel this game was planned because I truly believe USC was chosen. Bear Bryant chose John McKay. Bryant knew his fans would respect USC and McKay. So, however the game turned out, this factor would prevail, whereas I don't know if those people could accept losing like that to any other integrated team. But we just brought out that "student body right" and ran those sweeps, and that was that.

The fans saw teams playing together, and what they were holding onto was an anachronism, that was not what life was at that time. There were mixed teams already, but this was on their home turf, and so it was close to home. They relinquished what they held dear. That was the truth that came home. It was something that was on different fronts, but it was not hitting home. But after that, they thought, *We have to join the rest of society.*

What the Trojans meant to black kids was that now we could be heroes to all kids, white and black. I had white and black heroes: Gale Sayers, Jim Brown, Elroy "Crazy Legs" Hirsch, all exceptional athletes, but I can totally understand where they were coming from: growing up while holding onto the mold of racist sentiment, where your only heroes are white. But now whites could admire heroic black athletes. For black kids up until then, you're told you cannot do that, you've dreamt of scoring touchdowns, of being a star, and now they think, *Yes, I can.*

Don't say, "I can't do that." After that, folks knew you *could* do it. Fortunately, Alabama was willing and able to take significant steps. Before that, there were no blacks on these teams. It's hard to understand what kind of message this was. But Bear Bryant had the courage to make this change. I admired his integrity and the high standards he insisted on for his players and himself, the great dignity with which he carried himself. I was excited to understand that it was his idea to do this, which was a great American concept. Nobody forced him to. He did what was right because, in this country, we usually do that.

In 2003 Pete Carroll invited Sam Cunningham and John Papadakis to go back there when USC played at Auburn. I spoke to Sam and John about it, and they said the black folks living there now had a sense of awe about the whole thing, which makes sense, because it was history.

My career at USC was disrupted by an injury. It was a freak accident. I had size and speed, and I'd been a top player coming out of Baldwin Park High School, which is east of L.A. out on the 10 Freeway, near West Covina. Coach John McKay lived out that way. My injury prevented me from achieving what I was capable of in football.

The reason I chose USC out of high school was, I knew I was good, but you knew that if you play football, USC was the place to do it. I met the likes of Mike Garrett, O.J. Simpson, Craig Fertig, and Coach Dave Levy. An image was projected in which USC was more than a university, it was really kind of iconographic. You had heroes everywhere—the Kennedys in politics; in music there was Stevie Wonder and Marvin Gaye, icons like Frank Sinatra, Tony Bennett, and Dean Martin—and USC fit into that whole thing. Bob Hope was like John McKay, he was like the "Rat Pack." McKay was this larger-than-life personality. He had this old office, this big cigar, and he'd be sitting there relaxing, sharing what they would do. I thought, *This is settled. This is where people win Heismans, make All-America.* People had achieved the dreams that I had for myself. In North Carolina, there were limits, but USC meant there were no limits.

In my family, I had eight brothers and sisters, older brothers, and there was a lot of discussion about how USC was the favorite law school, that most of the judges had gone there, because there was this possibility that I would go into law. My uncle was an attorney in Los Angeles, and he suggested USC to position myself with the judges and attorneys, most of whom were from USC.

I was right on track after breaking Mike Garrett's freshman rushing record, and I won the job as the starting tailback. I was having a good day on the last scrimmage of spring practice, but on the very last play, I suffered this freak injury when a guy jumped on my back and turned my foot around, dislocating my hip. In most cases, that injury makes you damaged goods, so I thought I would have to find a different role beyond football, beyond all my plans to be a star. But I fought through it and attribute this to God. I was in the hospital for six weeks, but God kept me positive.

One doctor told me the injury I had suffered was similar to what paratroopers would do to themselves during World War II, and he said I'd never play football again. But it went in one ear and out the other. I was not going to let anything stop me. I was not the same after that, I lost a lot of flexibility and mobility, but I fought through it. I started even though I was not 100 percent, and Coach McKay may have felt he owed me something.

What does it mean to be a Trojan? That's what it meant. It meant "Fight On!" To me, USC is something that existed before I ever got there. A spirit exists there. It is a place of exceptionalism and exudes excellence. The root of the whole university may be the fact that it was a Presbyterian or Methodist seminary, but there is this feeling that *it can be done here, it can be you, Fight On! Don't give up.* You could see us come back, miraculous things, never give up.

USC attracts those kinds of people, people who are willing to fight through adversity. What comes first, I think, is the school just attracts those kinds of people. Part of it is guys who come to USC are guys who want to find out if they're the best, and they go to 'SC to test their mettle. As a result of this process, I saw guys I admired. I saw guys like Jimmy Jones and Bobby Chandler, great athletes, but I also saw guys like Marty Patton, who was a great athlete in high school. Our freshman year, he said he went to Notre Dame and Stanford on recruiting trips, but we both knew USC was the place to best test ourselves. Marty never became a superstar, but he was an example of a guy who wanted to be there because he wanted to see if he was one of the best, and that was an attribute of his regardless of whether he became an All-American or not. This is what Pete Carroll looks for today. We had guys willing to compete with each other instead of going to a second-rate school and starting, but not being a winner.

As I say, God was with me, the USC experience was a spiritual one, and part of that was the Notre Dame week of 1971. This was the midpoint between the big win over Alabama in 1970 and the "all-time greatest" 1972 national champions, a real seminal moment in the school's history, in the rivalry with the Irish, in McKay's career, and in the lives of the boys who became men. If you want to truly know what it means to be a Trojan, you cannot do better than to learn about the events of the week of October 23, 1971. They say that on certain teams, adversity that might bring ordinary players down will carry extraordinary players to great heights. The Yankees had that. Some argument or event that would cause a tailspin on other teams would mean a pennant-winning drive for them. The same with USC. We had a strength of character, a willingness to sacrifice, to go the extra mile, and to bear a greater burden than our opponents. It marks why USC is above and beyond the ordinary.

I was not suiting up that week, but McKay wanted me to go on my first trip to South Bend. After beating Alabama in 1970, we thought we would cruise from victory to victory, but instead we were mediocre. Our talent was incredible, but we played well below our capabilities. Remember, that 1970 team was filled with lots of dissension. It was racial in nature. The white quarterback, Mike Rae, or the black quarterback, Jimmy Jones? That was tough, to win when there is divisiveness. In 1971 it was still a cancer eating away at us, and on a team filled with All-Americans and future NFL draft picks, we were 2–4. McKay, the man with all the answers, was perplexed. Announcer Tom Kelly was puzzled, like, *What's going here?*

Notre Dame was 6–0 and contending for the national title. They were lying in wait for us back there. We'd had our way with the Irish for a few years, and this was their chance at payback. Ninety percent of other teams would have folded, but we're 'SC. Dave Brown, a little-known, little-used offensive lineman—quiet, not a team leader, but a member of the Fellowship of Christian Athletes—approached John McKay.

Brown, who is white, knew we were racially divided and that only Christ could bring us together. He asked McKay if he could arrange a "demonstration." McKay was Catholic and figured at 2–4 it can't hurt, so he said, "Yeah, as long as it's voluntary." There may have been a few stragglers, but most of the team was there, and it was very spiritual, very emotional. Guys gave themselves to the Lord, tears were shed, and the team was given new life. We went to South Bend, and I sensed something different. We played with reckless abandon and won. It's important to understand, this was 1971. This was still the '60s generation. We were college kids in an age of long hair, drugs, and acid rock, so a relationship with Christ was a real departure from normal college life, especially back then.

We won that game 28–14. Afterward John Papadakis and John Vella told reporters we had won, "With the glory of Greece, the grandeur of Rome, and the undying pride of the Trojans." Can you imagine some guy from Cal saying anything like that?

So after that experience, we beat Notre Dame, we came back, and that team was now together. And we never lost again. We were unbeaten the rest of the 1971 season and were all back as seniors in 1972. We had been together four years, we'd gone through Alabama together, the Notre Dame week together, and this team was primed and ready to go. The opener was at Arkansas—they were supposed to contend for the national title, and they had a hotshot quarterback, Joe Ferguson. The way we saw it, it was like a mini-Alabama, all their fans wearing red and white, just like 'Bama. That experience helped that 1972 team. There was this anticipation to show a southern team and the world that we were a great football team. Football was king down there, and we, a bunch of guys from California, went down there and won on their home turf. That set the stage for us. It was a carryover from the 'Bama experience. Nebraska lost to UCLA that night, and on Monday we were ranked No. 1. We held that spot all season.

USC has tradition. The question is, what is it about USC's tradition that separates it from so many other colleges? It's not just about winning more than anybody else. It's deeper than that. When I was on campus, USC had a smell, a feeling, a sound. I recall the bells going off there, which reminded me I was at a premiere university with incredible opportunities. I was part of something huge, and USC has that feel to me. I was recruited and spent time at other places. Dick Vermeil recruited me for Stanford, and I went up there, but nobody had that feeling. All the guys would say the same thing, but at USC it was like we had God as coach. McKay was bigger than life.

163

It's like what Vince Evans said, that he was watching USC on television and just got caught up in the colors, the band, the cheerleaders, the blue sky, the fans, the incredibly great team. He had this idea of what USC would be long before he ever got there. When he arrived, he saw that it really was what he thought it would be. It's really like that.

The 1972 team was so good, so very athletic, we knew from day one with the frosh that we were special as juniors. And by the time we were seniors, we were physical specimens. I mean, we had guys who were among the top 10 athletes in the world in terms of their capability. We had guys who were great in basketball, track, and baseball. We were ranked second in the nation to UCLA in basketball the previous year. It was not just from football, it was a happening place. The football team was stacked; we had guys with the attitude that we couldn't lose.

In the time I was there, we had these kinds of guys—guys like Charlie Weaver, Jimmy Gunn, Tim Rossovich, Greg Slough—they all had the attitude that we were going to win. Nobody was going to take it from us. We got to that '72 season, and the trainers had us work on new training techniques, running 800 meters (and I smoked that), and it was totally different. We had new coaches, a quality control guy named Joe Marducci, who was a "Dapper Dan," always well dressed, and he'd make sure our huddle was perfect. We made sure plays were perfect. McKay understood we had everything in place. It was special, and we attended to minor details. The opportunity was there and then, and the attitude was special—*this is the year we roll, we're unstoppable*. We were lining up Anthony Davis, Allen Carter, Shelton Diggs—great athletes, *holy moly*. Everybody was for the good of the team. It was a pretty strong atmosphere.

When we played UCLA, they were just plain scared. My brother, Fred, was playing there. He knew us, and I knew their guys. There was an acknowledgment that we had something different, a touch above the others, and even UCLA knew that. They had white shoes, they were a finesse team, but none of their gimmicks worked. They all knew they'd lose.

Versus Notre Dame, our defense was scary. Artimus Parker, Marvin Cobb, Richard "Batman" Wood, Charles Anthony, Willie Hall—all of these guys were super strong, all played pro football. We had prospects everywhere and needed no gimmicks. We never tried flea flickers. McKay would go through the game plan and understood what our team was looking to do, and we always knew we could stop the others. McKay delivered a message on how to beat opponents, and we went out and did it.

He was always right on. He shored up his coaching staff, and we had total information, it was like a professional team. We changed our practice facility, moved from the "dungeon." Heritage Hall had just been built, and it was an extra added attraction. We had this aura, this thing we had. We got back to where we'd been on defense with the "Wild Bunch," where we'd seen Charlie Weaver go nuts. Other teams were just, like, you don't want to go against these Trojans.

Against Ohio State in the Rose Bowl, I recall that McKay did not like Woody Hayes much, and he really wanted to win that game. To me, it was so important, a culmination of an incredible year and a reward for doing what we had done, a finishing mark on that year. McKay had changed a few things up, but at halftime of the Rose Bowl, he said, "Gentlemen, we're just going to go back to what we do well." And we came out and lambasted a very good Buckeyes team in the second half to wrap up the national championship. I'm not sure if it was personal, but McKay wanted to beat the Buckeyes.

McKay took umbrage with Hayes' idea that West Coast football was soft, that our style of football was not as tough, so he took the onus on himself to prove that incorrect. He made some comments that could not be shared with the public. You don't say things you must retract. You back it up and base it on facts. You took it that he had disdain for Hayes with those comments.

Rod McNeill's college and professional career as a running back was shortened by injuries, but he was a significant member of the 1972 "all-time greatest" national champions, earned the Trojan Club Award for most improved player, and was selected for the 1974 College All-Star Game. He went on the the NFL to play for the New Orleans Saints and Tampa Bay Buccaneers.

MANFRED MOORE

FULLBACK

1971–1973

As far as Coach John McKay is concerned, I didn't bring my handkerchief because when it comes to that man, I cry. He means so much to me, what he did for me. I'm so blessed. Life is full of cycles—you begin one and then another one. You draw on other trials, beginnings, middles, ends. So much of what I am blessed with today stems from my relationship with him.

When we were freshmen, you would see him on campus and walk on the other side of the street, and he would put his head down. Others got offended, but on the field he looked at you and said, "Get in there and run the play how it is supposed to be run." The lessons from Coach McKay apply to business and to life. I was voted by my teammates as the most inspirational and most improved player, but when I first came, there were hurdles, and Coach McKay helped me overcome them.

As a married man—a black man married to a white woman—at the age of 18 with a son, Jason, on campus, I was worried how this would be received, how it would affect my position on the team and my scholarship. I'd take Jason to some classes and to football practices, and he'd be waiting for his daddy after practice.

McKay could have said, "Don't bring that kid around here." He could have made it hard on me for any number of reasons. But one day after practice, McKay called Jason over and told Pat Haden to call a play, and he handed it to my son. I told him to run that way, and my wife and I cheered. Coming

166

in, McKay could have ignored me, but I had a meeting with him, and he told me, "Don't worry." He got me a job, got me admitted to married-student housing, and helped make everything smooth. Oh, that was a weight off my mind!

The racial thing was not an issue. It was not the way I grew up, worrying about that, and he never let that be an issue. We won the national title in 1972, and in 1973 we went to the Rose Bowl, but lost to Ohio State. He could have criticized me, but he said in the paper, if there is one last thing he does, "Manfred Moore will get a pro contract."

The San Francisco 49ers drafted me in the ninth round, and I played for them for two years. Then in 1976 Tampa Bay came into the NFL, and McKay took over as their coach. I was with them at first after the expansion draft. I was there when we lost all the games, and the writers asked Coach McKay, "What do you think of your team's execution?" He replied, "I think that's a good idea."

But near the end of the season, the Oakland Raiders needed to find a replacement for an injured player. They could have chosen anybody to replace a kid injured on a punt return, but McKay arranged for me to go to the Raiders. Al Davis was a former Trojan assistant coach, and there was a connection between USC and the Raiders, so I went to a team that won the Super Bowl. I had family in the East Bay, and this gave me a chance for my grandparents to see my games. They didn't really know football and got upset when they saw the other team hit their grandson.

There were other influences at USC. I was separate from most of the guys on the football team, not living on campus, and I was taking care of my family, so I was not getting together socially except during away games. Home games we stayed in a hotel prior to the game and would just hang out. That was the "Big Five": Edesel Garrison, Charle "Tree" Young, Rod McNeill, Sam "Bam" Cunningham, and me. Then Lynn Swann tried to get in on us, and we tossed him from the room. He was good, but we were seniors. I have a picture of us picking Lynn up and tossing him after we won the Pacific-8 title. We tossed Lynn up.

He just wanted to hang out and tried to force his way in. He was a mouthy guy, but we just laughed. There was some arrogance, and he thought he was good enough to hang with the seniors. He was the "pretty boy" from the elite Catholic school in the Bay Area, Serra High, and he was more like a ballet dancer than a football player. He had a big reputation, and so we felt the

167

need to keep him from getting too big for his britches. It was all in fun. We all liked him and, of course, he earned his way in. The camaraderie we shared was incomparable.

When Lynn made All-America, we appreciated what he did on the field. Being in a position to play and be active on the team, and have other team members pay attention, it gave me a chance to mentor others on how to be aggressive, to contribute to the team. What a thrill.

Sam "Bam" Cunningham could consume defensive ends and run right over them. His talent was incredible. He could have been one of the all-time greats, but the team had so many weapons that he was not spotlighted. He was a complete team player whose only concern was to win.

When USC traveled, we always dressed professionally, in a coat with a white shirt and tie. In the hotels, it was a controlled environment, no intruders, only family. We'd come in a day ahead of the game. We'd take a bus to the stadium, all together. When we went to Alabama in 1970, there were expectations. From the reaction from fans, they were surprised to see us. It was the verge of a significant game. We heard no cursing or people giving us the "victory" sign (as in the middle finger). They just looked at us, and this was what the game was all about.

They saw blacks and whites, together, a team that cared for each other. They saw discipline and esprit de corps. They saw a sense of professionalism—young black men, college students with futures, not porters or baggage handlers, who were not there to bow to them. We were there to be respectful, but we came to beat their team. At Alabama we executed on the field, and fans saw this sense of discipline, players of all colors playing together with discipline and with McKay in control, the leader.

McKay was once on a scaffold while Marv Goux was down on the field coaching, and we ran a sweep. Some of the players didn't understand the coach, and one guard didn't block, and the play was disrupted. McKay had this megaphone and called the shots, and he explained what went wrong. Then he just put down the megaphone, climbed down, and the whole world stood still. He calmly walked over to the quarterback and described how the play was supposed to be executed. Then he stepped back, and Haden called the play, but there was another mistake. Craig Fertig tried to intervene, but McKay continued to control the play and kicked Craig in the rear. I said, "Whoa, I don't ever want that to happen to me."

He was in command. When he said something, you paid attention, on and off the field. He was in charge of every detail and implemented everything on or off the field. He said it, and it got done. We never got smashed. Even if we lost, we never lost control.

There were some black players who felt that McKay had put us in harm's way at 'Bama. I didn't relate to the game in that way. Obviously, there were issues, but I was not worried about shootings or guns. It was just a game we had to win. There was one big question: how would we be received? That was on my mind. Ninety-nine percent of us expected bad racial events, so we kept our heads up, looked around, and saw how people reacted. People got out of the way as the bus came to the stadium, but they just looked at us in there. Fans saw us dressed professionally. Afterward, when the people down there were in transition, you understood that it was a unique game. But at the time you don't know what to expect. We'd been taught how to handle ourselves. If you know how to handle yourself, you can deal with it. After the game, nothing happened.

Mike Rae was the starting quarterback in 1972. He came in with us, and Jimmy Jones was ahead of us. McKay respected him enough to make him the starter. Rae was at the point where he had to build up to the position, but Jimmy was the senior quarterback. Mike had more physical tools and could throw the long ball, but McKay was in charge and never put Mike in the position to show all his talents. Mike never let on that he was having any troubles about his situation. He got to play in 1972, we won the national championship, and he got drafted by Oakland.

Other teams looked at the 1972 Trojans, and the thing I saw most often was that they were almost scared. They were certainly nervous. We had a swagger, a confidence, and the opponents would be gritting their teeth. We would race back and forth, we showed fire out there, and we'd see trepidation on the other team. Each player was so good, had such inner confidence. We'd look up at our opponent, and there was an unanswered question on his face. There were some defensive players who just threw up their hands. We were never stopped. If it was fourth and short, we attacked with the sweep. Clarence Davis was fast, but Anthony Davis was quick, and Cunningham was unstoppable.

Sam did not do that over-the-top touchdown dive as much during the year as he did versus Ohio State in the 1973 Rose Bowl. He did that as a dive. On the DVD, *History of USC Football*, McKay just stared across the field at Woody Hayes and used his hands to indicate, "Hey, Cunningham's going over the top, and you can't stop him." That sums up their relationship right there.

Hayes and McKay were kings of the college game, and consider that USC built the best record in the Rose Bowl, not in the "Frito-Lay Bowl." We built it versus those great Big Ten teams: Hayes and Ohio State, Bo Schembechler and Michigan.

John Robinson used the same skills as a head coach that he used to build himself to that point as an assistant. Robinson was a fine assistant, but he changed the way he handled things, and in 1972 he said, "I'm not your friend. You do it my way or you get benched." He conformed to McKay's tactics. "Do it as I say." Robinson was a friendly guy and *was* your buddy, but he recognized that to be a good coach he needed to change the player-coach dynamic. He handled it well, and it was better.

Marv Goux was a defensive coach. When we saw Goux do his thing, it was two weeks prior to the season, and he'd get on those guys, grab them by the ear if they had no helmet, and he'd get down himself and forearm an offensive lineman. He'd hit him like *this*, you'd see him coach, his tenacity. John Papadakis was a fireball, and you did not want to run that way. They were tough guys. John mimicked Goux's tenacity, and he backed it up. That's where he got his respect, he was so aggressive.

170

But Goux noticed your performance against his defense in practice, and he'd take the time later to tell you what a good job you'd done. It just made you feel like a million bucks. What an experience, to be a Trojan.

Pat Haden was a great contributor. There was a great deal of talk about Haden, who was the California state passing-yardage record-holder. He came in with his best friend, his favorite receiver at Bishop Amat High School, who was John McKay's son, J.K. They had a lot of pressure on them, golden boys and all. But this is USC. This is where we separate the men from the boys, golden or not. Both J.K. and Pat were excellent players who went above and beyond expectations.

From our perspective, to see a young guy come on and conform to McKay's requirements, Pat Haden did it magnificently. He was not big, but he was tough. But most important, he was smart.

J.K. McKay could take a blow. He was not a big guy, but he took strong hits. He'd catch the ball and be bleeding, but he'd go right back in. One time

J.K. took a savage hit, and Coach McKay was very concerned for his son on the sideline. Craig Fertig was calling the plays, and McKay told Fertig to check on J.K. Coach McKay didn't want to show emotion over his son, but he was concerned. But J.K. didn't give up, the same with Pat. They were surfer boys from a fancy private school, Bishop Amat—just like Lynn Swann had gone to Serra—but J.K. McKay and Haden connected with their team-mates, they proved themselves as leaders. J.K. McKay started calling me "Manny." My mom had called me that, then others started.

Malcolm and Kenney Moore are my brothers. Both played at USC. We were all a part of the great San Fernando High School connection. In our day, San Fernando High School was the best prep football program in the United States. It was the Long Beach Poly of its time, in that we were a con-glomeration of black kids, Hispanics, and kind of "pick-up truck" white guys like Allan Graf. Anthony Davis and I played there. Charles White and Kevin "Bug" Williams, God rest his soul, played there. Kenney was at USC with Charles White. Malcolm was there with John Robinson in the early 1980s.

How blessed I am! I played for the CIF–Los Angeles City Section cham-pions at San Fernando, the national champions at USC, and the world cham-pions at Oakland. I cannot separate my belief in the Lord Jesus Christ from what it means to be a Trojan, because I was blessed to be a Trojan. It was a gift from God. The people I met, the friendships, associations, experiences, memories, and family: praise be to God, His blessings are forever. Amen.

171

Manfred Moore was a running back on the 1972 national champions. He won the Sam Barry Spartan Award given to the junior varsity player who con-tributes the most to the varsity (1970) and the Davis-Teschke Award for most inspirational Trojan (1973). Moore was selected for the 1974 College All-Star Game, was drafted by San Francisco, and played for the 49ers (1974–1975), Tampa Bay Buccaneers (with John McKay, 1976), and Minnesota Vikings (1977). In 1976 he was traded to Oakland and was one of seven Trojans on the team that won the Super Bowl championship at Pasadena's Rose Bowl. His broth-ers, Malcolm and Kenney Moore, also played at USC.

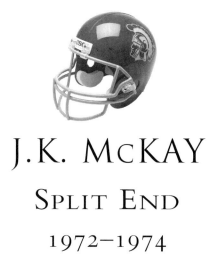

J.K. McKay

Split End

1972–1974

MAN, LOOKING BACK AT MY YEARS as a student–athlete at USC, it was just so great, so much fun, that in some ways it's a blur. But for all the fun, having my dad as the coach, it was great and in the end worked out perfectly. But there were pressures. Take the UCLA game. That's a big game, we all want to win it, it's for bragging rights. But in my family, at least for a number of years, that game meant my dad's job, literally. We had to beat them, or we'd have to move.

What it means to be a Trojan is a shared experience, the old alumni and the young have this common bond. I always hated that old guy getting up to speak, but now that's me. You go with it.

The school, especially then, was so small. It's a private university, and you know everybody. It's not 40,000 kids at a commuter school. We all know the same things, the apartment buildings we lived in, frat row, the 901 Club. Over the years, there have been so many guys like Craig Fertig, great alumni who have been great friends. Pat Haden and I still speak regularly in front of all these groups, and people remember things that happened 30 years ago. I've just learned to entertain audiences from watching my dad. Now people say I hold a crowd like he did. I don't know, but it's an honor to hear that.

To the rest of the world, John McKay is a legend, king of the mountain. He and his competition, guys like Woody Hayes, are considered monuments to the sport. So I have to constantly adjust my thinking from, *He's my dad*, to, *The world wants to know who Coach John McKay was.*

Well, he was a competitor. That's what the rivalry with Woody Hayes and Ohio State was. Two giants who hated to lose. Hayes and my dad, they were not friends, but they were not unfriendly. Hayes complimented my dad. Woody said my dad did the best job of combining the run and passing in offense.

USC just ran an offense that did both things well in an era when teams were either "three yards and a cloud of dust" (the Big Ten), the wishbone (Oklahoma, Alabama), or pass-happy (like Stanford). Those two were competitive, but they respected each other. I think the reason some have speculated that they didn't like each other was because of the regional rivalries, which still exist today.

Woody got in trouble bad-mouthing West Coast football, saying it was not as rugged as the Big Ten. Then he made it worse by making inferences about Hollywood immorality, equating the news media with a sense of political bias against his team, which manifested itself in his taking a swing at an *L.A. Times* photographer. But his opinions were contradictory. He supported Richard Nixon, a Republican from Los Angeles. If Woody saw Hollywood immorality, he was not seeing it in USC, a conservative, traditional school that remained patriotic, as he did. And my dad was a conservative Republican. Where you separated the two was in offensive styles, my dad being more free-wheeling, while Woody just wanted to run the ball off-tackle. The other difference was in their disciplinary styles. My dad changed with the times— the hairstyles, he was not real big on bed checks, and we were always loose— whereas Woody would hide his team in a monastery, and they'd come into the Rose Bowl tight.

Ara Parseghian and my dad had more in common. They were good friends. I was recruited by him, and going back there, it was like seeing God. He said, "I know you're probably going to go to 'SC, but if you decide not to, we'd love to have you here." You'd be surprised how much genuine thought I gave to that, coming out of Bishop Amat. Haden was also serious about it. His mom was kind of pushing it, so it was not as sure a thing as people believe. If I had not gone to 'SC, I would have gone to Notre Dame. They had a great tradition.

I must admit, the rumors are true. Pat and I roomed together. We lived in the dorms as freshmen (I think you had to), then moved to the Twin Palms,

173

J.K. McKay poses for a photo with his father, Coach John McKay, during USC's dominant 1972 season.

174

which was an off-campus apartment of about 10 units. I think three of us lived together—Pat, Allen Carter, and myself. We knew Allen because he'd competed against us when he was at Bonita High School, the same school that Heisman winner ("Mr. Outside") Glenn Davis of Army had gone to. Pat, Allen, and I, about 14 guys overall, most or all football players, lived there. Pete Adams was living there. John and Chris Vella were there, plus some other friends.

The rumor is that I would be in the front room partying, drinking beer, have some girls over, whatever, and Pat would be in the back, studying. Yes, that's about the size of it. He was a serious student who had the ability to compartmentalize leisure from business. He liked to have fun; he just took care of his studies and quarterback responsibilities before he let himself do that. I took the view as an undergraduate that if you got an A in a course, it meant you'd spent too much time on it, but Pat only got As.

In my sophomore year, 1972, I got a lot of playing time with Edesel Garrison. Garrison was a 400-meter guy who could really run. I'd played some at cornerback in high school, but mostly I was a receiver. I'd come in as a quarterback, but Haden was there, and as soon as I saw what he could do, it seemed like a good idea to play receiver. I met him the first day of practice at Bishop Amat. The two guys I copied were Fred Biletnikoff and, more so, Bobby Chandler, who was already at USC, a great guy and a great receiver. He didn't get as much notoriety because of the ground game, but he had a great game in the 1970 Rose Bowl and later was a great star at Buffalo and Oakland, although he died tragically young.

The one big pass I caught in the 1975 Rose Bowl—the winning touchdown in an 18–17 thriller over Ohio State—I caught in what we called the "Chandler corner" of the end zone. I copied that play. Neal Colzie, an All-America defensive back from Ohio State, was on that side a lot, but not on that last play. Colzie was talkative, a demonstrative guy on the field, and you wanted to get the best of him. But he was nothing like the current chattiness of players. He had a few words to say, but not like the modern stuff we see today.

There were no bad feelings. We had played three Rose Bowls in a row against Ohio State. We all knew each other well, but we had no issues. After we made a fourth-and-one, Coach McKay called timeout with two minutes left and said, "Run 64-X corner." I thought they were too far out and I couldn't beat my man on that corner. I told him that, and he just said, "I don't care what you think, get back in the huddle, call '64-run X corner,' and make the play." I had to take seven to 12 extra steps to get open and stay within the end zone. Pat pumped three or four times. Watch the tape, it's amazing how much time he got to throw that ball. Pat pumped into that end zone, and it was literally where I stood as a kid. I'd always thought how cool it would be to catch one down there.

My dad never told me about a letter he received after the Notre Dame game with cutout letters saying, "I'm gonna kill you and your son." So these FBI guys were there, these guys in suits who did not seem to belong there. But after the game Marv Goux grabbed me, and these FBI guys surrounded me, and I wondered, *What's going on here? How come I can't hang out on the field and celebrate with my teammates and the fans?* We never found who it was.

There was something about that 1974 team. We weren't as strong as the 1972 national champions, and you wouldn't rate us as one of the best teams of all time, even though it was our second national title in three years, and my dad's fourth (compared to Bear Bryant, who at that time only had three). But we played some of the most memorable games in USC football history, the last two games I ever played at 'SC, and it may just have been the most *exciting* team ever!

We never lost to UCLA in my four years, and I made the best catch I ever made for a touchdown against them, but it was luck as much as anything. I made a one-handed catch. We won two national titles, so, in the hierarchy of Trojan football alumni, we kind of had the "edge," so to speak. But under

175

Pete Carroll, they're up there or better. A lot of things have changed at USC and in L.A. The campus, the city, the neighborhood. I grew up in the San Gabriel Valley, at the foot of a huge mountain range that I never saw except after it rained in January.

The air quality when I was in school was so bad there were days one side of the Coliseum could hardly see the other. Not anymore. The air is unbelievably cleaner now than it was then. The neighborhood is cleaner and safer. It's a real revitalization.

J.K. McKay is the son of Coach John McKay. He was a member of the 1972 and 1974 national champions, two Rose Bowl champions, and after making the winning touchdown catch to beat Ohio State, was named co–Rose Bowl Player of Game in 1975 and later to the Rose Bowl Hall of Fame. After selection to the Hula Bowl and Senior Bowl, McKay was drafted by the Cleveland Browns and played three years for the Tampa Bay Buccaneers. An attorney in Los Angeles, he has been part of the group trying to bring the NFL back to L.A. His younger brother, Rich McKay, has been the general manager of the Tampa Bay Buccaneers and the Atlanta Falcons.

RICHARD WOOD

INSIDE LINEBACKER

1972–1974

GIL CHAPMAN. He's the reason a relatively unheralded kid from Elizabeth, New Jersey, became a Trojan. Gil Chapman was a great running back at Jefferson High School in Elizabeth. Gil went to Michigan. Gil was the reason why we were looked at. He was an excellent running back and a great student. Everybody wanted him. I would not have gotten recognition without him.

I'm not all that physically imposing at 6′2½″, 210 pounds. According to everybody else, maybe I was a little small, but I didn't pay attention. USC had a linebacker before me named Adrian Young, and he wasn't that big, but he was awfully good. There weren't many linebackers as strong as I was. We had strength training in high school, and I was lifting weights on a regular basis. They had no real strength and conditioning program at USC, though. I had to do it on my own.

My coach at Jefferson High met Coach John McKay at an Atlantic City football clinic. He looked at Gil and asked if they'd send film, and that's how it got started. They liked what they saw and recruited me.

Sam "Bam" Cunningham always talks about the first time he met me as a freshman. Hudson Houck, the offensive line coach and the freshman coach, first met all the freshmen at a get-together at Julie's. He asked everybody to tell a joke, so when it came my turn, I said, "Listen up, I'm Batman from Gotham City." My nickname was "Sergeant Rock" in high school, from the comic book. My brothers were all in the military, and everybody called me "Sarge." But when I envisioned what my nickname should be, I saw *Batman*. It was like, "I'll take on anybody, anywhere." I was 17, 18 maybe.

It's been said my first game ever as a Trojan, a 31–10 win at Arkansas, was the best first game any college player ever had. I just wanted to win, to get to double-zero seconds and have more points. I don't know how many tackles I had, maybe as many as 17. To have the opportunity to start as a sophomore was fantastic for me. A big part of it was that nobody respected us from our record the year before, but we knew going in it would be a much better season, that our goal was the Rose Bowl. Whatever happened from there was not just about Richard Wood. The bottom line is the Rose Bowl.

I went out, did the best I could, and tried not to make mistakes in a hostile environment. Joe Ferguson was their quarterback, and I hit him a couple times, but my job was to inflict pain. I made sure I was not blocked and could not be stopped. I was an individual, but *we* as a defense, nobody was going to run over us, not this evening. We got off to a great start and had a great finish, on a high note, to go 12–0 and win the national championship. To win the conference and the Rose Bowl, that's our goal, that's all we talked about. That's all the seniors talked about. They'd not been to one, and they wanted to go out on a good note. We kept the crowd out of the game and wanted them to see Trojan football at its best. Everywhere they went, they got a taste of it.

There was a revolution at the linebacker position before and during the time I played. It became a speed position. Jimmy Gunn, Willie Hall, and Charlie Weaver at 'SC were all great. We had the best athletes in college football, all around. In the late 1960s, when I watched football, I'd watch Nebraska, George Webster at Michigan State, but when I looked at USC, I saw good athletes: Mike Garrett, Bob Chandler, Steve Sogge, O.J. Simpson. A lot of these guys were multiple-sport stars who played baseball, volleyball, basketball, ran track. Through the years, that was how USC approached it.

Even the linemen there—that's what impressed me about Coach McKay, he didn't go for these big clodhoppers. Charle Young revolutionized the tight end position from a hybrid lineman to a skill receiver, runner, and athlete. Morris Stroud of the Chiefs was 6'10", but Charle had the most athleticism. Nobody looked like Sam Cunningham. He could play tailback or fullback. There was no better team around. The 1972 Southern California Trojans are the best team in college football history. I can respect somebody who knows

USC Trojans linebacker Richard Wood was the school's first three-time first-team All-American and a member of the 1972 and 1974 national champions. He went on to play 10 years in the NFL.

Photo courtesy of Getty Images

his stuff comparing the 1995 and 1971 Nebraska Cornhuskers, the 1947 Notre Dame Fighting Irish, and even the 2004–2005 USC Trojans. Those teams have their fans, and they're entitled to their view, but in my opinion, our team in '72 was No. 1.

When we played UCLA in 1973, I broke through the line and made a sack on the game's first play. I stood over the guy and said, "You're playing with the big boys now." They talked too much, and I don't think they knew whom they were playing. Little children suffer the consequences. We respected them and prepared for their wishbone. I don't know what they were told, but you don't antagonize us in the paper. It becomes cannon fodder. This wasn't training camp or high school or some other college opponent. I respected Mark Harmon, and he respected us. John Sciarra was excellent, but certain players mouthed off. Guys had gone to different high schools, but you're playing in the big time now, this is not high school. One of the officials told me when I came out for the Notre Dame game, "This is a game that makes men out of you."

People ask me, what was the better performance, Anthony Davis in 1972 or A.D. in 1974? You've got to talk about Red Grange and Tommy Harmon when you're talking the best day a college player had. But with both of A.D.'s games, you could make the argument on his behalf. For my money, 1974 was the game. That will go down in football history.

We played terribly in the first half and we knew it. No way Notre Dame comes to our stadium and beats up on us like that. At the half, McKay gave a little talk. He said, "A.D.'s gonna take this ball back and score." I know people think that's been exaggerated, but he actually said he'd run it back and score. The talk was three or four minutes only. He said, "Fellas, we played bad in the first half," and, "There's no rule against blocking," and, "We're behind." On the *History of USC Football* DVD, McKay says, "Then a couple math majors rose their hands."

Then Coach Goux got up and spoke, and I don't even *want* to repeat what *he* said. Come game time and practice, it was a different story. Goux was tough. We'd lost the year before at South Bend. I couldn't understand how they kept getting in field position and scoring. They had this kind of single wing that confused us, but it was nothing we shouldn't have handled. Then our offense caught magic in a bottle. A.D. ran the second half kick all the way back. J.K. McKay, Pat Haden, Jim Obradovich, Dave Farmer, everyone clicked, and everything just started to change. The skill guys started making plays. Charles Phillips made a couple interceptions; we recovered a fumble, made a few stops, and we were on our way. Now we were making plays on defense. When we started making progress, we needed things to happen in our favor.

180

Woody Hayes was announcing the game up in the booth, and he was our next opponent, in the Rose Bowl. The fans were chanting, "Woody, you're next!" The way he commented on the game, he wanted nothing good to happen to Southern Cal. He had beaten us in the 1974 Rose Bowl the previous year. But, come on, comment in a fair manner. I can understand his animosity, but it was blatant in his comments as an announcer.

In 1974 A.D. should have won the Heisman Trophy. It was a travesty to do him like that. That was before online voting, and we played Notre Dame in December, a late game. Writers were making sure their ballots made it into the mail on time and voted before the game. But, of course, had they voted after the game, A.D. would have won for sure. Archie Griffin knows he shouldn't have won that. People like to see us mad, and it's hard to fathom the winning that 'SC has done, but just look at the history books. Most of the schools are jealous, that's just part of it. We've won more national championships than the Gators and Seminoles *combined*. Combined times three.

We thought we'd blow Ohio State out. We stopped Woody on their first series, but he did his best to fire up his team after what we did to Notre

Dame. He's a great motivator and managed to make our win over the Irish work to their advantage. They took A.D. out of the game with an injury, and Allen Carter came in. If not for Allen, I don't think we'd have had a chance at winning. We all came in together—Pat, J.K., Marvin Powell, Dale Mitchell.

Allen was quite likeable, and most of us had respect for him. He does not rate with the great Trojan tailbacks, but he was a good player, and that day he carried us. Neal Colzie, bless his soul, always said about the final play, "How did J.K. McKay beat me?" Bless his soul, Neal died a few years ago. He took his eyes off J.K. He did what receivers try to do, to deceive the defender and make him think one thing, then do another. Colzie was not mouthing off on the field. You always had mouthy people trying to intimidate with their mouths. The camera showed Neal getting exuberant, but he was classy.

The line held, so Haden had a long time. McKay needed every second and every inch of the Rose Bowl end zone to break free and make the touchdown catch. We went for two—because McKay and USC did not play for ties—and made it to win 18–17. It was pandemonium, excitement like few games you can imagine.

Ohio State was the toughest school I played against. Notre Dame and UCLA with its wishbone were wicked, but the most physical was Ohio State. In 1973 we tied Oklahoma 7–7 when they called one of Obradovich's TDs back. I'm not sure how we stopped them. We stopped Joe Washington, but their fullback had a great game.

In 1974 we won the UPI national championship, but the AP gave it to Oklahoma even though they were on probation. They were 11–0 but played no bowl game, whereas we had to beat Woody and one of his best Buckeye teams, so we were cochampions. They won the national title with us, but they shouldn't have been voted champions after being caught breaking NCAA rules. Why even consider them?

I played for John McKay in Tampa Bay. Those were tough years for a time. They asked McKay, "What do you think of your team's execution?" and he replied, "That's a good idea." But we improved and went to the NFC Championship Game at the end of the 1979 season. Al Davis never liked me, so I guess I did something right against the Raiders.

Thirty years later, I love USC. I met my wife there and have been married 32 years. It's not only football, but the friends, my teammates, the people I

181

went to school with. It's an honor and it's humbling that so many great things happened there. I was elected to the College Football Hall of Fame, won two national titles, and played in three Rose Bowls. Lots of hard work paid off. I'm not a millionaire or anything, but there are other things in life—friendships, every day on campus, and it's a small campus, so you know more people with USC, the camaraderie. There's diversity at USC. People call it a "BMW school" or the "University of Spoiled Children," but that's garbage. USC is a school where minorities were always welcome, opportunities were available, and we had people from all kinds of countries and backgrounds in school. It was a period I'll always recall fondly. I'm proud to be a Trojan. I tell the guys they can't take anything away from us.

The guys I respect most are the tough ones. You have to give it to Archie Griffin. For three years, he gave as well as he got. He was the best player I faced. I've seen him interviewed, and whenever he talks about playing USC at the Rose Bowl, he always says, "Man, those guys were like a pro team." He gives and deserves respect.

That's the beauty of sports, and I give credit to those guys at Ohio State. They were tough. Oklahoma was very physical and fast, but we only faced them once. I have to rate the Buckeyes the toughest. Woody's teams were always ready, plus he had them believing there was a superior nature to Big Ten football. He'd say, "You don't wanna go out there. There's earthquakes out there, and the California sunshine makes 'em not so serious." I said, "Excuse me!?"

Hayes and McKay were way ahead of the curve on the issue of progressive opportunity for black athletes. You'd see that, growing up in the 1960s. There were schools that caught your eye, and you thought, *Now there's a place I'd like to play.* A friend of mine talked of Southern Cal, and I watched TV and saw Mike Garrett and Steve Sogge. I looked at these guys, but never in my wildest dreams did I think I'd be part of that.

I'd look at games on TV, but I didn't understand it until they recruited me. Gil said California was too far away for him, but I told him, "I'm going. I wanna see California, it's pretty out there." My brothers told me to take a look at it. They were all in the military and had left home and wanted me to have the same opportunities.

I look at some of these schools: Florida, Florida State, Miami. Michigan played Appalachian State. I give them due credit, they were Division I-AA champs and had some great athletes, but Michigan took them lightly. USC consistently plays the toughest schedule in the country. We'll play anybody, anywhere. We'll travel into the South, play an extra game, play on neutral fields. Plus every year, it's UCLA and Notre Dame.

What gets me is they talk of "Title Town." What city has won more titles than Los Angeles? The Pacific-10 Conference has won the most national championships in football, basketball, track, tennis, volleyball, gymnastics, swimming, water polo, golf, soccer, rugby, rowing, women's softball—you get the point! Then add other West Coast schools like USF's basketball and soccer titles, baseball championships at Fresno State, Fullerton, and Pepperdine, and titles in all these sports California dominates like volleyball and swimming. Add in the Lakers, Dodgers, and Angels, and talk about Title Town!

Coming from outside New York to the West Coast and hearing people call athletes out there "soft," it's like, "Excuse me?" The state has produced by far the most pro football players, big leaguers, NBA players, tennis, track, and Olympic athletes. USC and UCLA are like countries in the Olympics. I'm part of that.

Plus there were nice people there. Everybody was smiling and friendly, not all this unhappiness as in the East. I was not used to that, but I wanted to get along with my teammates and everybody. You don't have that at other places. McKay put on no acts, it was honest. Wayne Fontes was honest. Dave Levy was one of the nicest persons I have ever met.

Lastly, it's great to be a Trojan. It was great to be part of that history. I'm so proud to be a part of it. I didn't want anybody to beat me or my Trojan teammates. Maybe some people thought I was overzealous, but *Fight On!*

Richard "Batman" Wood was the school's first three-time first-team All-American and the first ever selected three times from a West Coast college. He played for the 1972 and 1974 national champions. Wood played on two Rose Bowl winners (both over Ohio State, 1973 and 1975) and was All–Pac-8 in 1972, 1973, and 1974. He made the Playboy Preseason All-America team (1973). He is on the short list of the greatest college football players, and most especially the greatest linebackers, ever to play the game. He was selected to play in the Hula Bowl, Senior Bowl, and the College All-Star Game. Batman is a member of the National Football Foundation College Hall of Fame and the USC Athletic Hall of Fame, and played in the National Football League for the New York Jets and Tampa Bay Buccaneers from 1975 to 1984.

CLAY MATTHEWS
INSIDE LINEBACKER
1974–1977

I PLAYED AT THE UNIVERSITY OF SOUTHERN CALIFORNIA from 1974 to 1977, two years for John McKay and two years for John Robinson. I had gone to high school in Arcadia, California, but in my senior year my father got a promotion, and we moved to Illinois. I went to New Trier East High School in the Chicago suburbs. We had lived in a lot of places. I was born in California, but we'd also lived in North Carolina around 1970. I had played linebacker, on the offensive line, and also at fullback in high school. But USC brought me in as a linebacker.

Coming into USC in 1974, I knew of Anthony Davis because of his great game against Notre Dame in 1972, when he scored six touchdowns. But I was not as familiar with the players as a kid might be today, where they know each other from camps and the Internet. I had just come back out with my family to Southern California, and USC offered a scholarship. At first, to be honest, I didn't know all the guys. But it seemed to be the right geographical area, and I became a Trojan.

I got a lot of playing time as a freshman in 1974. Until recently, freshmen had been ineligible, but Mario Celotto, who was also a freshman linebacker, and I got a lot of time. I came in with no preconceived notions about redshirting or playing time. It was a little different back then. You did what they told you. I came in and had some early success and, as the season went on, played more and more, especially on special teams. I was on the kick return team when A.D. made that touchdown return against Notre Dame.

That day was just incredible. We won 55–24. There's so many distractions in Southern California that the fans are not quite as vocal as other fans. There are more things to spread their attention to, but there could not have been a more incredible atmosphere than the Coliseum on that day. You couldn't have found a fan or a stadium in the country that commanded more noise and greater attention than in the second half of that game. It was almost electric.

We were getting killed, but scored late in the first half. McKay came in to the locker room. We were down 24–6 at halftime. He carried himself in a certain way, where he had a certain amount of clout. He says, "They're gonna kick it off to us, A.D. will run it back, and we'll proceed to win this game."

I thought, *What is this guy taking about? This is bold*. But that's what happened. Craig Fertig tells a story (or maybe it was McKay himself) where Coach McKay said something like, "Gentlemen, we're behind…" and three math majors raised their hands and said, "Yes we are." If Fertig tells the story, it may be subject to embellishment.

Anyway, after A.D. ran back the opening kick of the second half for a touchdown and David Lewis stopped them on an incredible play, we got on a roll where we were at twice the speed we'd been on. We became unstoppable and absolutely killed Notre Dame. That game gave us the momentum to beat Ohio State in the Rose Bowl, and after a couple of the right teams lost bowl games, we won a share of the national championship.

When it comes to my memories of McKay, he was not the "warm and fuzzy" type. He ran a good program. I came in, they brought me to him, and he said, "How's your visit?" I said, "Fine." He said, "I'm not one for big pep talks. I let the school and our players sell themselves." He asked, "Do you have any questions?" I said I didn't, and it lasted a few minutes, but he didn't have to put on a big sales pitch to get guys to play at USC.

Assistant coach Wayne Fontes did most of the recruiting of me. Later he became head coach of the Detroit Lions. I'd been in Illinois, but his brother was at Michigan State, and they recruited me. It was more regional then than now. Fontes' brother recruited me, but I said, "To be perfectly honest, I'm probably going to USC." He asked if there was anything he could do to change my mind, but I was set. Stanford was also in the running, but I chose USC.

Clay Matthews (60) helps block for Anthony Davis during his 102-yard kickoff return for a touchdown against Notre Dame to ignite a 49-point second half that gave USC a 55–24 victory in Los Angeles on November 30, 1974.

His brother had called Wayne and said that USC should take a look at me. Wayne Fontes said, "I've heard good things from my brother," and he offered me a scholarship. His recruiting pitch to me was, "You'll marry a cheerleader and get a job in the movies."

Marv Goux was a tough man who treated everybody the same. He was very fair, a real equal-opportunity guy who just loved being a Trojan. He was just a delight. You either loved or hated Marv, and I loved him.

I made All-America in 1977. My last two years, 1976 and 1977, I played for John Robinson. He was extremely well organized. He had been in the NFL and was very aggressive with his practices and overall approach, but I don't remember it being a difficult transition. I'd not really dealt with McKay that much. I'd already been recruited, and there was no real change. Robinson's personality was different, but the program was still run decently, maybe a little more progressive on offense.

In my senior year, 1977, our quarterback was Rob Hertel. He was the starter for only a year and is not one of USC's more recognized names, but he was a very good athlete. He was also a baseball player, whose father was a scout or something. That season we just missed having a really good year. We were 4–0 and ranked No. 1 in the nation when Paul "Bear" Bryant and seventh-ranked Alabama came to the L.A. Coliseum on October 8.

Bryant and his team had lost to McKay and Sam Cunningham's Trojans in that famed 1970 game that is considered such a big moment in integrating sports, so beating us was kind of revenge for their fans. They ran that triple-option, which you didn't see much of in the Pacific-8 Conference. They were good. They had great athletes like Ozzie Newsome and Johnny Davis. Alabama rolled out to a 21–6 lead in the fourth quarter, but Hertel did a great job and brought us back. It was a typical USC game, but we fell just short, 21–20. Two weeks later we traveled to Notre Dame, where Joe Montana and Notre Dame came out with their green jerseys and beat us on the way to the national title.

187

Hertel was a fine quarterback who later played for the Cincinnati Bengals. I remember he did a real good job, but I never analyzed what they did on that side of ball. At that time, I was not equipped to analyze the offense. He had a strong arm, and if we had won a game here and there, we could have made it different, but we got into a little slump, lost to Warren Moon and Washington, and finished 8–4. But we beat UCLA and killed Texas A&M 47–28 in the Bluebonnet Bowl to finish 12th.

I was drafted in the first round by the Browns and played 16 years with Cleveland and later for the Falcons. My brother, Bruce, was also an All-American at USC, although I didn't influence his decision to go there. By that time, our family was living in Arcadia, and he'd seen me play at USC, so the choice was an easy one for him. He played for the Houston Oilers and is in the Pro Football Hall of Fame.

My son, Kyle, played for USC from 2000 to 2003. My youngest son, Clay III, is enjoying his stay at USC. He was smaller, around 160 pounds as a junior, but he decided to play there and compete with the best. He dedicated himself, and now he's 6'4", 247 pounds, and doing really well.

Clay Matthews played on the 1974 national championship team that beat Notre Dame 55–24 and Ohio State 18–17 in the Rose Bowl. He was All–Pac-8 (1976–1977), played for two Rose Bowl champions (1975 and 1977), was team captain (1977), and a consensus All-American (1977). Matthews was selected for the 1978 Hula Bowl and is a member of the USC Athletic Hall of Fame. A first-round draft choice of the Cleveland Browns, Clay was a mainstay for the Browns and Atlanta Falcons (1978–1996). His brother, Bruce, was a USC All-American and Hall of Famer, a first-round draft pick of the Houston Oilers who played for the Tennessee Titans in Super Bowl XXXIV, and is a Pro Football Hall of Famer. Both of Clay's sons played for the Trojans: Kyle (2000–2003) and Clay III (2004–2008).

FRANK JORDAN

PLACE-KICKER

1977–1978

I GREW UP IN THE SUNSET district of San Francisco, a primarily Irish Catholic neighborhood that feeds high schools like St. Ignatius, Sacred Heart, and Riordan, which is where I went. Another man from the Sunset with the same name—Frank Jordan, no relation—was mayor of San Francisco in the early 1990s.

I was not recruited by Stanford. Cal was quasi-interested. I was in the *San Francisco Chronicle* my senior year of high school, but I was not offered a scholarship. Art Spander of the *San Francisco Examiner* later asked me how I didn't end up at Cal or Stanford after a USC-Stanford game I played in. Mike Parodi, my coach at Riordan—Bob Toledo was our coach my junior year—talked to Cal coach Mike White and was told I was not good enough to play in the Pac-8, so he told White to "stick it where the sun don't shine."

The guy who got me into kicking was Bob Toledo, who went from Riordan to UC-Riverside. I was recruited to Riverside with a few other guys from my high school and from St. Ignatius, so we had a city contingent and a great team. Calvin Sweeney and Butch Johnson of the Cowboys were on that team. Quarterback Dan Hayes led the nation in passing, and we were becoming a Division II powerhouse. I made all-conference in 1974 and 1975, but at the end of the season, we were told that they were dropping football because of Title IX. Guys with two or more years of eligibility were recruited by everybody. We had some notoriety because of our rising status as a Division II power.

Toledo was hired at USC and brought Calvin Sweeney with him. Toledo called me and said, "We'd like to get you to 'SC, but we have three kickers on scholarship." He tried to get me into other places. I had a nice chat with George Seifert, who had gone to Lincoln High in San Francisco. He was the head coach at Cornell and later the 49ers' coach. He said they needed a kicker, and they had a good architecture program. I was interested in architecture then, but the Ivy League didn't offer scholarships, so that idea went by the wayside.

I enrolled at San Jose State and was there during spring practice in 1976. I kicked the winning field goal in their spring game, and I went to the head coach, Darryl Rogers, and said, "I can't stay here unless I get a scholarship." He said they didn't have any available. Then in the middle of all this, he announced he was leaving to take over at Michigan State. Toledo talked to Lynn Stiles, whom they brought in from UCLA, to try and get me a scholarship, and *he* said they didn't have any available.

190

I told Toledo, who was at 'SC by now, and he said that Glen Walker was a senior, and when he was done, his scholarship would be available. So I'd have to sit out a year at USC. I went to City College of San Francisco and took 30 units in architecture classes. I went through the regular recruiting process after the 1976 season. I was invited to the Rose Bowl victory over Michigan. Toledo picked me up at the airport. Even though I was a "done deal," I was recruited along with the others. We stayed at the Wilshire Hyatt. The elevator came up to the lobby, Ricky Bell entered the elevator, and Toledo introduced me as a recruit. He was a huge specimen of an athlete, and he looked at me like, *What position does this guy play?*

My playing years at USC were 1977–1978. I got a diploma in June 1980, in business, not architecture. Not all the transfer units were allowed, so I was around 20 units short of graduating in the spring of 1979, which is when I should have graduated. So I took the business degree instead of prolonging the process in architecture, and it was still 1980 before I finished. I tried out for the Rams in 1979 while still in school. I managed my apartment building, and the school paid my tuition.

In 1978 we won the national championship, which was propelled by an early-season victory at Alabama. I could tell, when I got to Birmingham, that

Frank Jordan gets off a 37-yard field goal with just two seconds left to give the Trojans a 27–25 victory over Joe Montana and Notre Dame in Los Angeles in 1978.

in general it was much different there. We flew to Alabama on Thursday night. We went to bed, then to Legion Field for a walk-through. Then we had a couple of hours of free time. John Robinson said we were free to mosey around, so guys took off for the local mall, looking to get some souvenirs, until we had to come back for dinner.

Half the guys lined up for cabs—myself, Marty King (the punter), Rob Kerr (another punter), and Jeff Fisher. We jumped in a cab, and the cabbie was a stereotypical redneck—short, thick, fat, and beet red, with a crew cut, a big wad of chew in his mouth, and a hound's-tooth hat just like Bear Bryant's.

"Where y'all wanna go?" he asked. We said to take us downtown to buy souvenirs. He spit out the window and said, "Ya don' wanna go downtown," and his explanation of why that was included an unkind racial epithet. So we just said to take us to a sporting goods store instead. That was our introduction to Birmingham.

Actually, our introduction had been the trip from the airport to town. It was all these granny shacks. These were like photos in a sociology book about rundown, tough neighborhoods. The clock had seemingly never moved past the Great Depression. Our guys were taken aback and frightened.

For an hour or so before the game, the kickers, punters, and skill position players were warming up. I was kicking field goals. Bryant and Robinson were talking. Then Bryant wandered over to where I was kicking. He was standing right behind me, maybe seven or eight yards away with his arms folded. He watched me kick eight or nine field goals. I was kind of shaking until I hit my first field goal. This is *Bear Bryant*. Finally, he walked right by me and said, "Nice job, son."

Nice job, son! Was he trying to psyche me out in case I had to kick one with the game on the line?

Charlie White ran for 199 yards, and Paul McDonald audibled half of the plays in a packed, loud environment at Legion Field. Bryant called it the greatest job of any quarterback he ever saw. It was hot and humid, and Alabama had a good football team, but our guys knew how to turn it on. For me as the kicker, I did what I could, but our guys were amazing. They took the crowd out of the game and jumped off to the lead. We were up by 10. I kicked a 40-yard field goal in the second quarter, so we were always up by 10, and we won 24–14.

By the way, right after the Alabama game, before the Notre Dame game, we played Michigan State with Kirk Gibson. Darryl Rogers, who had been the coach at San Jose State, was now at Michigan State. So the game after 'Bama, we played Michigan State, and now I was kicking for USC. I was talking to him warming up before the game, and he congratulated me on my journey to USC. I think I kicked three field goals in that game. He commented on it after the game and offered congratulations.

The 1978 Notre Dame game was for all the marbles. It came one year after our loss in the "green jersey" game. I had no inkling of what to expect when that big Trojan horse came out onto the field in 1977. I thought it was kind of odd. Then they came busting out, the crowd got fired up, and they never were off their feet until halftime. They overwhelmed us. I don't know if they were better, but that day they beat us. We lost to Alabama by one point in 1977 at home, lost to Cal by three, and lost to Warren Moon and Washington for the Rose Bowl, 28–10. But we had a good team in '77. We clobbered Texas A&M 47–28 in the Bluebonnet Bowl, which was a sign of things to come.

In 1978 Joe Montana was back, but at the time he was considered an average college quarterback. His name at Notre Dame is elevated because of what he did afterward, but he was not regarded as the greatest quarterback ever. We were not focused on him. He was good, he'd led them to the national championship and obviously beaten us in the "green jersey" game, but we felt emotion had carried them more than Montana. Looking back, we should have given him greater due, but we didn't.

They had a good team, but we did a great job in the first half shutting them down. We had a great defensive scheme. But Notre Dame had good coaches, too, and they made halftime adjustments. Our defensive scheme did not adjust immediately to what they were doing.

You could see it unfold, and they got momentum. Montana started to find open receivers. It wasn't a lack of effort by our defense. They did a good job of adjusting, as we had at Alabama. What made us a great team, aside from great athletes, was we had a coaching staff that could make adjustments. Later staffs in the 1980s and 1990s didn't do that.

After Montana led a big-time drive, they went ahead 25–24 with a minute or so left, but missed the two-point conversion. If they'd made it, Coach Robinson would have had to make a decision on whether to kick and settle for a tie or drive for the win. Knowing Robinson, I think he would have opted to go for the score and not settle for a field goal. None of that mattered, however, because a field goal could win it, which put it all on me.

These huge guys, these behemoths, kill each other all day in the trenches, and now it's up to the place-kicker. But that's part of the game. It is called *foot*ball.

Earlier in the game, at the start of the fourth quarter, I kicked one from the right hash mark but didn't have enough angle to put it through. I remember coming back to the bench, thinking it wouldn't mean anything to the outcome. We had been so far out in front, I didn't think it would matter. But now it did, and Otis Page came over to remind me of that. I don't recall Otis saying anything like, "I'll kill you if you don't make it." He just said, "You get another chance."

How did it all unfold in my mind? None of that stuff was in my head. Robinson was calm as usual. I could hear the Notre Dame guys behind me. I could hear their comments, but it all happened so fast I didn't have time to think. I think more about it now. I see film clips of people in the stands going wild, but I didn't hear them. I just heard their guys. Over the years, the only thing I could equate it to was a college basketball game when the kid's on the free throw line and people are waving banners and foam fingers. I can tell you from being in that same position, those guys don't see people waving arms. It's like you've got blinders on, and you just do what comes natural. I tell my kids this now, and tell other kids the same thing.

By the time I got in the game, it was as natural as breathing. You throw or catch the ball, you've done it thousands of times, it becomes second nature.

I was worried more about the snap, the hold, whether something beyond my control would occur.

I had a little more adrenaline, knowing it was for the game. But it was just a kick, it was like putting a golf ball, which is all technique. A lot of guys have real strong legs and can kick it 50 or 60 yards. But, without the right technique, you won't make a field goal if you can't line up properly. Honestly, I can say I didn't think, *If I miss this, then this happens. If I make it, we win the national title.* None of that was happening. I lined up like I always did and kicked it through. All pandemonium broke out, and I was mobbed, the place was ecstatic. But it was a blur. We beat Notre Dame and we did win the national title. A picture of this hangs in the clubhouse at Harding Park Golf Course in Sunset, near where I grew up.

Over the years, it might have had more effect had I stayed in Southern California and lived off it. I did choose to come back to San Francisco, where I live now, surrounded by Cal and Stanford fans. The fact that I wear the national title ring gets some people to notice me. People on BART see it. At parties people see it, but it doesn't really open doors for me. I never wanted to have people do business with me by saying, "I'm Frank Jordan, who kicked the winning field goal against Notre Dame."

194

I'm most proud of being part of the rich tradition of USC, to have contributed to its good fortune, to play with the best of the best. I remember riding from the hotel to the Coliseum, sitting next to Ronnie Lott, Dennis Smith, and Anthony Munoz. I'm a part of their life experience. I can take to my grave the great tradition of Troy, to be part of these great players over the years and in the future.

Now Pete Carroll's revived the program bigger and better than ever. I came out for the spring game. It was a great game, and there were 35,000 in the Coliseum for a scrimmage. Pete's a great guy. I was in L.A. with my kids, and I just said, "Lets go by 'SC on the way back." I took my kids to the bookstore, and we walked out on the practice field to see the players up close. Tim Tessalone came by and said hello. My kids had their pictures taken with John David Booty and Mike McDonald. He said his dad talks about me all the time. Tim grabbed Carroll, and he said hello. He grabbed my two kids and took pictures with us.

I have a 1978 game scrapbook with photos and clippings in a box in my garage, but I can't recall all details of the games. I played for the people, my teammates, the coaches, the fans, and the school. That's what I remember.

Frank Jordan is one of USC's greatest heroes after kicking the dramatic field goal to beat Notre Dame in 1978, ultimately leading to a national championship. He works for New York Metropolitan Life in his native San Francisco. He is an amateur military historian who leads battlefield tours in France. His brother, Steve, also kicked for the Trojans and played in the NFL.

PAUL McDONALD

QUARTERBACK

1977–1979

I WAS AN UNTESTED FIRST-YEAR STARTER at Alabama in 1978, my third year in the program coming out of Bishop Amat High School, which had previously produced Adrian Young, Pat Haden, and J.K. McKay. We opened against Texas Tech and struggled, trailing 9–0 at the half, and we got booed off the field. In the second half, we played well and won 17–9. We ran all over Oregon. I only threw about eight times, so there's no question my first real test came at Legion Field in front of a hostile crowd against the No. 1 team in the country.

They utilized a lot of stuff with me, the idea being for me to get the best play called we could. Every play or every other play, Alabama did a lot of disguising on defense, trying to confuse me, but most times we got the right call off. Charles White had a great game. He dominated them, and we surprised them with our speed and physicality. I was able to get some key throws off. Kevin Williams made a spectacular play for a touchdown. It might have been tipped, but somehow he came up with it for the touchdown. I felt comfortable and poised in the pocket. If you look at my record, you'll see I didn't do a lot of scrambling. It was a really humid day. I remember after warm-ups just being tired. I walked into the locker room, and all the players were sprawled out on the concrete floor with ice packs on their necks. I thought. *We haven't even played a game yet and everybody's bushed.* It was 90 degrees with

Paul McDonald prepares to hand off in a 17–10 win over the UCLA Bruins on November 18, 1978, at Los Angeles Memorial Coliseum. *Photo courtesy of WireImage*

90 percent humidity, so it was a testament to our endurance, how we practice and conditioned. For some reason, I was very calm and comfortable. Sometimes you get in a state where you see everything clearly.

I called a lot of audibles, and apparently that is not the norm in the SEC. The stadiums are loud and discourage that. Bear Bryant later said it was the best quarterbacking job he'd ever seen.

The next week, we played Notre Dame at the Los Angeles Coliseum. The national championship was on the line. We took it to the Fighting Irish from the start, and it's a natural human emotion to start feeling good about yourself when you play well. I got off good passes, and it looked like we had this thing figured out. I knew something about Joe Montana, but I didn't know he was *that* good. He'd beaten us in the "green jersey" game the previous year and led them to the national championship, but there was no indication he was the player he would become. At least not until the second half of the 1978 USC–Notre Dame game.

In the first half, he was really lousy, missing guys by a wide margin. Most people don't know this, but on the second series of the game, I made a poor read and should have thrown the ball. I got sacked by Bob Golic on a blitz. The inside linebacker rolled up on my ankle and tweaked it. I hobbled off to the sideline trainer. He couldn't figure out what was wrong, so we decided to tape it up.

I went out for the next series after they punted. I hit Kevin Williams for 35 or 40 yards. We did a good job on offense, and I left the field feeling fine, no problem. But later in the first half, I threw a touchdown pass to Danny Garcia. Charlie had his usual great game, and we got things going on offense, but then my ankle started to swell, and I couldn't move well. By the end of the first half, I could hardly walk. They took me by cart into the locker, but I just decided, "Hey, wrap it up," and I ran out of the tunnel for the second half. That's when Montana got hot. We thought we were okay, but we couldn't put points up. By the end of the game, Montana led them down to score a touchdown. They didn't convert the two-point conversion, thank goodness, so they led 25–24.

There were 45 seconds left. I grabbed the offense and said, "Hey guys. I'm *really* not happy at *all*. We should be winning." We dominated most of the game but let a big lead get away. My ankle was killing me, but I said, "We don't need to go that far, Jordan's gonna kick a field goal to win it. Just keep them off me, so there's no pressure."

I hit Vic Rakhshani in the flat, but he didn't get out of bounds. On the next play, we had the ball on the short half of the field. I rolled to the short side, but everybody was covered, so I retreated and threw the ball away to avoid having to use the timeout, which we needed for the field goal. I'd thrown the football, of course, but most Notre Dame fans think I fumbled. Jeff Weston grabbed me and spun me around. The ball hit a Notre Dame player in the side hip pad and ricocheted back, so they all thought it was a fumble. They thought the game was over and started spilling onto the field, but the referee, thank God, ruled—correctly—that it was an incomplete pass. Most of my friends and players still think it was a fumble.

It happened so fast, and I had so many guys around me, that most people with the naked eye thought that, but they made the right call. You can see it on the *History of USC Football* DVD. You can slow it down, go frame by frame, and freeze-frame the play, and it proves it was a forward pass.

I called for Williams and Calvin Sweeney on the same side. Williams went short motion off the snap, and before he got tackled short, crossed to the right to keep the linebacker shallow. Sweeney went on a deep cross past the linebacker. The other guy ran a post to keep the safety deep. The free safety was Joe Restic. The last thing he wanted was a post pattern where he got beat deep, so he was very deep. Calvin did a great job and made the catch on the side. He ran the ball upfield before we called a timeout. We ran White on the field for an off-tackle. He powered seven yards to put the ball at the 25, thank goodness, and that put us in great position.

199

Frank Jordan kicked the winning field goal. It was the best game I ever played as a Trojan—an emotional roller coaster between two great teams and traditions. We thought we had the game won, and they thought they had it won.

We came back, and Frank kicked the ball through. Frank had nerves of steel. John Robinson also had a calm quality, he really did. He'd crack jokes and laugh on the sideline, making it easy for you to have fun. I said to him, "It's easy for you to laugh, I gotta go out there." He surrounded himself with good people and was not uptight.

At LSU in 1979 we were No. 1 in the country going in. Louisiana State had 78,000 people, and they had a good team. The most vivid memories I have were flying in on Thursday night, checking into the hotel, and taking the walk-through on Friday night at the stadium. We needed an escort to get into the doggone stadium *the day before the game*. People were hootin' and hollerin', yelling and screaming, and this is just the walk-through. I'm thinking, *These people are really serious about football.* That night I told Jack Ward, our head trainer, to give me something so I could sleep. He gave me half a sleeping pill and a muscle relaxant. In the morning, I was wiped out. I didn't really wake up until the second quarter.

I remember the Tiger outside the locker room was roaring. A lot of people were nervous. It was the loudest crowd I ever played in front of. I've played in the NFL, in domed stadiums—the Metrodome, Kingdome, Astrodome, Superdome. It was louder than any of them. All those people come out early and party all day, and they're out of control by nighttime. We got off to a sluggish start, and they had an early lead. They had the lead until the end of the game.

We kicked a field goal early in the game. It was one of those games where we audibled quite a bit. It was "check with me." I didn't decide on the play until I was at the line of scrimmage, based on the defense they showed. I remember it was so loud that Keith Van Horne had to turn and read my lips. It was hard to fire out on the defensive end when you're looking at the sideline and then at the quarterback. That was difficult. I could kind of hear myself in the middle of the field, but inside the 20s, you could not hear anything. We got called for penalties—offside, illegal procedure. It was hard to get a rhythm. They were pretty good at plugging up our running game and stopping our passing game.

We finally scored a touchdown when Charles White went "22-blast" over the top in classic White fashion, just as we've seen so many times. We came back in the fourth quarter. We were driving at the end of the game and needed only a field goal. We were down 12–10, but we wanted a touchdown if we could get one. On third down, we got a face mask penalty in our favor when a defensive lineman for LSU grabbed my mask, and that was amazing to me. An SEC crew threw a flag!

Speaking of the referees, on the first play, I knew it would be a long game. There was a new NCAA rule that said if the crowd's too loud and you couldn't call cadence, you could look back at the official, and he could let you go back and huddle up. They'd warn the crowd and assess a five-yard penalty on the defense.

On the first play, the crowd was unbelievably loud, so I turned back and looked at the ref. He put his hands in the air and pointed at me adamantly:

Run the play. So I forgot that rule. In the SEC, that rule doesn't exist. But in the end, I got a favorable call and was shocked. I threw a pass to Kevin Williams in the flat to win the game 17–12.

I don't recall any racial animosity from the LSU fans, but it would not shock me at all given the nature of the game itself—the scope of it and the fact you had 80,000 crazed fans. I wouldn't be surprised if a lot of that went on, but I didn't hear it. I don't recall.

In 1979 we went unbeaten and defeated Ohio State 17–16 in the Rose Bowl. I didn't realize at the time that Pete Carroll was their secondary coach, but I can say this: it was the best defense I ever played against in college. They were very well coached and showed a variety of different coverages, nickel fives, and the defensive backs were only in the flow. I thought, frankly, *Let's don't screw around. Let's stay on the ground.* White had a classic game. I played well. I made some good throws and some good decisions. I had one pick and one touchdown off an audible to Kevin Williams, but there were no easy throws. At the end of the first series, we were not doing well throwing the football for a variety of reasons. There were miscommunications between me and the receivers, so we said, "Hey, let's go to classic USC football." Dominate and wear them down. Stop screwing around. We had the best offensive line in college football, and we just ran on every play. We decided which guy to go to, and that was White running behind Anthony Munoz. He was dominant, unbelievable. All the linemen were on their guy, but "Munz" destroyed his guy.

Our team had always been poised. Those six seniors on that team said there was no need for surprises. We weren't new to each other. Our mindset was, *Just go out and execute.* The huddle was calm, matter of fact. We had big-time players.

Carroll's tutelage of Ohio State was impressive. We thought, *Those guys are good.* Go back and look at that tape, at the throws that had to be made, and there's no wide-open guy downfield. No one got in front or behind his defenses. There were no gimmes. He and I shared a funny story. When USC played in the Rose Bowl against Michigan in 2004, we talked about it once on the radio, and he gets sensitive. In Carson Palmer's senior year, USC averaged 6.5 yards a play. That trend continued and would be a record for USC football. The last team that averaged nearly that many yards was the 1979 Trojans at 6.3. We were in the Rose Bowl and he said, "Yeah, yeah, how'd

201

you like to play us now?" He was talking about the 1979 USC offense versus the 1979 Ohio State defense. He was still sensitive to the Buckeye defense he coached 30 years ago.

An amazing story was when USC got to the Rose Bowl in Matt Leinart's sophomore year. Carroll walked out early, and I was on the field cruising around. I said, "Hey, Pete." He was on the field, kind of running pass patterns, and he said, "Paul, I never should have called that blitz." He was talking about a play from our game against Ohio State, a play that happened 25 years earlier. That's how loose he is. He has this great memory. We talked about that, my audibles against his maximum protection.

Then there's Marv Goux. Marv was amazing. He was Trojan football, and was the real keeper of the flame, especially when we'd go to South Bend.

One of the great legends and fan favorites of Troy, Paul McDonald was a 1979 All-American, Academic All-American, recipient of an NCAA postgraduate scholarship, and a National Football Foundation scholar-athlete. Paul led USC on some of the most memorable late game-winning drives in school history, including victories over Notre Dame (1978), at Louisiana State (1979), and Ohio State (1980 Rose Bowl). He engineered the victory at Alabama's Legion Field (1978) en route to the national championship. McDonald quarterbacked two Rose Bowl champions, was sixth in the 1979 Heisman balloting, was all-conference, team MVP, and played in the Hula Bowl. He was the Cleveland Browns' starting quarterback before playing for Dallas, and was in the NFL from 1980 to 1986. His son, Michael, played quarterback for the Trojans. An investment banker, he is also USC's radio analyst alongside Pete Arbogast on football broadcasts.

The
EIGHTIES

KEITH VAN HORNE

OFFENSIVE TACKLE

1977–1980

I GREW UP WITH HOBY BRENNER, who was a year younger than me at Fullerton Union High School, a tight end at USC, and played for the New Orleans Saints. I showed him around campus on his recruiting trip and obviously talked to him a lot about it, and it helped him make his decision to come to USC. Fullerton had started a boys club, and when I was in the third grade, I played basketball and flag football. My brother, Peter, was two and a half years older than me and was already in it. One of the best coaches I ever had was Pete Liapis from the boys club. He was an old boxer, was missing three fingers on his right hand, and was a character. He was a tough guy, but he loved kids and worked us hard. He taught us the fundamentals, and Hoby was part of it. We both ended up at 'SC, which was unusual from our program at Fullerton, which wasn't very good.

I was always kind of tall and skinny. I hit 6' in the eighth grade, and I was 6'7" by my sophomore year in high school. I lifted weights, but not like crazy. I did what the coaches told me to do. I had good strength and was a late bloomer. My size at USC went from 6'7", 225 pounds, as a freshman to 265 pounds as a senior, from working out and growing into my body. Then I was 286 pounds drug-free in the pros, when I spent a lot of time in the weight room.

Anthony Munoz and I came in together. That was the first recruiting class of John Robinson—Munoz, Brad Budde, Charles White, Jeff Fisher, Pat

Howell. Myron Lapka was already there. Marvin Powell, Dennis Thurman, Rod Martin—they were there, and it was one hell of a team.

My left foot had to be fused, but when my left foot was back up to speed and I'd redshirted, I played on the 1977 team that beat Texas A&M in the Bluebonnet Bowl. In my third, fourth, and fifth years, I started.

Frank Jordan kicked a field goal in 1978, and any time you beat Notre Dame, it's a wonderful thing. We had some good kickers, and Frank came through on more than one occasion. He was a great kicker and a good guy.

I've always loved Chicago. I was born in Pennsylvania and raised there, but my dad moved us to California. It was a little rough at first when I played for the Bears, being a Trojan in Notre Dame country. There were only three or four schools that recruited me out of high school. Notre Dame had sent me a letter. They wanted film on me. Dan Devine then sent me a letter that said, "You don't qualify to be a player at Notre Dame." Years later, Devine was with the Bears, and I told him that in practice. All the Domers took it as being a smartass, cocky.

That's where Hudson Houck was a master. He could evaluate talent and project you. He turned me into a football player. He taught me the intricacies and footwork. He made it possible for me be a pro.

205

In my opinion, Munoz, who didn't play that much in college because he was hurt, is one of the top three tackles ever to play in the NFL. He worked hard and was a natural athlete, a ballet-type player who could move smoothly. His balance was great, he never lost balance even when he leaned forward, because he had such natural strength. He had quick feet, great hands, was technically perfect, and fun to play with.

The speed of the runner can be a problem when we ran "student body right" or "student body left." We were still a running school, not the wide-open passing team they are now, and we'd do it over and over. Repetition. Charlie White would sweep wide and get past the block, but hit the hole quickly, and that's what made him so great. He was a tough son of a gun who could take a hit and deliver one. It was a pleasure blocking for him. He always gave us credit, and when a guy wins the Heisman, you can't beat that.

Paul McDonald was our quarterback. The QB has to be a leader. When he comes in, guys look to him, and if he's not in control, if he gets flustered, it's not good. He knew the game and could read defensives. Paul had such a great arm. Paul Hackett was our quarterbacks coach, and John Robinson surrounded himself with great coaches. He let them do their job. The two Pauls together were a great team. He became that champion that we had to have, who'd say, "Okay, fellas, this is what we gotta do."

At Alabama in 1978, he read defenses. He'd see how they lined up and then call this or that way, and Paul played it perfectly. Charlie had a great day, and the way we ran the ball combined with play-action or roll-out passes, was simply unbeatable.

Robinson already had great players from John McKay, plus he had great recruiting classes. But if you look through the record, while that continued, against Missouri in the opener of his first year [1976], they trounced us, and we were booed off the field. It was one of those games, I don't know how they beat us. They were not all that great. They ran the opening kick back for a TD and beat us at the Coliseum. It was a shellacking and it was embarrassing. It was a game where people would see scores scroll across the TV and do a double take—it's got to be a mistake.

Afterward, Coach Robinson just stood up and said, "Gentlemen, I will never be booed in my home stadium again." If there was any question about his team, he made it a turning point. We practiced hard and went after each other.

Anthony Munoz came back in the 1980 Rose Bowl after sitting out the whole season with an injury. We started at our own 6- or 11-yard line, or somewhere down there, and it was Charlie right, Charlie left. We ran just about every play. I could be wrong, but I don't think we passed, and Anthony was a huge part of that on the left side. We switched—I was always on the strong-side tackle and Anthony was on the weak-side. Ohio State only needed to hold us to finish No. 1.

We had another drive like that at Notre Dame that started at their 4 or 6. They thought they had us buried deep. Ohio State felt pretty confident, and they had a tough defense. They were obviously a great team, and even Robinson just said, "We're gonna run this thing down their throats."

All they had to do was stop us, and they'd win, but they started to fade. When you keep running first down after first down, on the ground, right through you, it wears you down. Both of us were just as tired, but when you get pumped and motivated in the Rose Bowl, nothing against them, but it's deflating to be on defense and get run on all over the field like that.

I think we just ran until we got to the goal line and punched it in. It was a great moment. Remember, also, Pete Carroll was the defensive coordinator for the Buckeyes, and his specialty was stopping the pass. We chose to

Keith Van Horne, shown here in an October 1989 home game against the Houston Oilers, was a dominant offensive tackle for the Bears for many years.

Photo courtesy of Getty Images

avoid the air, we hadn't gotten much all day against him, and our decision to stay on the ground is a testament to his coaching.

By the way, that rose on the middle of the field was made out of some kind of hard, dried paint. I fell on that thing, and it hurt a lot. The pain was hard to overcome; it was like a bad turf burn.

The national title in 1978 was well deserved, but sort of came with an asterisk by our name. That's because Alabama was given a co-title, even though we'd beaten them on their field, which was ridiculous. At Arizona State, we lost five guys to knee injuries. We lost three centers and had to move two guys over from the defense. ASU took it to us; they wanted to prove they belonged in the Pac-10. After that game, knee braces were invented, and it made a difference.

Mike Ditka was my coach in Chicago. He was an intense individual. We called him "Sybil" because you were never sure of his personality. He was a great motivator, but not necessarily a great coach. He got the best out of his players and was a big reason we won the Super Bowl. Our team was fractured, and he made sure we came together as a team. The reverse was true about not going back later. We lost focus.

Our quarterback, Jim McMahon, was a nut. He was crazy, but he knew football. He partied a lot, but was ready to play. I don't know how he coexisted with BYU, but he was interested in passing, and they just wanted to throw the ball. They probably let him slide. If he had stayed healthy, we probably would have gotten back to the Super Bowl. He suffered serious injuries and wrecked his shoulder.

McMahon was looser than Paul McDonald. Paul was all business, though he'd crack a smile every now and then. McMahon would crack jokes in the huddle, but he knew what he was doing.

Vince Evans was a senior when I was a freshman at USC, and my teammate in Chicago. Thinking of him, that Notre Dame thing flashes back, and in my five years we beat the Irish four out of five times.

The loss was the "green jersey" game in 1977. I remember the crowd went nuts. They hadn't done anything like the green jerseys in 30 years. I'm not sure of the impact on us, but that Trojan horse was quite a spectacle. If you check the stats of that game, we outplayed them, but made seven turnovers. They took advantage. When that horse came out of the tunnel—they're masters of psychological stuff—it was quite a spectacle. They swarmed behind that horse and caused a delay. First there was a banner, and they followed behind that, and the place ignited. It was my first visit as a young sophomore. I knew who they were, and people are right about that rivalry, there's none better. It was a long dry spell when I was playing in Chicago in the 1980s and early 1990s, but Pete Carroll returned us to our glory. It's fun to watch. He's perfect in college, and I hope he stays.

208

Keith Van Horne was a consensus All-America offensive lineman in 1980, a member of the 1978 national champions, two Rose Bowl champions, and three bowl winners. An Academic All-American in 1979, he was a Playboy Preseason All-American (1980), twice All–Pac-10, team captain, and USC's Offensive Player of the Year as a senior. He played in the 1981 Hula Bowl before being selected as the No. 1 pick of the Chicago Bears, where he starred from 1981 to 1993. In 1985 he was a key member of the Bears' Super Bowl champions, considered by many to be the best pro football team of all time.

ROY FOSTER
OFFENSIVE GUARD
1978–1981

I WENT ONE YEAR TO TAFT HIGH SCHOOL in the San Fernando Valley, but before the 10th grade we had a death in the family, so my mom wanted to help comfort her dad in Kansas City. Carol, my little sister, went to junior high, and I finished at Shawnee Mission West High.

I was born in Compton. I was never even thinking about high school, I'd barely gotten out, so going to college was not big in my mind. But I made all-state, I was one of three black kids on the team and the only standout. I played running back and was recruited by USC as a fullback. That changed quickly when I got there. I went from being No. 30 on Tuesday to No. 64 (an offensive lineman's number) on Wednesday. About 150 schools had recruited me. I visited Colorado, UCLA, USC, Arizona, Arizona State, and at first had my heart set on ASU. I liked the campus but wanted to get back to L.A., to get back in town. Mom thought USC was the most prestigious, so I went there. I'd been a high school All-American, a "blue chipper," I suppose, but I was an obscure player coming out of Overland Park, compared to the national recruiting scene. I'd gained 1,100 yards as a running back, and I'd also played defensive end. I'd not been an offensive lineman.

John Marshall primarily recruited me. I entered in 1978 but barely played that first year. I was behind Brad Budde and Pat Howell. They put me on the offensive line after I had trouble with a pitch in "student body right." My

Roy Foster of the Miami Dolphins takes a breather during a game against the Pittsburgh Steelers at Three Rivers Stadium on September 30, 1990. *Photo courtesy of Getty Images*

210

future as a running back was limited, as I was in the same backfield with two Heisman Trophy winners—Charles White and Marcus Allen. That first year I didn't redshirt. I was asked to, but I passed it up and played sparingly, after a game was no longer in doubt or someone got hurt.

My first year we won the national title. I was in such awe of all that. I didn't realize the magnitude of USC football. I was there in a vacuum, it took a while to figure out the playbook. We played Alabama in 1978, and it was a giant game. Bear Bryant was their coach, a legend. Dwight Stephenson, later my teammate at Miami, was their center, and they had an incredible team.

Yeah, it was a big win, and it was in the hostile environment of Legion Field. Charlie White had a big game, he rushed for about 200 yards. Ronnie Lott, Dennis Smith, and Anthony Munoz all played great games, and we beat them solidly.

I was just a freshman, so I wasn't in it like the juniors and seniors. I was just along for the ride, but you could feel the emotion, how important practice was. Going back to 'Bama, there was a lot of racial tension. Somebody had done a spoof. We had a guy named Otis Page, who was the prankster in the group. He came in and woke us up early with a white sheet over his head like it was the KKK. Nothing came of the trip. It was uneventful, and we were treated well. But it got us loosened up, we were able to laugh about it.

By beating Alabama in convincing fashion on the road, we placed ourselves in the driver's seat for the national championship. But we got a little complacent after that big road win. After beating Alabama, we thought we were pretty doggone good. We traveled to Tempe to play Arizona State. It was hot, and they had a very good team, with Mark Malone at quarterback. I don't think we let down after Alabama. I think Arizona State was playing to prove themselves. They had just been admitted with Arizona to the conference, which went from the Pac-8 to the Pac-10. In those first four-plus years, both ASU and Arizona upset us. They had talented players and belonged in the conference. Some of their players had not been offered scholarships to USC, so they played with extra incentive. But that loss proved to be a valuable lesson after that.

We featured Charles Ussery, Dennis Edwards, Byron Darby, Herb Ward, Dennis Johnson, George Achica, Charlie White, and Paul McDonald. It was a great team, but we played some games we should have won by larger margins. Jeff Fisher almost gave away the UCLA game when he committed a big penalty late, but we held on. It was a thriller at the end of the Bruins game. We won 17–10, but we'd led 17–0 at the half.

Joe Montana came to town with Notre Dame. It went into the evening, a thriller that went back and forth. Kevin "Bug" Williams caught a deep ball, and we were able to get into their end zone. But in the end it took a winning Frank Jordan kick to beat those guys 27–25. The Irish had a really good running back, and Dan Devine was their coach. But that game was all about how to stop Montana. Notre Dame gives scholarships, too, and they did what we do. We had a big lead on them, and the Coliseum was a big celebration. All of a sudden, our running plays weren't working, and they were opportunistic. In the heat of a game, pressure busts the pipe. Here was Joe Montana, who was "Mr. Comeback," and that day he showed exactly what he later did in the pros. We could not stop him.

Coach John Robinson was a bit conservative, and perhaps that conservatism caused us to split the title with Alabama. Nobody could understand that, because we beat them on the road, but we sat on the ball and barely won at the end of our two rivalry games. And Alabama was good. There were enough people who voted for the Crimson Tide.

Looking back, how we did not crush UCLA in '78? And let Notre Dame back in before Frank's field goal? We beat Michigan in the Rose Bowl in a defensive struggle, 17–10. But we had the ability to win by bigger margins. Bryant was a popular legend, the Joe Paterno of that era. We walked off the Rose Bowl field figuring we were national champions, but the AP went for 'Bama, and the UPI went for us.

In 1979 I started at offensive guard, still not really knowing which way was right or left, but knowing it was my time. But it's feast or famine. I wanted to contribute, people were counting on me. The adrenaline was up. Hudson Houck was my coach. Marv Goux was teaching his boys on defense to tear my head off, and Myron Lapka lived in the weight room. I was strong, but not that strong. I had to battle every day, and we taught each other how to play. But Goux would catch me in the lunch room and give advice. He'd tell me that he appreciated a block I made. I was coming from a single family and got that from Marv; he was a father figure.

That's what it means to be a Trojan. It's the Trojan family, it was a sense of camaraderie, a family atmosphere. We all policed each other. We watched each other's back. Coaches were father figures. Marv was the head of all that. He'd make sure you dressed properly on road trips. It was an elite group, and we had a style about us where we felt we were better than the Bruins across the street and acted that way. We were not cocky, but we had a swagger and an assuredness, and we never came off that.

It's hard to believe now, but I'd seriously considered quitting. Calvin Sweeney told me not to quit, to stay in school, that I'd never have an opportunity to do anything better. But at first I was not grasping the playbook. School was a difficult adjustment, the social scene, and every day it seemed like there was a brick wall that needed to be knocked down. I had family close by, but my mind, my thoughts were in other places. Putting that uniform on, slugging it out every day, I could not see progress. You don't look ahead and see what you'll see looking back. But my mom just said, "Do you wanna dig ditches?" I never had any idea of playing pro football. She knew I had an opportunity to make something of myself if I stayed.

I was in an unsung position on the line. Other guys were getting the recognition. We had these glamour guys getting the interviews. Charlie White, Marcus Allen, Ronnie Lott, Paul McDonald—these good-looking guys whom the reporters liked to interview—the camera loved them, they were golden boys. But I was sweating it out on the line so they could get recognized, and it took a while to adjust to that.

In 1979 we traveled to LSU, and it was another Alabama-like atmosphere. I'll tell you, some other schools load up the Ball States and the Bowling Greens, but not 'SC. Not then, not now. LSU was pretty cocky. We came from California and showed them what we could do, but it was unreal in that environment, "Death Valley." We rallied late, and Bug Williams caught the game-winning touchdown pass to win 17–12.

But the Stanford game I have to give some responsibility to John Robinson, who sat on the ball. We were up 21–0 at the half. But they had Ken Margerum, Darrin Nelson, and John Elway, a Hall of Famer. We got complacent and figured a field goal or two, how could they catch up? But they did with 21 unanswered points. And we turned the ball over a few times. Lott was scrambling to get after Elway, but he just could not pin him down.

We beat Notre Dame four times in a row when I was at USC. South Bend is like no other setting, it's like playing basketball in a small gym with the crowd right on top of you. The crowds were about five feet from the field. It's packed, loud, and historic. I don't know where it comes from, but there are certain teams you gear up for. For Notre Dame, it's Michigan and us, those are their big games. For us, it was them, UCLA, and the Rose Bowl. It's that game you put your stamp on, like playing your big brother. There's a competition, a win factor, the whole country is watching, and you don't know where you find it, but we just gear up for certain opponents. You can't explain it, but at USC you have to understand that *every* opponent you play is geared up for *you*, and it takes a lot of pressure.

Marv Goux never let us take anybody lightly. The man ate raw meat before games. I'm serious. Marv would heat-steam meat and eat it with salt and pepper, drink two beers before bed, and sleep like a baby. He told all these stories. At Notre Dame he'd lead us onto the field and point to "the spot" where he'd injured himself and probably lost out on an NFL career. He'd cry and scream. He named a dog after a Notre Dame player.

I made All-America in 1980 and 1981 and played with Ronnie Lott. Lott was really serious; he was stern, no fooling around. He had this game face from the time we woke up. Lott would hit you with a lot of leverage, and sometimes the velocity was so bone-crushing, even in practice, that you could just feel it from his shoes. We'd have to pull him out of drills. We'd try and develop a play, but he was so tenacious, so relentless that he would disrupt it. He was not really heavy, but he had a *willingness* to hit with full force that cannot be taught. Once he had his pinky finger *amputated at halftime* so he could continue to play! It was not over 'til it was over to him. He was like an animal, like a medieval figure. Off the field: smart, nice guy. But he had a quality you just don't teach. The great ones!

There was just something about that snapping of the helmet, he became a robotic figure, like a different mindset. People like that, they are on a mission they're trying to complete. After the game, we'd have a beer and tell stories, but between the lines he had business to take care of.

Joe Montana was an opponent at Notre Dame in 1978. And when he and Lott were with San Francisco, they beat my Miami team in the 1985 Super Bowl up at Stanford. Then he was my teammate when I went to the 49ers. He was just special, as cool as the other side of a pillow, a magician. He had an attitude about him that he was a competitor. He was always thinking. Joe was a field general, he could control the huddle. We all looked up to him. There was a sense of comfort when he was in the huddle. Harris Barton once said, "If he's healthy, we're going to the playoffs." Joe led by example.

What does it mean to experience USC? Needless to say, it was very special. I was regarded as one of the top guys, the "big man on campus," but there was a sense of humility when you dealt with others, even those who did not have the same success or play as much. You didn't treat anybody differently, you tried to be equal. John Robinson had a unique way of not letting us get ahead of ourselves. He treated us with respect and demanded it in return.

My son went to USC. I left him alone to do his thing and enjoy the 'SC experience. I didn't want him to feel pressured. But none of this would have come about had it not been for my mom. Mom always liked the finer things in life, and when it was a toss-up between USC, Arizona State, and UCLA, she knew the prestige of a private university, and the greatness of the Trojans. She had this inner sense of knowing it was the best place for me. Early on, I didn't want to go out to practice, but after a while we almost anticipated success. I had coaches who told me that it was new for the others, too. I didn't realize that. I didn't think I belonged at first. You could tell who didn't belong, the guys who didn't stack up, but thanks to Mom I stuck it out and eventually did stack up.

Roy Foster was a two-time All-America offensive guard, a member of USC's 1978 national champions, and two Rose Bowl champions. A three-time All–Pac-10 selection, Roy won the Morris Trophy in 1980 and 1981. He was USC's Offensive Player of the Year in 1981 and received the Howard Jones Incentive Award for greatest increase in grade-point average (1980). After playing in the 1982 Hula Bowl, he was a first-round draft pick of the Miami Dolphins, where he played in two Super Bowls for Don Shula (including the 1985 game at Stanford Stadium, a loss to Ronnie Lott and the 49ers) and was All-Pro before a three-year stint in San Francisco (1991–1993).

JEFF BROWN
INSIDE LINEBACKER
1980–1983

I WAS RECRUITED BY CAL AND ASU. Coach Sweeney at Fresno State also wanted me, as I was from nearby Porterville. Bill Sharman (a great Trojan) was originally from there. USC recruited me, of course. UNLV and Cal Poly recruited me, along with some of the smaller Division I programs. I saw a game at Stanford, but threw their application away.

The sport I prefer is the one I'm playing when it's the season. I just loved to play. If it wasn't football season, it was baseball season. You didn't have the all-year training programs like you have now. My older brother played in the Angels organization. His son played for the Chicago Cubs in the big leagues.

I was decent at baseball, but it's nothing like the one-on-one conflict of football. There's a difference in the preparation, the way you train. I loved the team aspect of football more. I signed with the Dodgers and played minor league ball, but everybody's out for themselves. I loved my football teammates. But in pro baseball, in the locker room, you couldn't talk to people like at USC. I made it to Double A and signed a Triple A deal that gave me an option, but I was going to be a bench role player. I went to Mexico City and played my last year there. It was fun. The travel sucked, but the people were kind. They had an owner there who owned all the public utilities. He was generous and forthcoming with perks and benefits. I played with Willie Mays Aikens. He was one of the guys I grew up watching. Mexico City then was a place you could run players back and forth between the big leagues and Triple A.

Rod Dedeaux was the most influential coach I've ever been around. Later I was a head baseball coach and assistant football coach, and the things he taught me I carried into those programs. He was always teaching. Coming off the bench as a freshman, I probably learned more about the game in that first year than in my entire life. Some people discounted his knowledge. He got a bad rap for not doing enough—he was getting old—but he treated you like a man. He treated you with genuine respect, and that's something about USC. The people I met were real, and he was at the top of this list.

Marv Goux was also very influential in my life. My brother, Steve, played for John Robinson in a College All-America Game. Marv came, and I was introduced to him. He looked at some 16-millimeter video of me, came back, and said, "You can play for us." I said, "Count me in." Talk about influential! He set high standards and had ways of getting on you where you still knew he respected you. My memories are of him in the locker room at Notre Dame, and talking about his back injury. He said in 1954 he got hurt at South Bend but, "I got the SOB back." He'd say, "Get the piano wire out and sharpen the bayonets; we're going to war."

217

I can remember driving up on the Golden Dome. He had all kinds of sayings and enthusiastic expressions for us. His father died in the Battle of the Bulge, and he was as patriotic and hardcore an American as ever lived. He loved God, America, USC, and his family—and we were all part of his family. It sometimes seems they don't make them like that anymore.

Mark McGwire was my baseball teammate. What I recall were his dad and mom, and that's where you see what he was all about. He was a good guy, and he could have fun and enjoy himself, but he had a sense of urgency about what he was doing. He came in as a pitcher. The guy who was most influential was Marcel Lachemann, who managed him in Alaska and put him at first base. He made him into a hitter and changed the course of history. He had a great arm like his brother, who played quarterback for the Seattle Seahawks. He could throw the hell out of the ball as a pitcher. Mark had a sense of cockiness. He was confident, but he was a team player who cared about others. He'd pick others up. When you meet a person's folks, that tells you a lot about who they are, and he came from a family that valued hard work and discipline.

Jack Del Rio was my teammate in football and baseball. We were both catchers. He was a serious athlete about his business, but a joker too. One of his great attributes was he never played uptight. He was relaxed and in control. He had an air about him. He was a leader, and I'm not surprised where he's at now as head coach of the Jacksonville Jaguars. Jack and I roomed on the road in baseball. I met his folks, and he came from real humble beginnings. His dad was a hard-working man. Jack was a very good athlete and a good person.

One of the things about Jack was that you could enjoy a laugh with him, but when it was time to get serious, he could make it count. Del Rio was probably as good at baseball as football. He just liked to play the game. Heck, he enjoyed playing basketball. He'd been a high school All-American or all-state in basketball. He was a good all-around athlete, which was not new at USC. Anthony Davis, Anthony Munoz—we've always had people who played two sports, a lot of guys. Jack had a great arm. When he caught, he could throw above-average runners out. Hitting is a skill that eludes you if you don't do it often, but by season's end he'd be mashing the best of anybody on our team, and that was without playing in Fairbanks in the summer or fall ball. He'd just improve as the year went on. He just figured it out and was as good a hitter as anyone we had. Plus he handled the pitching staff really well. I thought he could have been a major league player, a two-sport athlete like Dave Winfield.

218

When he was with Dallas, I'd go to St. Edwards where the Cowboys trained, and Ernie Zampese followed me as a grad assistant with 'SC. Jack never changed. In pro football he moved up but stayed true and maintained friendships. Another Trojan, Kennedy Pola is with him in Jacksonville.

I was team captain my senior year and played from 1980 to 1983. When I got there, we had guys like Marcus Allen. That's how I learned to play, from examples set by people like that. Keith Van Horne, Jeff Fisher, Tony Slaton, Don Mosebar, Ronnie Lott; you either got really good or they ran you off the field. Man, Chip Banks, Riki Ellison, Dennis Smith—it transcends into this level of expectation. The difference between USC in the 1980s and the early 1990s was the level of competition on the practice field, and it had a lot to do with John Robinson. He never cut you any slack. It was helmet to helmet to helmet seven days a week.

What it means to be a Trojan is to be part of a family. There's few places where a blue-collar guy who grew up on a cotton field in central California can fit into a metropolitan city at a school mostly known for BMWs. But I was able to do that. It's not just the people but the culture, and what it meant is something I still carry every day. It's a sense of accomplishment and confidence you can't buy.

In 1983 senior captain Jeff Brown won the prestigious Davis-Teschke Award for most inspirational Trojan. A top baseball star for Rod Dedeaux, Brown played in the minor leagues for the Los Angeles Dodgers.

MICHAEL HARPER

TAILBACK

1980, 1982–1983

So how does a kid from Kansas City become a Trojan? For me it was pure circumstance and coincidence. I was blessed with talent and speed. I lived in a place that didn't mention the Pac-10 or the Pac-8. Where I lived, it was the Big 8—Missouri, Kansas, Nebraska, Oklahoma. Those were the big schools. But Brad Budde's father had played for the Chiefs, and Brad played in Kansas City. He got married, and the wedding was in Kansas City. He had played at 'SC. Hudson Houck, John Robinson, John Marshall, all those guys came back for the wedding. During their visit, they took the opportunity to do some recruiting. John Robinson came back to my home. John Marshall recruited me. He was the linebackers coach.

Now, I don't know for sure, and it's never been explained to me, but it may have been a matter of Budde's dad mentioning some of the high school stars in the Kansas City area, and my name came up. I was a blue-chip All-American, so it's certainly possible they knew about me ahead of time, but it's never been explained to me. It was a combination of things. I was blessed to have had a great high school career and put up big numbers. I was recognized statewide and nationally, but I had no clue who or what USC was.

I raised some eyebrows as a freshman at USC, because I wasn't understanding or appreciative of the tailback or the tailback position, but it was *quickly* brought to my attention who and what that was built around. It was pointed out to me that the Trojan tailback had been Mike Garrett. I knew who he was because he'd been All-Pro with the Chiefs on two Super Bowl teams. I hoped to run like Garrett.

Then there was Charles White. In my freshman year (1979) he won the Heisman Trophy and was one of the greatest running backs of all time. I'm remembered for replacing Marcus Allen, but as far as competing at tailback when I came to USC, White was a Heisman candidate. It was a fairy tale of a freshman year, to come in and witness the greatness of White firsthand. Plus I got a chance to play.

It wasn't until this year that it was brought to my attention, but only a certain number of freshman tailbacks ever ran for 100 yards in game. White is one. There was a guy a couple years after me, maybe Ryan Knight or Aaron Emanuel, and of course Reggie Bush and possibly LenDale White, but only a few players ever had a chance to play behind Charlie White. I was the second-string guy. Marcus was the fullback, and I'd come in to substitute—this was before Allen replaced White at the tailback position. Against Oregon State, I scored two touchdowns and rushed for around 126 yards in a 42–5 win in front of 32,000 fans in Corvallis. In my first carry from scrimmage in an 'SC uniform, I ran 47 yards behind "student body right." I got one or two more pitches and was starting to think, *Oh, my goodness, this is gonna be easy. Is it that easy?* I had Bruce Matthews, Don Mosebar, Fred Cornwell, and Tony Slaton blocking for me. We were all freshmen. It was incredible. Heismans, All-Americans, All-Pros, Hall of Famers. It was insane! What a special team, and here was Charlie White running to the left, running to the right. It was a great opportunity to play behind White, knowing he was gone after the season and I'd have a chance at playing, until my injury.

After we beat Ohio State in the 1980 Rose Bowl, I saw there was favoritism to Marcus Allen for the next year. Well, I wasn't the California kid, but I had an opportunity to compete for the position. Marcus and I did split time in 1980 for a few games until I was injured at Minnesota, a 24–7 win where I had my ribs broken. It was difficult.

Marcus had a good season, but he was injured when Notre Dame came to Los Angeles in the final game of the season. We won 20–3. I honestly can't recall all that much, but they were ranked second and hoping for a national title. We'd lost a fluke game to UCLA. Gordon Adams was our quarterback. I don't recall the specifics of that game, but I had some good runs, some good kick returns, and I played a key role in our winning.

I redshirted in 1981, the year Marcus Allen broke every college rushing record known to man. In 1982 I was a junior and suddenly the starter at Tailback U. We were intent on winning the Notre Dame game. We trailed 13–10 and were driving in the last couple of minutes. It was a typical USC comeback of the era. The Trojans always seemed to be winning games on the last drive like this, and we were stubborn about sticking to the running game. It was just like Pete Carroll, where we had the mindset that, if it's fourth and one, we're not going to give in, we're going to go for the first down. We had a great series of plays, a couple of passes, but mostly run to the left, run to the right downfield. We pressed their goal and called timeout on the sideline. It was typical 'SC—a tie was out of the question. We play to win.

The last thing I recall was the thing nobody wants to hear. Somebody said, "Just hold onto the ball." We called "22-blast," one of our staples, and it was like a "29-pitch tailback up the middle." We were behind but were taking it to them, and we were going to punch it in. Nobody was going to stop us. We'd picked up steam, and I think Notre Dame had lost steam. Also there's the telltale sign of USC's former dominance in the running game, the same way 'SC would come back in the fourth quarter against Ohio State in the Rose Bowl, or at LSU in Baton Rouge.

Ted Tollner or Norv Turner just said,"Hold on to the ball." What a thing to say! So I got the ball on "22-blast." The fullback went to block the DB, and maybe it was Bob Crable or Mike Golic who dove over the fullback, stuck an arm out, and tagged the football I was carrying. He knocked the ball loose. The million-dollar question became, *Was I over the goal line or not when the ball came loose?* It was a very controversial call, and we know the result, of course: touchdown, USC 17, Notre Dame 13. It was a big statement for John Robinson in his last game at USC as head coach, for us to come from behind and win it for J.R. as well as for Marv Goux.

I don't think Notre Dame was in contention for a national title—we didn't knock them out—but it was a real sore spot in the Notre Dame fan base for years to come. But it was great. Tony Slaton was in on that play. He picked me up off the ground, and I remember going before the band. I was elated.

What it means to be a Trojan means a lot more than current players can understand. It was not until after I left the university that I looked back and appreciated what was done on my behalf. They helped me as a student-athlete and as a person to go forward in life with a quiet confidence about what I could potentially achieve.

I couldn't recall any times at all when there was not a winning attitude, even when we had a losing season in 1983, which was the first in a long time. We had that winning attitude. And it wasn't until after I left that I recognized the distinction between a winning and a losing attitude. We had a winning attitude with the Rams, and guess what? John Robinson was the head coach; Marv Goux was an assistant. I had an opportunity to play in Canada, and later I was a receiver with the New York Jets. I learned to appreciate what a "winning attitude" program we had at USC because we had it there, but not on all those professional teams.

For me as person, I was able to overcome significant odds because I remained around winners. At USC people around you do so many things you don't recognize as a player. I can only say thanks to the boosters, the professors, the coaches, the parents, my friends, the students. It was phenomenal. Even today I can't say how strong that tradition is. It's an ongoing family thing now, to experience this for the first time with my kids. My children are now a part of it. I go down for "Salute to Troy." I've gotten to know Coach Carroll and introduce him to my kids, and it's just great.

Michael Harper is a unique figure in the school's football history, in that he was tasked with the daunting task of upholding the impossible standards set by his predecessors at the tailback position. He replaced Marcus Allen when Allen was injured and missed the 1981 Notre Dame game, then took over full-time in 1982 with the Heisman winner's departure for the NFL. While Harper may not be a legend, he nevertheless starred in two wins over the Fighting Irish (1980, 1982), earned the Marv Goux Award for best offensive player in the 1983 UCLA game, was drafted by the Los Angeles Rams, and played for the New York Jets from 1986 to 1989.

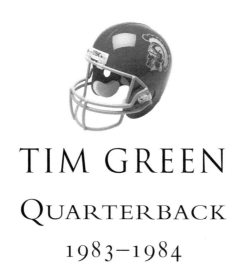

TIM GREEN

QUARTERBACK

1983–1984

STEVE SARKISIAN IS A GREAT COACH, even if he did break my records at El Camino Junior College. I've never seen more talented guys on the same team as the Trojans under Pete Carroll—Mark Sanchez, Mitch Mustain, Aaron Corp. They're blessed.

Jack Reilly was the coach at El Camino. He'd coached in the pros. It was like the 49ers' offense of the '80s. We emulated ourselves after the 49ers with shifting and sending people in motion, illegal picks, shooting people out in the flat, sending them behind them with quick hits, then spreading the field vertically with long bombs. History says I peaked too early. I threw for 30 touchdowns in 10 games.

I played my high school ball at Aviation High in Redondo Beach. Paul Westphal went there, but they closed the school down. TRW or somebody took it over. It's next door to the federal building where the FBI and, I guess, the CIA and the NSA are, so my guess is that whole block is "spy central" now. If you want to knock out our intelligence assets on the West Coast, that's where they'd hit!

It's tough to have your old high school shut down. You don't have games to go back to, you miss all that. My girls will go to Mira Costa High School in Manhattan Beach, our old rival. A couple guys on my staff at the architectural firm I have went to Aviation—Don Morrow, some great guys. I can remember going to the Aviation High gym on rainy Saturday mornings, and Paul Westphal would be there. I wanted to be like him.

Mike Roth and his brother, Tim, went to Mira Costa. Mike was my team-mate at USC. Tim went to Nebraska. Tim went back to El Camino and got his real estate license. Mike has a company in the South Bay called the Mike Roth Company, a real estate firm. He and his wife operate the company down there.

Norm Katnik was a center for us. He was great except for this one fumbled exchange. Mike Roth was opposite of Jeff Bregel on the offense. In practice, after a few hours, we needed to put him in a straightjacket. I was more like a Jim McMahon–type than a Pat Haden–type. The beauty of that team was that we were not a bunch of Matt Leinarts or Carson Palmers.

In 1984 we'd come off a 4–6–1 season, but we had a few good J.C. transfers, a good group mixed with the guys left over from the John Robinson team. We knew we'd be good. It was not a great season by USC standards, but it was a nice recovery from probation and 4–6–1. Had we not slipped up the last part of the regular season, losing to UCLA and Notre Dame, they'd be making T-shirts about us.

I never had a chance to compete with Sean Salisbury. John Mazur had seen his job handed over to Salisbury, an unproven freshman. They touted Salisbury as the next Heisman winner, and rightfully so. He was talented, 6′5″, athletic, and could do anything. I was coming off a pretty good season myself at El Camino, but it was, like, exit lefty No. 11. I came in to compete for his job, and it was like I'd invaded his territory, but they had every intention to play him.

One story most people don't know is, after he got hurt in the second game of the season, I came in, and we were 5–1. Before the Arizona State game, he decided to come back and take over the team. He walked into [head coach] Ted Tollner's office and announced that he was healthy enough to play. Tollner just told him, "You're redshirting now. This is Tim's team." People think I got lucky, that I just wandered on the field and was the MVP in the Rose Bowl. There was not a player on that team who'd have traded me for anybody else. Everybody backed me.

It was slim pickin's in the '80s for Rose Bowl victories. Paul McDonald on January 1, 1980, and me in 1985. Todd Marinovich won on January 1, 1990. All three were lefties. But there were only two Rose Bowl victories in the

Tim Green triumphantly salutes the crowd after the Trojans defeated the Ohio State Buckeyes 20–17 to win the 71st Rose Bowl on January 1, 1985. Green threw for two touchdowns in the Trojans' win.

1980s. I feel good when I go to the Rose Bowl and they talk about past games or what have you. There's these UCLA banners. UCLA's got a lot of banners in the '80s. Tom Ramsey's is there, but they're missing a Pac-10 championship in 1984. You buy a Rose Bowl program, and it lists the past games and Players of the Game. It's a page or two—it's a pretty short list—and there's my name.

We had some disappointments. In 1983 at South Bend, I played the whole second half of that game and brought us down for a score or two, but we just didn't have enough that day.

I remember the 502 Club. I knew Terry Marks, who became the president of Coca-Cola, North America. We'd drink beer in there. The "Five-O" was the place to hang out with the guys. The "Nine-O" [901 Club] was the place to look for sorority girls. But the Five-O was our place. We'd get off the plane late at night, 2:00 AM, they'd open the place for us, and we'd spend the rest of the night in there. It was just us. That was pretty cool. I was there only four semesters, but it was very impactful on my life. There's few things in life that satisfy you like that. The crowds, people asking for autographs, all the accolades. Now it's pretty good, it's not bad, but those were some memories.

I had the privilege of meeting Pete Carroll. I go to the "Salute to Troy." Sam Anno is on that staff. He's a good buddy.

Going to USC goes beyond football. One of my favorite sayings is, "I won the Heisman Trophy." What I mean by that is my friendship with Rex Moore is like winning the Heisman. He's one of the greatest Americans I know. He'd be a surefire Hall of Famer if he didn't break his legs. I wouldn't trade it for anything. I'm so grateful, all for one guy. We were in each other's weddings, and we have lunch every week. I'm tight with his kids, and we have an interest in each other's families. I'm also Sigma Chi. I lived in a house. I lived in a nice environment with a variety of nice fraternity brothers and teammates. It was a nice mix of the social row and football. I had relationships that were complete opposites with guys on the team. There was a lot of stimulation on the social scene.

As far as doing business with USC people, whether it's trucking or architecture, if they're tied to 'SC, nine times out of 10 they'll do business with me. That's been wonderful, too.

As far as history goes, Haden, McDonald, Rodney Peete—a lot of those guys are more political and social than I am. I keep my groups small and intimate. I don't go and try to get the hero's welcome at USC. I'm uncomfortable with it, but those guys all know who I am, they shake my hand. My heroes are Vince Evans, Rob Hertel, Gordon Adams. McDonald and Pete are friends of mine—it's a little fraternity. It's special. I didn't go on to play pro football, though I got close. It's something I can live with. But to not ever play at USC—lots of better athletes than me go there and never see the field. I'm thankful to have had that one season and have it be a Pac-10 title and a Rose Bowl victory. Little did I know it would be the last time I'd play, but it was a good way to end it.

What does it mean to be a Trojan? I would sum it up like this: growing up in Southern California and watching USC football throughout the 1970s and early 1980s, we all witnessed greatness with McKay's and Robinson's teams. And, as a young man, I would do anything possible to be involved in any capacity. This is a legendary group, and only the very best are asked to join. My dreams came true—being the starting quarterback at USC, winning the Pac-10 championship, and being named co-MVP of the 1985 Rose Bowl game. No matter what I do or don't do in life, this will carry on, for my family, for many generations to come. I was in heaven for two years and walked away a cardinal-and-gold champion for life.

A product of Aviation High School in Redondo Beach and a record-breaking All-America quarterback from El Camino Junior College, Tim Green quarterbacked the ninth-ranked Trojans to a 9–3 record in 1984, capped off by a 20–17 Rose Bowl victory over Ohio State. Green was named co–Player of the Game with Jack Del Rio.

STEVE JORDAN
PLACE-KICKER
1981–1984

ICAME IN AS A FRESHMAN and played alongside Marcus Allen in 1981. Things change, the years have passed, but what I remember most fondly was how nice a guy he was. He'd trained with perhaps a track coach at UCLA and was a bruiser at 6′2″, but he came back a slender 6′2″. He was blocking for Charles White in the early years. In the later years, those were still great days of USC football. What I'm most fond of was our first game at home against Tennessee. He rushed for about 300 yards, and we crushed the Volunteers 43–7. I'd watch him not just run but glide. He was a slasher, it was hard to tackle the guy. He was the first guy to shake my hand after kicking a point-after. I'll never forget that. Years later, the 49ers played the Los Angeles Raiders at the L.A. Coliseum, and the first thing I said to him when I saw him was, "I remember you always shook my hand after a point-after." He said we needed every point possible. It didn't matter whether I was freshman—that was Marcus, a true winner.

Jack Del Rio and I were very good friends. He also played baseball and came from the San Francisco Bay Area where I'm from. We'd grown up going to concerts together. I knew his family, and it was like living with a brother. My senior year [1984], I remember at 8:00 in the morning there was a knock at the door, and in walks Mark McGwire. This was before a double-header. What it means to be a Trojan is to be part of what we were doing while we were there. The camaraderie with other athletes was the best part.

Big Mac liked to play video pong, so I played with Big Mac for hours. He was gold on Atari, we'd play for hours and hours. I remember sitting on that parking structure out beyond right field watching his games. I think he hit more than 30 home runs. He played in the Olympics and with the A's, but was just "Big Red," a normal guy who always remembered me by my name.

This theme repeats itself. Clayton Olivier was a big redheaded kid, a good friend of mine, and a fine basketball player. I was 5'9" or 5'10". James Fitz-Patrick was a great friend, and he was 6'8", 300 pounds. No matter who you were, it was the same little deal. USC was like an island, scrutinized by the neighbors around us. Part of the reason for our mystique was people looked at our guys to figure out how we were thinking and living. It didn't matter whether you were a man or a woman. I was friends with a lot of the girls, athletes like Cheryl Miller and the McGee twins, who were fantastic basketball players. I drank many pitchers of beer with them, me howling at their stories.

We'd go to Heritage Hall every day on a mission. We were all trying to win the national championship. It's unfortunate for us that we didn't get that opportunity. We were fit to be tied our senior year. It was our chance, and we played in the Rose Bowl. The only reason to be kicker is to have a chance to win for your team. I played in that game, had the chance to kick two long field goals, and we won by three.

Going to USC was incredible. Everything about it. I remember Lynn Brombeck, the head cheerleader. She was beautiful, but she was just like us. All those girls, they were just fun-loving, playing pranks. They had a team and camaraderie just like the players. We were all Trojans.

Over the years, at every stage of my life, no matter what I'm doing, I still get goose bumps just *talking* about USC. I brought my daughter, Amanda, down there, and we met Richard Saukko. He trained Traveler, USC's mascot, whom we also got to meet. My daughter loved it, she loves horses, and we were told all about his breeding and upkeep. We went to the USC-UCLA game, and she was just in awe of the people around us. She's been to concerts and knows what it means to me.

[Head coach] Ted Tollner was like a second father to me. He'd put his arm around me because he knew I was money for him. He'd put his arm around me and ask, "How you feeling?"

"I got a test, Coach," I'd say. "I'm kind of nervous." After I'd ace that, I'd head straight to his office and say, "I'm so ready for this week's game."

Steve Jordan, younger brother of Trojan legend Frank Jordan, made his mark in the 1985 Rose Bowl win over Ohio State with two field goals of over 50 yards.

He was passionate. USC's not an easy place to be, and he was under fire. Everybody knew it. You were on stage all the time. I knew I could play any-place, but I wanted to be on that stage. I'd known since I was a kid. I'd walk over to St. Ignatius High School and kick field goals for hours. I wanted to go to USC after watching my brother beat Notre Dame in 1978. I'd grown up watching Notre Dame, and the camaraderie, the rivalry between the two schools is second to none.

Marv Goux was what he himself would call a "mother." Brian Luft was on the travel squad. He's from Fresno. I looked over and he was with Goux and a few of his guys at Notre Dame Stadium. It was kind of snowing. The kicker has free run, so I was playing catch, checking out the facility, looking for Touchdown Jesus. The defensive linemen, George Achica and those guys, seven or eight of them, were on the Notre Dame side hunched down. Goux was looking down and saying, "Fucking this and fucking that…this is where Notre Dame broke my fucking back." I was a 17- or 18-year-old freshman and was just staring at this spectacle. The thing about Marv was once you proved to him you could do it, he loved you to death.

Steve Jordan, the younger brother of legendary kicker Frank Jordan, was a four-year starter from 1981 to 1984. Jordan entered the history books at USC with 23 field goals of 40 yards or more, and eight field goals of 50 yards or more. In 1984 he was a cocaptain of the special teams and kicked field goals of 51, 47, and 46 yards versus No. 1 Washington, earning Pac-10 Player of the Week honors. USC won the conference title and then the Rose Bowl, where his two 51-yard field goals made the difference in the 20–17 win over Ohio State. He made honorable mention all-conference and played in the Japan Bowl. Named Offensive Pac-10 Player of the Week four times, Jordan was drafted by the Los Angeles Express of the USFL and played for the Indianapolis Colts (1987). He is the recipient of Congressional Recognition for his contributions to football history and is owner of Jordan Kicking Services.

JEFF BREGEL
OFFENSIVE GUARD
1983–1986

I WAS A TWO-TIME CONSENSUS ALL-AMERICAN, but I shot up and played with a lot of pain. I hurt my back at Stanford Stadium before the East-West Shrine Game. I earned two Super Bowl rings in San Francisco, but the whole time my spine was fused.

I was an Academic All-American and maintained a very high grade-point average at USC. I was pretty disciplined, more so through football. The schedule became a routine, and it was a well-run program. Ted Tollner took it seriously. I excelled in the business school. Some classes, like anthropology, I didn't care for, but the finance classes interested me. I'd put things off, but I made sure I had enough time to study or cram for a big test.

I liked the business side, and knew I was going to be in something like business securities analysis, and also real estate investments and securities. I know how to value a company and have been doing that the past six years. I've been in mortgage consulting. I do splits-and-referrals. It's been a growth period for me.

At age 44 I should have been more successful, but once football was over, I was depressed. It didn't work out the way I thought it would. I had a real vision of where my career would go, but my back injury caused problems. I'm over all that now, and I'm getting rolling financially. I got a lot out of business school and have knowledge that probably can allow me to work for several different companies.

Two-time All-American Jeff Bregel was a throwback to the tradition of rugged football toughness.

I saw Coach Carroll in May 2008 at the Rod Sherman fantasy camp, and I see that program *Trojan Rewind*, and he really does it like a reality show. It's just like the season.

I loved Ted Tollner. He was a big Jeff Bregel fan. I started four years and was always improving as a player. Ted's son, Bruce, is a big sports attorney and sports agent now, I think he's with Leigh Steinberg and handles top prospects.

Pete Carroll was with the 49ers after I left. I left the Niners on bad terms from my back surgery. They rushed me out when I was in pain and was not in good shape. I said I wanted to just end it. Maybe I jumped the gun. Later, without all my football routines, it was a difficult transition.

I heard a lot about Coach Carroll when I was in the NFL. They all talked a lot about him, and you knew he would go on to bigger and better things. Mike Holmgren was our offensive coordinator. He loved 'SC guys—he'd been a quarterback there in the '60s. We had a lot of Trojans—Riki Ellison, Ronnie Lott—and we had great camaraderie. Things changed as we switched head coaches from Bill Walsh to George Seifert. He was less personable.

Mike Holmgren found his path in coaching, winning the Super Bowl with Green Bay and coaching the Seahawks. But I'm told that when Mike was a high school quarterback in San Francisco, he was considered a far greater prospect than Jim Plunkett, who was at another Bay Area school at the same time. I knew Plunkett when I was in the Bay Area. Joe Montana was my teammate. He recently moved his kid to Oaks Christian High, and there was a competition for quarterback there between Montana's kid and Wayne Gretzky's kid. There's something "only in L.A." about that. He was a great teammate.

I met a lot of great folks at USC. We'd hang out at the old 502 Club. Jerry Buss' daughter was there, I think. I was there with Jack Nicholson's daughter, Jennifer. That place was incredible. It was across from Webb Tower. The girls would find us there. We'd go to the 901 for the sorority girls.

The football tradition at USC is such that when something goes wrong, they correct it. After [head coaches] Tollner and Larry Smith, they turned it around and put on a show. Carroll has created a great advantage, a great program, and with recruiting he's gotten back to the traditions—the Heismans, the linemen, the days of Ron Yary winning the Outland Trophy, Brad Budde the Lombardi. The list of All-Americans on that campus was unreal. We joked that if 'SC was in the same neighborhood as UCLA, it would turn the screws on recruiting. Now the campus has improved, it's cleaner, the smog's been cleared, and the whole neighborhood, from Staples Center to Galen Center, is safer. They have safe housing down by the Coliseum where, in my day, you didn't think of going. This has happened just as recruiting's become the best in the country—and that's because the campus is so much better and Carroll created an atmosphere that's just great for that team. I give Carroll credit for going into the inner city to try and make things better, but honestly, that's gotten worse; but he tries.

235

Usually the USC–Notre Dame thing is the rivalry that evokes the most passions among the guys in pro football, because there's more players from those two schools than anywhere else. Ronnie Lott would get on Joe Montana; Joe would razz me; but I was a part-time starter, so I was not as much in the mix. With Joe around, and others, we'd have the same effect on each other talking about the rivalry. It was really neat at team meetings, or we'd watch games on TV in the hotel on Saturday before games the next day. There wasn't any serious betting, but there was good-natured ribbing. It was fun—"We're gonna do it…we're gonna beat you guys."

USC, Notre Dame, and UCLA all had great athletes back then. The difference between college and the pros was we played against some inferior guys in college—Oregon was not a powerhouse, and Oregon State was at the bottom of the Pac-10—but in the NFL, everybody has burners. The pass rushers move around well. The big difference was in the quality of opponents week in, week out. Practice was a stepping stone for those types of games.

I was on the sideline when we beat Cincinnati in the 1989 Super Bowl. I had a bum knee, my ACL needed to be repaired. We beat the Bears to get there. I'd gotten hurt against San Diego blocking Keith Browner, a former Trojan teammate. It was a trap play. I blocked out the other guard, but he rolled into me, and we got jumbled. In my third year, I had started but then had back problems.

I've been trying to help this doctor who has a fantasy camp for the Living Heart Foundation. He does these screenings, so it helps guys. I've helped him set up several conventions. We do screenings for ex-NFL players. I'm told the average age of death for NFL guys is 56 or something. Lots of guys have good medical care, but not all. The glamour of pro football gives way to this life after the game, and the burdens of ill health are the price we pay.

San Francisco was great, but it was nothing like USC. I go to reunions once in a while, but pro football is nothing like "Salute to Troy." I see all these guys I played with or who were alums.

Baseball players at USC had a blast, too. I knew a lot, many of them were friends. Guys like Rodney Peete also played baseball. USC's been to the College World Series many times. Rod Dedeaux was there when I was there, and I know his son, Justin.

Jeff Bregel was a two-time consensus All-America offensive guard (1985–1986). A member of the 1984 team that won the Rose Bowl, he was also an Academic All-American, twice a member of the Playboy Preseason All-America team, and played in the 1986 East-West Shrine Game. Bregel played for the San Francisco 49ers and earned two Super Bowl rings as a member of the 1988 and 1989 world champions.

REX MOORE

INSIDE LINEBACKER

1984–1987

USC WAS GOOD TIMES AND GOOD FRIENDS. It was the 502 Club. It was teammates.

Brent Moore, a defensive end, was a real good friend. I've stayed in touch with him. He played for the Packers. Brent was a real free spirit, an intellectual who made good grades. We had a few guys with a real academic focus—Brent and some other guys from Northern California, John Berry was a lot like that—but it was not a priority for a lot of us. Football was my top priority.

Brent is from Marin County, and that's where Pete Carroll is from. There are similarities I see in their personalities, and you can argue that maybe their approach works best in football. Some of us from the Southland were from the old school, tough-as-nails school.

Tim Green was old-school, a quarterback with a linebacker's mentality. He was an entrepreneur who had a moving company in Pasadena. Then he went back to school to become an architect, and now he has an architectural firm in Los Angeles. He was the co–Most Valuable Player in the 1985 Rose Bowl.

Kennedy Pola was a heck of a warrior and a real Trojan. He got into coaching.

I live in the Newport Beach area, Corona Del Mar. I'm a nursing home administrator and run football camps. I had some injuries, and maybe I could have had a pro career, but I'm okay with it. USC was the best experience of my life.

In 1984 I was a backup. I started two games because the guy in front of me was injured. But I had played some during my redshirt year in 1983. Keith Biggers was in front of me. His strengths were my weaknesses, and my weaknesses were his strengths. I filled the middle. He was more of a sideline-to-sideline player. He was sometimes too fast and would get beyond the point of attack.

Jack Del Rio was more than a great player. He was a great teammate and champion. He definitely was a leader on our team and the defense. When he spoke, everybody listened. He was like E.F. Hutton. I root for the Jaguars because of Jack and Kennedy Pola, who's with him in Jacksonville. When I see him, it's like old war vets, we just pick up where we left off. I have a lot of respect and admiration for him. He was a fierce player who had real desire. That is the standard.

Green was like a linebacker in the quarterback position, a guy you wanted in the foxhole next to you, in a dark alley, when the bombs go off. I was attracted to him as a teammate because of those qualities.

Sean Salisbury was a drop-back quarterback. Green could run a bit better. He was more of a ball control–type quarterback. Our style was that the defense would shut them down. Fred Crutcher would get four yards. He was a durable back. Tim would play within the system. In 1984 he played that way in our big win that year, which was at the Coliseum against No. 1 Washington.

The Huskies were awesome, the best team in the nation, a major college powerhouse, but we rose up and earned one of the great upsets in USC history to beat them 16–7, and that gave us the conference title and a trip to Pasadena.

Ted Tollner was full of integrity and loyalty. He was a tough man, and I can't say enough good things about Coach Tollner. I'm thankful and appreciative to him personally, for myself and as a team.

It's tough to be the head coach of any USC team. As loyal as I am to USC, it bothers me how quickly alumni can turn on guys. Ted did not get a fair shake. There were key people who lacked patience.

Nineteen eighty-six was a difficult experience. UCLA beat us badly, and we blew a huge lead in the fourth quarter against Notre Dame at home. Every time you lose, part of you dies. It's what champions do in adversity that differentiates them from non-champions. Champions come together and *Fight On!*

Non-champions start to blame each other, and the wheels come off the wagon. We'd hunker down, this was tradition through the ages, it's how we'd deal with losses and adversity. It's what I tell my team in the youth leagues. Kids today seek out alibis.

The toughest opponent for me was UCLA's Gaston Green. In the five years I was in the program, UCLA beat us three times (1983, 1984, and 1986). We beat them in 1985 and 1987. It seems like Green always had 200 yards rushing. As a middle linebacker, I found him pretty tough. USC respects them. That's what it means to be a Trojan. When a running back is moving on you, that deflates you, and I had to respect his toughness.

When you're 18, it's different than now, at 43. Football was my fate, USC my country. Football was my priority. Now I have family priorities. It's different now, I have faith in a higher power. I think about the men and women fighting for our country. This is the greatest country in the world, and I love it. I have my own family, so some things are down the list for what is important, but I'll never show disloyalty for my alma mater. I look at these World War II guys and see people who made it possible for me to raise my family in the land of the free and the home of the brave. Without them, there is no USC, no football.

Nineteen eighty-seven was my senior year. We opened with Michigan State on a Monday night. We got beat, and I blew out my ankle. I broke my fibula and missed the whole year. We had a good year as a team but lost to the Spartans again in the Rose Bowl.

We beat Troy Aikman and UCLA to win the conference when Erik Affholter caught a touchdown in the end zone. At the half, we trailed 13–0 and were at the Bruins' goal line with one play left. Rodney Peete got intercepted, and the guy started to run it back, looking like he was going to score. If they scored, they would have been up 20 at the half. It would have been over. Rodney chased him 100 yards and tackled him a few yards from our goal. The gun sounded, so they had no chance at a TD or a field goal. Rodney showed his heart and what he's all about. That turned it around, and we won 17–13.

The difference between the Notre Dame and UCLA rivalry is, when I think of Notre Dame, I think of a longer history. There's history on both sides. But UCLA's more territorial. It's between Southern California guys.

Even at El Modena, it was a local battle for our neighborhood against Villa Park—the west side of town was a better neighborhood, and the other side was tougher. I was interested in the tough part of town. That was our history. It's a fight for respect and territory. The same was true at USC. For me, there was never a question that I'd go out of the area. I had a brother at Stanford, but I was a Southern Cal guy.

Orange County is considered Trojan country. It produces the best prep athletes in the nation. People ask why this is so. It's a combination of things. We have good weather, and it's a middle-class community of parents who support their kids and schools. Competition is not frowned on. Winning is not a dirty word. It's a patriotic place where tough coaches are admired, not fired.

Sports competition makes everybody better. It raises the bar. At USC we practiced hard. A lot of times on Saturday it was easy compared to the guys I went up against all week. Competition raises you to a higher level.

USC is so special. I've known my wife since the sixth grade. We did not get along particularly well, but we had a class near each other at USC. We'd see each other at the VKC steps and talk. We each found out the other was not that bad. After class, after a couple of weeks, we'd look forward to seeing each other. We became friends, we'd have lunch after class, and the next thing we knew, we fell in love. That, along with having kids, has been the biggest paradigm shift in my life.

Sam Anno, Tim Green. These are good friends. Tim McDonald was a great defensive back. We shared a day on a boat and discovered we liked each other and didn't want to leave each other's side. I heard that the line, "Show me the money!" from *Jerry Maguire* came from Leigh Steinberg asking Tim what motivated him to play. But that guy would play for nothing. He had a huge heart and was one of the best players I ever played with. McDonald was a quiet leader.

The Trojan family comes together. There are many different demographics, but when you pay the price together, it bonds you. It's a little like going to battle. It's different from basketball or baseball. There's a fear you go through, and that makes the bonds maybe just a little closer than other sports. The physical and mental demands and the adversity bring you together. I remember we had this new juke box in the locker room and somebody would play "Little Red Corvette." Somebody else would push a button for Willie Nelson. There was this big fight over what was played, but after that fight, there was cohesion. After the confrontation, we worked it out among ourselves. You don't have to listen to one or the other. We could listen to both.

Rex Moore was a "blue chip" recruit whose high expectations were cut short by injuries, but his reputation for audacity and football toughness are legend among his teammates. In 1986 Moore won the Davis-Teschke Award for most inspirational player, as well as the Marv Goux Award (offense) for greatest contribution in the UCLA game.

MARK CARRIER
SAFETY
1987–1989

I PLAYED AT LONG BEACH POLY HIGH. It was a power then. It had a lot of history in athletics, especially football, but it didn't have the notoriety then that it has now with the Internet and print media. They get more public relations. It's amazing how many good people have been there. Poly has produced tennis players, baseball players, golfers.

Billie Jean King and Tony Gwynn played there. Chase Utley was a Jackrabbit. So many people came out of there over the years. I forget everybody. I'm pretty proud of that history, of the people who came out of there, and the diversity of the school.

I was a pretty highly recruited high school Parade All-American and all that stuff. I considered Notre Dame. I even made a verbal commitment to Notre Dame, then changed my mind. I woke up the next day and thought I would be best served at USC.

I came in the fall of 1986 and redshirted. Larry Smith came in 1987. I started at defensive back that year. We bottled up Troy Aikman and UCLA to win the Pacific-10 title and advance to the Rose Bowl. It was one of those storybook games you hear about, made for TV. They were No. 5 in the country, and we were just coming into our own. We'd won three in a row but were getting beaten by Aikman and all those All-Americans. They had a 13–0 third-quarter lead, but we came back. One thing after another

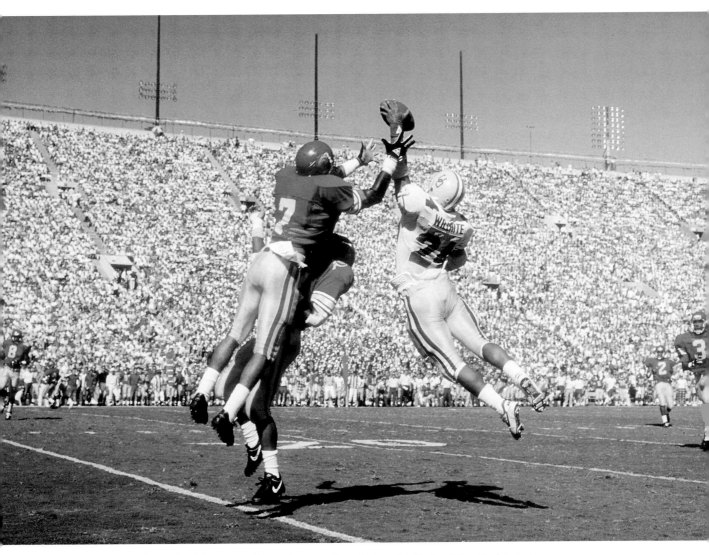

Mark Carrier (7) goes up for an interception during the Trojans' 42–14 victory over the Oregon Ducks in October 1988. *Photo courtesy of Getty Images*

happened, but the key thing was we kept them out of the end zone and got some turnovers. We kept pressure on Troy and won the game.

One of the things I'm asked about many times is, do I have any regrets? I don't, but I was 0-for-3 against Notre Dame. The toughest was in 1988 when we were No. 2 and they were No. 1. That was to play for the title. We were favored but lost at home. They soundly beat us. It was very disappointing to me and the whole team.

It's hard to say we let down against Michigan in the 1989 Rose Bowl a month or so later. I don't think so. Michigan had a good team in their own right. We had the lead and were going in for the winning score, but we fumbled the ball away. Don't get me wrong, though. We couldn't stop Leroy Hoard, so it's too easy to say we let down.

I won the Jim Thorpe Award in 1989. I beat out Nathan LaDuke of Arizona State and Todd Lyght of Notre Dame, and made the All-America team in 1988 and 1989.

Tim Ryan was like a brother to me. We came together and hit it off. He was like the leader of our group. He was outspoken and very confident. He never lacked for enthusiasm. Behind the scenes, he was our leader. He set the tone and had that desire.

Tim, Curtis Conway, and I were all teammates with the Bears a few years later. Keith Van Horne was there with us his last couple years. In Chicago, the Notre Dame guys knew who you were, the school you were from. I got that everywhere I went. They let me know what the record was.

I played seven years for the Bears and made All-Pro three times. I've heard maybe I'll be selected to the College Hall of Fame. I see people going in and wonder what the criteria are. I just got into the USC Hall of Fame two years ago, and in some ways it's bigger than some other Halls of Fame. It's an elite group, and I was taken aback to be selected, because you're in contention not just with fellow football players but Olympians, major league stars, basketball players, track stars, women athletes, coaches. You look at the list, and it's perhaps the greatest list of all-around athletic greats assembled anywhere!

I had the privilege of knowing Jim Murray of the *Los Angeles Times*. He was a very smart and knowledgeable man, easy to deal with. Reporters come in all different kinds, but he was just a guy. He and Mal Florence were nice guys who made you feel comfortable. Tom Kelly has the best voice I ever heard. I can listen to him all day.

I was involved in sportscasting after retirement but got into coaching. I'm in my third year coaching. I was at ASU. I'm not sure if coaching is what I'll do for 20 years. I'm not sure I want to. I need to master what I'm doing and let it go from there. I enjoy what I'm doing and don't think about it that much. The hours during the season are what they are. In the off-season, it's more like an eight-to-five job. But in season, it's at least 12 hours a day. You lose a great deal of sleep. You can work from 6:00 in the morning until after midnight and come back early the next day. If you can't deal with it, stay out of the coaching profession.

Mark Carrier was a two-time All-American and winner of the Jim Thorpe Award for best defensive back in the nation (1989). Twice named All–Pac-10, Carrier was a 1989 Playboy Preseason All-America selection and was elected to the USC Athletic Hall of Fame in 2007. He was selected in the first round by the Chicago Bears, playing in Chicago (1990–1996,) Detroit (1997–1999), and Washington (2000). Carrier was selected to the All-Pro team three times. After pro football, Mark became a radio sports commentator, then went into coaching as an assistant with Arizona State University and the Baltimore Ravens.

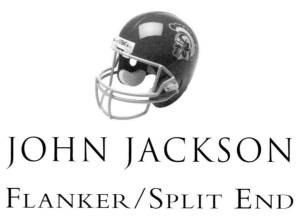

JOHN JACKSON
FLANKER/SPLIT END
1986–1989

I'M FROM DIAMOND BAR IN EASTERN Los Angeles County. Jim Edmonds, who played for the Angels and Cardinals, is from there. I attended Bishop Amat High School, which was still a big-time power when I was there. Mazio Royster, Eric Bieniemy of Colorado, and Ron Brown all played there. Bishop Amat produced Adrian Young, Pat Haden, J.K. McKay, and Paul McDonald of USC. J.K.'s brother, Rich, now a GM in the pros, went there. John Sciarra of UCLA was a Lancer. Phil Cantwell and Gary Marinovich coached at Amat. It was a great era, but in recent years they haven't been particularly good.

I came to USC for football mainly and hoped to play baseball. I was always the kid who loved whatever sport I played in whatever season it was. It was never clear-cut. I liked them both. There's pros and cons, and it's hard to choose one over the other.

I played for Ted Tollner as a freshman in 1986 and for Larry Smith from 1987 to 1989. We had great quarterbacks—Rodney Peete my first three years, and Todd Marinovich my senior year. They were polar opposites in many aspects. Rodney was obviously more mobile. He had the intangibles a quarterback needs as a winner. You can't teach a lot of it. Quarterbacks who are good but do not have that intangible don't become great. The lack of it is a factor with comparing the two. Rodney was a more mobile quarterback and a more vocal type of leader than Todd. Todd led by example. I knew Todd at a younger age. Todd was extremely accurate. He could knock a soda can off a trashcan from 40 yards away. Todd was as accurate a passer as I ever played with. I was a senior when he was a redshirt freshman and, ironically, caught the most balls in my career from him, more than from Rodney. I never took a "kill shot"—he could keep his receivers out of harm's way, which was a testament to his accuracy and field vision. Both quarterbacks loved pressure and played better under pressure. When the heat was on, they were at their best.

When there was media criticism, both played better the next week. Once, when Rodney Peete had the measles and didn't practice the whole week, he played one of the most inspired games in the history of the USC-UCLA rivalry, beating them in the Rose Bowl. They were loaded. In the first game after Todd had a poor performance in a tie with UCLA in 1989, he played great in the Rose Bowl, beating Michigan 17–10.

I played on some great baseball teams, and we were loaded with talent. My teammates included Damon Buford, Murph Proctor, Jim Campanis, Bret Boone, Jeff Cirillo, Mark Smith, Brett Jenkins, Mike Robertson, Randy Powers, Phil Kendall, John Cummings, and Bret Barberie. Barberie married Jillian Barberie. He met her in Chicago when she was an aspiring TV personality and hooked her up, helped advance her career. Rodney Peete was my teammate and a great ballplayer.

Mike Gillespie is the best coach I ever played for in any sport, for several different reasons. First, he knew how to attract talent. Second, he knew how to deal with and manage disparate personalities—talented players' personalities. Boone and Cirillo did not have a great friendship, but through Gillespie, players that did not mesh did not hate each other. Different personalities do different things. With Gillespie, we had football players on the team, guys whose fathers had played in the bigs or at USC or were wealthy alums, families who were well off, and those that were not well off. He handled it all and coordinated it extremely well.

So Gillespie was the best football or baseball coach I played for. We had unbelievable talent offensively. We could hit with anybody and scored a *lot* of runs.

After USC I played in the NFL, for the Cardinals for three years and the Chicago Bears for one. I was drafted in baseball by the San Francisco Giants, and played two years in their organization, then three years in the Angels'

John Jackson snares a touchdown pass against Oklahoma on September 24, 1988, in Los Angeles. The Trojans defeated the Sooners 23–7. *Photo courtesy of Getty Images*

farm system. I wish I'd had a chance at playing in the major leagues, as I would have been one of only three or four guys to play in the NFL and the big leagues.

I have great memories that I can't compare to anything, and it helped me in becoming a broadcaster. I'm truly blessed. I got an opportunity with Fox Sports and have been fortunate to be with them during a period of tremendous growth. Multiple-channel cable TV, the growth of college football, and the incredible growth of televised high school football all occurred during a time when USC's been the dominant program in the nation. It has given me opportunity and exposure beyond just the local market. I started my broadcast career with Fox Sports after my NFL career, and I give Tom Kelly credit for bringing me in. What it means to be a Trojan is that Trojans help each other, we extend a hand for each other, and that's what Tom did for me. I saw him and joked with him, told him that he had a good gig, that it would be nice to look good and get paid for it.

He sent me to the guys at Fox—Jerry Garcia, Gary Garcia, and Jeff Proctor—and it was like, "What do you want to do?" I said I wanted to be on camera. I started with USC baseball as Tom Kelly's partner. He carried me. Fox then launched a high school sports package, and it grew from there: Pac-10, arena football, college baseball and football, major league baseball. Each was a building block along the way, and my timing was great. Kelly got me started, one Trojan helping another. Tom is 100 percent class, a great guy. That mantra repeats itself over and over at USC. Every other school, you're there four years, but you're a Trojan for life! To have somebody reach out and mentor me was great. I'm so thankful to Tom for the opportunity. He made me what I am today, which is more than just an ex–football player. It's been great.

Pete Carroll, in my case I can attest, you are part of the Trojan family. He gets that. I've never held a "regular" job. I've never interviewed or gone through the hiring process for any job I've ever held. It's always been a Trojan who said, "Hey, come work for me." People would get to know me personally and say, "Let me see what you can do." I'd never been in front of a camera in my life when I got the job at Fox. How do we get you trained? Those opportunities are at USC and set it apart from so many schools. We have organizations, alumni clubs. It's a big reason why anybody should go there. It's a great school but part of a huge fraternity.

As an athlete, we have a huge advantage when it comes to working in the media. It's a big media market, and we get interviewed a lot, much of it broadcast nationally. Our network is huge, and kids at USC get used to it, they're comfortable in that environment.

John "J.J." Jackson was a first-team All–Pac-10 wide receiver in 1989, won the Theodore Gabrielson Award as the outstanding player in that season's Notre Dame game, and was selected for the East-West Shrine Game his senior year. J.J. was an NCAA Postgraduate Scholarship winner, an NCAA Top Eight recipient, a National Foundation Scholar-Athlete, and two-time Academic All-American (1988–1989). Jackson played for the Phoenix Cardinals (1990–1992) and Chicago Bears (1996) in the NFL. One of the best all-around athletes in Trojan history, he also was a center fielder on the USC baseball team and went on to the San Francisco Giants and California Angels organizations. He is now a popular, well-regarded sportscaster for Fox Sports, where he specializes in USC, sideline reportage, and major high school games with Jim Watson. His father, also named John Jackson, was an assistant USC football coach.

The
NINETIES

TODD MARINOVICH

QUARTERBACK

1989–1990

I WAS HIGHLY RECRUITED, but it was always assumed I was heading to USC. I really didn't go to any other schools, but I almost rebelled and went to Stanford. I like Northern California and identified with the lifestyle up there. I went on a trip to Stanford and two "trips" to USC. Jack Elway asked me, "On a scale of one to five, what are the chances you'd come to Stanford?" I told him "four." But Larry Smith put on his best suit during the recruiting process, and it came down to playing in the Rose Bowl. I just didn't want to come down to the Coliseum every year and lose like John Elway had done. There was that allure of the quarterback history at Stanford, plus it appealed to my artistic interests, which had started ever since I was a freshman at Mater Dei High School. I transferred to Capistrano Valley High School as a sophomore.

What a dream to have played for Pete Carroll and Norm Chow! I went to practice, and he's a quality guy. I told him what a dream it would have been. That atmosphere is alluring and attractive. He makes it fun. They stopped practice while warming up, and he introduced me to the team. I waved, and they acknowledged me. I've not seen any other group that is so classy.

I redshirted in 1988. With the Rodney Peete situation I walked into, it made all the difference in the world. I had a year to mature and learn from a guy like Rodney, who's a quality person, to watch how he handled himself on campus and with the media. You learn through experience. You can't put

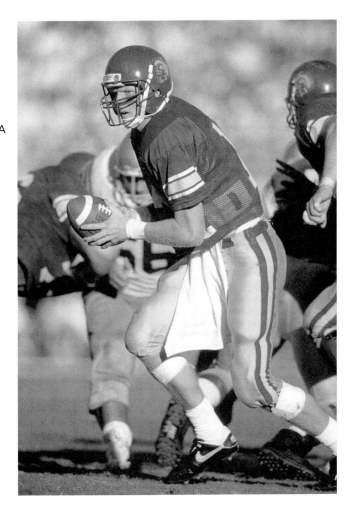

Todd Marinovich prepares to hand off to his back in the annual crosstown rivalry game against UCLA on November 18, 1989, in Los Angeles.
Photo courtesy of Getty Images

a price tag on it. I traveled that year, though. They took me to all the away games to give me a feel for the road.

My first start was the 1989 season opener with Illinois at the Coliseum. The game was scheduled for Moscow, but plans fell through for political reasons. The Berlin Wall came down two or three months after that game. We ran a very conservative offense but seemed to have it won until Jeff George got hot, and they upset us 14–13.

A few weeks later came the defining game of my collegiate career, at Washington State's Martin Stadium. It was an intense game, and we trailed 17–10 with a couple minutes to go in the fourth quarter. The noise was phenomenal.

The comeback was unbelievable. We were getting ready to stop them and give ourselves the opportunity to drive for the winning score. Cleveland Colter was standing on the 50-yard line waiting to catch the punted ball—he was an All-American, so I figured we'd have great field position. But the punt goes *off his head* and just bounces and bounces and bounces until we recover it on *our own 8-yard line.*

That took all the wind out of my sails, and we started out the series 0-for-3. Then I hit Gary Wellman for a first down. Wellman pretty much did it all. Wellman and Leroy Holt. We did it all with passes and converted *four* fourth downs on that drive. We just advanced until we scored a touchdown from three or four yards out. I looked to Ricky Ervins in the flat pattern and then came back to Wellman. That made it 17–16, and we decided to go for two and the win. We stayed with the same play as the TD and made it.

I didn't call any audibles on that drive. I love two-minute situations. I always enjoyed it because I was in the shotgun. I loved it because I could see the field and was more comfortable back there calling my own plays. The coaches called the plays except in a two-minute drill. They gave me the green light to audible and call my own plays because, although most of the plays came in from the offensive coordinator, with two minutes we didn't have time to run plays in.

We returned to Los Angeles after the game, which was played at midday. I was downstairs at Heritage Hall putting my stuff away when Smith's secretary came down and said, "You've got a phone call from President Reagan." I thought it was a joke. Reagan had been out of office since January but was at the height of his popularity with communism on the verge of defeat.

Larry walked out and gave me his office, and I thought that was different. It was Reagan. I immediately recognized his voice. He was the in hospital recovering from surgery and had watched the whole game. He had this distinctive way of saying, "Way-uhl, Nancy and I enjoyed your game today. You inspired us…"

He played the Gipper, and a lot of people thought he was a Notre Dame guy, but President Reagan's a Trojan all the way. I was quiet and grateful for the call. The others, they thought I was full of crap. As I told the story, people still thought I was full of crap, but guys who were with me at the 502 Club that night all had been there and verified it happened.

The energy at Notre Dame Stadium in 1989 was one of the greatest experiences of my college career. It's similar to the Rose Bowl. There's not a lot of room between the field and the stands there. The bands and the crowd are right on you, and their crowd is knowledgeable about when to get loud and when not to. I was wearing a turtleneck and two shirts. I was calling the signals from behind center, and I saw Chris Zorich, their All-American, and he was wearing a cut off-jersey with steam coming out of his face mask. The helmets are cold, but they were used to it. It was in late October, and it was the first cold game I ever played in. It was not a real factor, but they were all baring their arms and looking beastly. It was one of the most exciting games in the rivalry's history, but they prevailed 28–24 to knock us out of the national title hunt.

We played Michigan in the 1990 Rose Bowl. It's funny, I don't know how I can sum it up except there was not much excitement. I played well, but they thought Ricky Ervins was the MVP. We just broke their backs and controlled the ball at the end to win 17–10. What stands out about that game is that it was Bo Schembechler's last game. As a kid, I watched him all the time. On the play that sealed it, we made a big punt, and he threw his headset to the ground. I knew it was over then.

In 1990 I was a Heisman contender, and we were vying for a national championship. We opened at the Kickoff Classic near New York City. Prior to that game, at the pregame afternoon meal, *USA Today* was spread out on the table, and the sports page had my photo and the headline, "Marinovich Swan Song? Is This His Last Year?" I hadn't even thought about it, but third-year players were coming out for the first time. We'd lost Junior Seau and Mark Carrier, and the paper brought attention from the coaching staff, but it wasn't my idea, it was the New York media. We beat Syracuse and looked really good.

255

We had an all-time shootout with Tommy Maddox and UCLA at the Rose Bowl at the end of the season. A lot was going on with Coach Smith and me, and he was playing games. He played [quarterback] Shane Foley against ASU, and we only beat them 13–6. The reason given was my attendance, missing classes, which was a joke because all they go by is GPA. But this was the thing he used to make a pit for me. For what reason, I don't know.

They didn't announce I would start the UCLA game until that day. I wanted to make the most of it to prove my worth. That is the best stadium I ever played in. That Rose Bowl energy is the best. We didn't do much in the first half. I didn't do much, but we broke out in the fourth quarter. Johnnie

Morton was the youngest receiver I threw to in my era, and he just beat this guy on the cover to give me a chance. The main receiver wasn't clear, so I went to the right guy on the sideline and gave him a shot at a great catch.

On the last touchdown, I was going for Gary [Wellman] while he made a timing/crossing route from the 14 or the 17. We called a timeout, and I said, "Let's try Gary up the middle between the two safeties." But he got bumped at the line of scrimmage, so we had to go to the "mack" side for Johnnie Morton. It was just like the catch made by Sam Dickerson to beat UCLA in 1969, and J.K. McKay's catch to beat Ohio State in the 1975 Rose Bowl. It was my favorite route since Pop Warner, the corner station.

What does it mean to be a Trojan? The deciding factor on why I went to USC was my grandfather, "Chief" Henry Fertig, who ran the Huntington Park police department. Chief asked me, when I was done playing college football, where did I want to live? I said I wanted to live in Southern California.

He said, "Why make your name in Miami or someplace? It doesn't make sense to go out of state." That was the deciding factor. I found out over the years that the Trojan family extends long and far. Wherever I go, I am welcomed with open arms. The love and support of my fellow Trojans, along with my faith in my Lord and Savior Jesus Christ, has sustained me through some really tough times.

256

Todd Marinovich set national passing records and was perhaps the most highly recruited, sought-after, and heralded prep football player of his era. His father, Marv, was the captain of the 1962 national champions. His uncle coached Pat Haden and J.K. McKay at Bishop Amat High. His mother was the sister of Craig Fertig, hero of the 1964 USC–Notre Dame game. Nicknamed "Robo QB" because he had been raised and nurtured on a steady health food diet and workout regimen by his father, he was a freshman All-American who led the Trojans to victory over Michigan in the 1990 Rose Bowl and the next year engineered a stunning 45–42 win over UCLA in Pasadena. Todd was a first-round draft choice of the Los Angeles Raiders. Today he coaches high school quarterbacks in Orange County.

SCOTT ROSS

INSIDE LINEBACKER

1987–1990

I WAS A LINEBACKER AT EL TORO HIGH SCHOOL in Orange County, which is really Trojan country. I was being recruited by the University of Arizona, coach Chris Allen and their then–head coach Larry Smith recruited me. They were pushing hard, and Allen came from Arizona to my house. I had been recruited by USC coach Ted Tollner's crew, but Tollner was not recruiting me as hard as some other schools. Then there was a switch. Tollner was fired early in 1987, and Larry Smith got the USC job two weeks later. So now Coach Allen was in my house, again having traveled from Arizona, only this time he's recruiting me for USC because he'd come over with Coach Smith. I was already set on USC. I had been polite and listened to Coach Allen and to Arizona, but I was going to USC.

I was a freshman in 1987, but I got playing time. Rex Moore was the starting inside linebacker. Delmar Chesley backed him up. I didn't travel. We played the Kickoff Classic in East Rutherford, New Jersey, against Michigan State, and I was in Ensenada watching the game. I watched Tony Mandarich break Rex Moore's ankle, and it was like a Joe Theismann thing. I looked at my friend and said, "My redshirt season's over with."

On Monday, Coach said, "Delmar's ahead of you. You're No. 2. Get ready." I played on special teams, and five games or so into the season we traveled to South Bend to play Notre Dame. I was 218 pounds. Notre Dame was running up the middle. Delmar was getting his butt kicked, so the assistant coach was furious, he was spitting mad.

"Get me a linebacker who can fill that hole!" he screamed. He just looked at me and said, "Ross, get in there." I was a freshman, and it was my first game—versus Notre Dame. I played the rest of that game and stopped the run. We lost, but I never lost the starting position after that.

I was starting, and I got accepted by the upperclassmen. Though there were exceptions. Marcus Cotton didn't appreciate a freshman running the huddle. I'd worn No. 64 because of Hacksaw Reynolds, but Rex Moore said No. 35 was a longstanding linebacker number at USC, so I went from wearing No. 64 to No. 35.

Our quarterback was Rodney Peete, whom I describe as the most modest "Hollywood player" you could imagine. He fit the image of the USC football player—good-looking, charismatic, a leader, articulate. He was like a movie star, like what a casting agent would recommend to play a quarterback in a football movie.

Rodney never looked down on anybody. He knew I was insecure, but he propped me up. He was one of the best players I ever played with. He was a senior in 1988. He always had a smile, always encouraged you. Rodney was so versatile, a superior athlete, a great baseball player. At first he'd been a running quarterback, but he could throw the ball, too. I played with Junior Seau, Willie McGinest, and Tim Ryan, but Rodney was the best all-around athlete and leader. He was more like the Bo Jackson of USC, very versatile, and he was the politician of our team. He knew how to talk to everybody, how to encourage people. He was diplomatic and helped make the team work. Junior was quiet, not a leader of the team the way Rodney was.

In 1987 we were trying to establish ourselves. UCLA was in the middle of a strong run. Troy Aikman was their quarterback, and under coach Terry Donahue, they had beaten USC four of five years and won the Rose Bowl a few times. There was talk in Los Angeles that the Bruins now had the better football program. We'd gone through the firing of our coach and were struggling. We entered the UCLA game at the Coliseum underdogs but with a chance to get to the Rose Bowl with an upset.

That game was the best thing in the world. We rallied and came from behind against them. At the end of the first half, Rodney had a pass picked off, a heartbreaking play where we could have been right back in it, but it was picked and run back almost the length of the field. But Rodney chased him down and tackled him yards from the end zone before the gun sounded. It was a swing for us, and they couldn't score with time expired. Rodney brought us all the way back in the second half. We won 17–13 and went to the Rose Bowl.

I didn't realize the magnitude of that game when I was 18 or 19. But we'd beaten Troy Aikman, and Terry Donahue was curled up in the fetal position, crying in the tunnel after the game. I felt for him, but I did laugh, I gave a little snicker, because it was a sweet win. We knew what it was like to be humbled.

In 1988 we had national championship aspirations. Rodney and Aikman were on every magazine cover, the two Heisman hopefuls. Early in the season, we beat Oklahoma, and UCLA beat Nebraska, and we ascended to No. 1 and 2 in the polls. So the whole season there was this anticipation of a showdown for all the marbles. It seemed like it was one of those California seasons that happen every so often. The Lakers won the NBA title, Stanford won the College World Series, the Dodgers beat Oakland in the World Series, and the 49ers won the Super Bowl. So it seemed like USC-UCLA was a natural in '88.

259

Finally, we got to the UCLA game at the Rose Bowl. It was going to be Peete versus Aikman for the Heisman Trophy. The winner of the game would be conference champion, probably be ranked No. 1, and play in the Rose Bowl for the national title. People were talking about the 1967 USC-UCLA game, O.J. Simpson versus Gary Beban. You couldn't play a bigger, more high-pressure college football game. The intensity, the media buzz, was over the top.

So what happened? Rodney Peete got the measles. It couldn't have happened to a better guy. We rallied behind Rodney, like we knew we'd have to play as a team and not rely on our star in order to win. For the defense, we increased our intensity, our urgency to get to the Rose Bowl game on New Year's Day. Our best guy was sick, so we figured we couldn't let it get away. We had to stop Troy Aikman.

We did just that. It was kind of a mediocre win, not a big crushing, but we controlled them, 31–22. Rodney's statistics were not great. He recovered enough to play, but we won as a team. No sooner did we win that game than we had to play Notre Dame at the Coliseum one week later. This is a unique aspect of USC football. Other teams play one big rivalry game. Ohio State gears up for Michigan, Auburn for Alabama. Even Notre Dame is gearing up for us at the end, at least in even years. But in those years we had to play UCLA and Notre Dame in consecutive weeks. What other program in the country would ever put itself through something like that?

All season in 1988 it was USC-UCLA, Peete versus Aikman. Now we'd beaten them, and it was like, *Oh, man, Notre Dame's unbeaten, too. And we have to beat them now, if we want to achieve our goals.* It's hard to say it was a letdown versus Notre Dame. It was still Notre Dame. I think as a team, as a whole, we had won the "Super Bowl of L.A." and then had to play a great Notre Dame team. Trojans don't make excuses. Many USC teams have done what we had to do. But it's sort of like a baseball team that gets on a hitting streak, peaks, then hits a lull. A lot of guys were still on a high.

It's not so much a factor in the pros as it is in college, where you still play on emotion. You play in front of 80,000 to 100,000 fans. An average player plays exceptionally, and an exceptional player plays out of his mind. In the pros, you have to play exceptionally all the time. But for 20-year-olds, it's a lot to ask.

Peete hurt his shoulder in the 1988 game with Notre Dame. I remember him getting hurt. But, to tell the truth, as much as we were a team, the defense is consumed with defense, so we didn't meddle in the offense. We were down three at the half, and it was anybody's game, even though Rodney was hurt and not playing great. But they dominated us in the second half, intercepted a pass and ran it back, and we lost 27–10. It's tough to be more down than we were, because the national championship was taken from us, and our biggest rival, the Fighting Irish, now had the inside track at it. That was Lou Holtz' team. I remember screaming at Holtz on the field. We knew each other. The intensity gets up, and it's hard to lose to them, especially on our home turf.

So much was lost that day. The national title, and all of a sudden Rodney's Heisman. It seemed like he was going to win it after beating Aikman, but out of nowhere Barry Sanders at Oklahoma State had been quietly putting up incredible rushing totals. Now that Rodney had a bad game on the big stage, Sanders won it.

We still went to the Rose Bowl against Michigan. It got to be the norm for me, going to the Rose Bowl. I went after the 1987, 1988, and 1989 seasons. I can't say we let down against Michigan after losing to Notre Dame in '88. We led 14–3 and seemed to be in control, but they rallied and beat us. People said we were uninspired because we were not playing for No. 1, but it's still the Rose Bowl, so I doubt that.

Larry Smith was unsung. He took me to three Rose Bowls. He was a tough coach. We went full speed in practice if he thought we were getting soft. He was great with Peete—the two of them communicated well. They were on the same level, but he was a little conservative. He got conservative with Todd Marinovich.

I competed against Todd in Orange County high school ball. I was at El Toro, and he transferred to San Juan Capistrano, where he set every national record and was the biggest prep recruit maybe of all time. The expectations for him were off the charts. His dad, Marv Marinovich, had played at USC. Todd was literally a "SCion," Trojan royalty on both sides of his family, born and bred to play quarterback for USC. His dad controlled every aspect of his life, what he ate, his workouts, his preparation. But when Todd left home, he was going to do what he wanted.

Smith and Marinovich didn't communicate. If Todd would have had his way, he'd run shoots, trick plays, and change plays in the huddle. Larry would go nuts even if it worked and Todd gained 20 yards.

In 1989 no one remembers the season opener versus Illinois. Todd was a redshirt freshman, and he started. Jeff George was Illinois' quarterback. We led 13–0, but Smith didn't let Todd open up. We just ran the ball and held them on defense. But late in the game, George started to bring them back. We went into a prevent defense. With 2:30 left, they had a third down and needed a touchdown. Jeff threw a lightning strike over my head. I jumped up and got hold of the ball, tipping it, and Mark Carrier was behind me, ready to intercept the ball. But their receiver went up, caught the ball, and went into the end zone. If I'd let it go, Carrier would have intercepted it, and we'd have won.

Todd's best game at USC may have been the 28–24 loss at Notre Dame in 1989. That was a tough pill to swallow. Smith's conservative approach never really meshed with Todd, who was more of a West Coast offense guy, a free-lancer who was good at reading defenses. We beat Michigan 17–10 in the 1990 Rose Bowl to finish 9–2–1. It was a surreal experience. There was a picture of me in the *Los Angeles Times*, on the front page, and that was the highlight of my career. We beat Bo Schembechler in his last game. We couldn't have beaten a bunch of better guys. We ran into those guys from Michigan out in L.A. a few nights earlier, plus there was the "Beef Bowl" at Lawry's. It was a good win. But my senior year we went to the John Hancock Bowl, and the season was a disappointment.

We had high hopes for a national championship, and Todd was a Heisman candidate. We opened with a big 34–16 win back in New York over Syracuse in the Kickoff Classic, but we ran into that great Don James team at Washington. They beat us in Seattle, and everything crumbled. Todd and Coach Smith argued. Junior Seau went into the NFL after his junior year, so he was not with us. We beat Tommy Maddox and UCLA 45–42. That was Todd's greatest moment. But we lost again to Notre Dame and then were uninspired in the Hancock Bowl. Todd and Smith argued on TV, and that was that.

What does it mean to be a Trojan? I don't think there's a better club or camaraderie other than the U.S. military when it comes to a helping hand. There's no one better when it comes to that. They all want to help, to catch a game with me. I have friends in the alumni who are 80, and there is a connection with people there. We break down walls with each other. Open up, and they help you.

When I had to come back to USC to get my degree, I called the Orange County Trojan Football Club, and they came up with money from the John Wayne Scholarship Fund, which paid my way to get my degree. I never would have graduated without their help.

The generation gap totally breaks down due to the USC connection. I became best friends with an 80-year-old guy who's 45 years older that me. But he lived through the Great Depression and could relate to my problems, and we just hit it off.

Pete Carroll is remarkable. He intuitively understands the USC connection and incorporates it into his philosophy. I was with some of the younger guys last year before the season, and I couldn't believe the discipline. It was not harsh, but it was something they wanted and needed, and he gave it to them in a way they accepted. The things they do in the off-season—I thought it was wonderful that they get up at 6:00 in the morning to go running. He makes sure they're not out partying, running amok, and I couldn't believe the discipline they impose upon themselves and upon each other.

I attended a football event at Phil Trani's restaurant in Long Beach, and they were disciplined in that environment. They had this great demeanor, there was no alcohol, and it was all because of Carroll. I was amazed. The old-school wild boys would get in trouble and run amok at the old 502 Club, but Pete's got a complete handle on that. I had a hard coach, but this guy is hard. Yet he makes it seem like you are imposing his discipline on yourself. The ability to do that is something you can't teach, but Pete's got it.

It's a brotherhood. To this day I look around in society and see 'SC people. They're all over the place. I never met a bad USC guy. They just rise to the top.

When I was a player, I went to the 100-year reunion at the Coliseum. Aaron Emanuel and I butted heads all the time. *Sports Illustrated* said he was supposed to be a Heisman candidate, but he wasn't. We were in the locker room, and these old cronies came in. We had a keg of beer, and Aaron and I got into it. And we were in suits, were supposed to be respectful. We started to get after each other, and Pat Harlow grabbed me. I heard a couple of the older guys chuckling, saying it hasn't changed since they had played there. We went out and had a good time at dinner, and the next day we laughed and shook hands. We're all Trojans and respect each other.

Scott Ross was an All-American in 1990. He was All–Pac-10 in 1988, 1989, and 1990, played in three Rose Bowl games (1988, 1989, 1990), was selected team Most Valuable Player, Defensive Player of the Year, and was the recipient of the Davis-Teschke Award as a senior. USC's record was 35–12–2 in his four years. After selection to the East-West Shrine Game and the Hula Bowl, he was drafted by the New Orleans Saints and played for them in 1991.

DERRICK DEESE
OFFENSIVE GUARD
1990–1991

I PLAYED AT THE UNIVERSITY of Southern California from 1990 to 1991. I came from El Camino Junior College, which is one of the best J.C. football programs in the nation. John Firestone, a legend, was my coach there. Between him and the offensive line coach there, they made great names for themselves. They do a great job of getting kids to the next level. The good thing is they're still sticklers for getting kids an associate's degree. They make sure you get it whether you needed it or not, and it's one reason I still stay involved.

I played at Culver City High School, which was not a very good program, but it's getting better. I see they've been making it to the playoffs more the last seven years. My senior year was the first time they'd been in the playoffs in 15 years or something. Carnell Lake of UCLA and myself, we came from there.

Clarence Shelmon recruited me for USC out of El Camino as an offensive guard. I also played on the defensive line in high school and at El Camino. The funny thing is coach Gene Engle was not sure if I'd play on the offensive line or not. He recruited me to play there. They give you an envelope detailing your position responsibilities, and mine was for both sides of the ball. I think it was hard for Coach Engle, who's still there, because there'd been a disruption of coaches because of what happened my senior year. He told my mom, "I never make promises," but he guaranteed he'd get me to a

Division I school. My situation was, I wanted to play football and get an education. To be honest, I wanted to be a police officer, so I went to El Camino, and Clarence Shelmon talked to their coaching staff. My tapes had been shown, and they said I had great speed and technique. I spoke with a lot with coaches, and I signed with the Trojans in the spring of 1990.

Mark Carrier and Junior Seau would have been seniors that year, but they were two of the first players to leave early after their junior years. Now it's common, but then it was rare. We expected to compete for the national championship that year, and had we had them, it would have been much more possible.

I got to USC, and you have an air about yourself there. Basically, you felt like everybody wanted to be at that school. As an offensive lineman, you get hyped. It's Tailback U and it's Linebacker U, but we've had a lot of offensive linemen, and that was the thing 'SC was known for. Unless you are a real football addict, you don't pay attention to offensive linemen, but you have to have them in order to have the running game USC's always had.

I was an L.A. kid, so growing up I knew a lot about it and all about the USC-UCLA rivalry. When I got there, I found out we were kicking off the season for college football and had a chance to win a national championship. The opener was the Kickoff Classic at Giants Stadium in East Rutherford, New Jersey. It's a pro stadium, and that was a big, hyped game. No one else was playing, so all the focus at the beginning of the season was on us. You want it to be like that at the end of the season. You want to be playing for No. 1. That was our focus, to show what we had worked for all spring and summer.

Our quarterback was Todd Marinovich. The funny thing about Todd is I played with some of the greatest quarterbacks ever to play the game. I think if he'd stayed focused, he would have been a great quarterback. But coach Larry Smith had a spat with him over control issues, over who had the power, and it affected Todd. He came out early, and looking back, if he'd stayed another year, he could have changed USC as a whole. He was up for the Heisman for most of the season. He'd been a freshman All-American and led the Trojans to a Rose Bowl victory. So if he had come back, I think he could have won the Heisman.

We lost to Notre Dame 10–6. That was after our big offensive game with UCLA. I don't think there's a big physical difference between the Irish and the Bruins. I look back, and both teams were well coached and had great guys

Derrick Deese settles into his stance during a 1997 playoff game as his 49ers took on the Minnesota Vikings.
Photo courtesy of Getty Images

266

on both sides of the ball, who went on to play in the NFL. In big games, the first team that makes a mistake is usually the team that loses. We fought back as well as we could and felt we had a chance to win. Some people thought that coming back from the high of the UCLA game caused us to lose, but great teams keep that level of play consistent.

The UCLA game in 1990 was one of the greatest games in USC history. It was my first year coming from junior college at El Camino, where we had a semi-horseshoe of a stadium. It seats a few thousand. Then we played the Kickoff Classic in our first game. This is after I'd played in the Cardinal and Gold spring game, which can get a few thousand in one section of the Coliseum, which to me was like *wow*, and now New York.

At Giants Stadium we warmed up, and I was thinking, *This isn't so bad.* Then I heard the introductions, and after we'd rested in the locker room and heard the roar of the crowd, we went out there and saw this big, full stadium, 40,000 or 50,000 people. It was shocking for a junior college transfer. Then we went to the Rose Bowl to play UCLA. Being an L.A. kid, that's the granddaddy. If you're in the Pac-10, you want to play in the Rose Bowl, bottom line. USC owned that stadium for quite some time. Now we get to play our rivals there. They're the enemy who are going to have bragging rights all year, and you know all those guys. We follow them, they follow us. They see us out in J.C. or high school, we know each other. We got to the game, and I remember they had Scott Miller, a receiver from Saddleback whom I had played against. He was a pretty good guy, and I knew he could take the game and control it if given the opportunity. We entered the game, and it's the biggest game aside from Notre Dame. We got out there and saw 100,000-plus going crazy. That is phenomenal. Even in the NFL, you don't experience that type of crowd atmosphere. That's a true football game. It became a definite game of mistakes, a game of inches in which the lead must have switched hands 10 times or more. I've talked to people from UCLA, and they're always asking, "Could Johnnie Morton have made it if not for the one-foot rule in college?" Or, "What if he needed two more feet in the end zone?" That's where it becomes fun. We both showed up to play, and obviously the best team won!

I started with the San Francisco 49ers in 1992 and played with both Joe Montana and Steve Young. We won the Super Bowl in 1995. I played with Jeff Garcia. Those quarterbacks show how much more you need to think, how much they achieved, but they've all had different reasons why they succeeded. I've played with two Hall of Famers, both Joe and Steve.

Montana was extremely smart. He could read defensive players. He had an air about him and was able to lead guys to a higher level. In his case, he had good athletes around him, and his confidence rubbed off on everybody. He had a swagger, no matter who was coming into the game, no matter where you played on offense, it rubbed off and made people around him better.

In 1994 I think Steve Young put the pressure on himself to win the Super Bowl and to be the best no matter what. He was not going to be satisfied with his accomplishments and accolades. It's easy to say, but basically he took the bull by the horns and decided what he was gonna do with the horn. He had to play a long time behind a quarterback considered the best in the game.

To replace somebody like that is pressure, but he put the same pressure on himself. The 49ers have always been a team where nothing less than winning the Super Bowl is good enough. It's like that at USC. We could go 11–2, win the Rose Bowl, and finish No. 2, but it was a disappointing season because the expectation is a national title. That breeds excellence. When you put the pressure on yourself and play with that, you carry that on and off the field. Nothing breaks you. There's nothing you cannot attain, and you will do it.

Pete Carroll came to San Francisco in 1995. When he came there, he was a guy who'd been fired by the New York Jets. He was our defensive coordinator, and our defensive players loved him. Merton Hanks, Tim McDonald, they all loved him. Guys loved to play for him, and you thought he could be our next head coach. He definitely had a great defensive mind. When he left, guys were in shock but happy he got a head-coaching position in New England.

When he was hired at USC, Tim McDonald and I went on the air and said they'd made a great hire. I think he was a great hire, and it can't get any better for USC. What was funny is later we found out that Mike Garrett thought he was not going to hire him. You've got to be kidding me. He was thinking about going in a different direction.

Players who played for him knew how good he was. I saw him coach every day, so I knew. The alumni and the media were not excited, but you knew players wanted to play for him. The thing is, when I was playing for him before he was at 'SC, I would say, "I bet this guy's a good recruiter." You'd look at Carroll and never see him highly upset. He was always smiling, there was always something good on the other side, and a kid can see that.

Either he has it or he doesn't. He could get an NFL job, but frankly, as a past Trojan, I hope he never takes another job. He's good for USC. He has a great staff. Look at the way he runs his system. Yeah, some kids leave early, but they have to understand that it's not just one person who's that good, but a lot of intangibles in a team game that makes you that way. The fact of the matter is that Carroll, even with kids who leave early, is still able to take it to another level.

Carroll has made a name that will live on for decades. He'll be talked about when my kids are old enough to have kids. Does he want to accomplish more at a higher level? You mention college legends like Knute Rockne, Bear Bryant, and Bud Wilkinson—Pete's there now, I think.

Steve Spurrier tried it his way, in college and the NFL. But who does the recruiting in the NFL? Look at the questions a general manager asks. Do we want to pay him? In college it's, "Do we have a scholarship?" Carroll can get 10 "first-round draft picks" in one recruiting class. In pro football, you can't do this, you've got a budget. Jerry Jones will put the money out. Dan Snyder and a few others will spend money to get the players if they have to.

Announcing is great. I've done radio since my second year with the 49ers. I've done a lot of Elvis and JayVee on KMEL "Hot 97," then 94.9 and so forth, and I liked it. On radio I get a chance to be able to talk to someone who can't see you, so you have to give them a visual. On TV it's all on the screen. But it's just you on the radio. You have to keep people listening. I like things difficult more than easy. That's the road I travel.

I did *In the Trenches with Derrick Deese* with Rick Barry on KNBR/68 in San Francisco. From there I went to Tampa and did an ESPN show. Chris Visher got me on weekly, and when got hurt, I got a try-out on 570 in Los Angeles and got hired. "Big Joe" from Northern California was on when I came to L.A.—that's Joe Grande from "Power 106." They hired me, and 570 let me do this show, and I stayed there a year. Fox Sports had me sit down in there. They liked what they heard, and it's been that way ever since. It's difficult because I've had a lot of injuries, and I can't sit as long as you need to.

269

Ultimately, you don't want to be a guy who walks the fence. I pick one side or the other. *In the Trenches* gave some glory for the linemen. The "pretty boys," the blonde guys like Boomer Esiason, the Frank Gifford types, they get lots of these post-career media jobs. But Mike Golic gets to do those things. You look at it, and offensive linemen are big guys, but we get to put it forward. Lincoln Kennedy has his opinions, and they're different.

Why do so many USC athletes do so well on the radio? There's a media perimeter around the campus. It's tradition. You have no choice but to talk to *somebody* every day. Los Angeles is one of the top three markets in the world, so you're going to be seen and heard. Some guy from a small town may talk to five or 10 people in a week before you bring him to L.A. I guarantee, Jason Sehorn was like that, coming from a tiny town like Mount Shasta, but he became a celebrity in New York. He learned how to handle that, like Gifford did, at USC. There's so many people around you at USC, celebrities coming by, and the last thing you want to see on TV is you saying, "Uh…I uh…let me see…"

You don't have to like it, but you have to appreciate what someone says. Disagree with my opinion, but I know what I'm talking about. I've played and I'm knowledgeable, that can't be denied. That's what I can do because of what I did at USC. They have speech classes, communication classes, plus psychology and sociology. You have to be able to get yourself out there and be a guy who can speak to anybody. You have no choice, you had to do interviews, we had to do that. Even if you just got here, they'll say, "Get here and speak." You learn that, and it's not just football.

Jim Rome interviews USC athletes all the time— basketball players, baseball players, women athletes like Lisa Leslie—and says that far and away our people are the most articulate. Baseball players like John Jackson and Tom Seaver are well-spoken. Years ago when Tom Seaver was a young celebrity/superstar in New York, he knew how to handle it. He'd say, "That's a journalistic trick you're trying to pull; I learned that in a journalism class at USC." Or, "I took public relations classes in college and know what you're trying to do."

Plus I learned what not to do from people in the media when I was a player. I never respected Ralph Barbieri on KNBR/68 in San Francisco. He was dogging me even though he never played, so I told Mark Ibanez, who did a postgame show on channel 2, that I didn't appreciate certain members of the media trying to discredit me, especially when they had two DUIs in a couple months like Barbieri did. Ibanez laughed so hard they had to do a second take, but I repeated it on air. After that, Barbieri had all kinds of praise for Derrick Deese. Whatever.

Derrick Deese was selected for the 1992 Hula Bowl, then starred with the San Francisco 49ers from 1992 to 2003. He was a member of their 1994 world championship team and was with the 49ers when Pete Carroll was an assistant with them from 1995 to 1996. After playing for Tampa Bay (2004), he became a national sports radio host.

MATT GEE

INSIDE LINEBACKER

1988–1991

I CAME FROM A SMALL TOWN, Arkansas City, Kansas, and went to USC, where I played inside linebacker. I was a highly recruited player out of a town of 10,000 people, and they tracked me down. We had a historically great high school program down there, so scouts knew to come there.

Coaches Larry Smith and Ted Tollner both recruited me after they found me, and they really loved me. I was on their list, but not excited about California. I was all for going to the University of Oklahoma, because my town is near the Oklahoma border. I was a good track athlete and had set a high school javelin record. I was asked by the Olympic Committee to try out for the javelin at a camp with track and field athletes, for the Seoul, South Korea, Olympics. So there I was, along with these track veterans, and it was held at USC, so I was at Heritage Hall. I'd dodged USC, but they came out. I ran the 40 in 40.6 seconds but fell on the track and scraped my hand. I went into the training room, and the coaches just went down there and talked me into coming to 'SC. I did my research on 'SC and saw all their linebackers were in the pros. Back then, for linebackers, it was by far USC.

I went from a tiny town to L.A., so it was an awakening culturally, but my expectations were centered on football, to win a national title. They also said I could run track if I wanted to, as long as I played spring ball, because others had done the same thing. USC has a long tradition of dual-sport athletes—football/track, football/baseball—as does UCLA, who also allows dual sports. But I couldn't keep up with the javelin and track and still play football. I came out for some points in track meets, but not full time. We went to two Rose Bowls when I was there.

I think to be a Trojan is everything. Coming from the Midwest, I had no idea how big it was to be a Trojan, to have that connection for life. In Southern California, people's eyes get big when they hear you went to USC. "So did I." As time progressed, I became tight friends with so many USC people. Even my business today is centered around USC people. They stick together. As you progress from freshmen to seniors, you don't realize how important it is until you leave school. I can't emphasize enough, so many things happened when I was there, it's unreal. I can't imagine something else. I go see coaches I haven't seen in years, and it's just great. And it's a small school, a tight area to have to know a lot of people.

I didn't really get to know Coach Smith until my senior year, when he was under stress. I stayed close with my position coaches. He had nothing to do with the defense. I was the captain my senior year, and we got closer, but he was a standoffish guy. He never bothered me. His nose was always to the grindstone, and he worked constantly. Some people didn't like him, but I did.

Coach Tom Roggeman was my linebackers coach while I was at USC. He had a real Marine drill sergeant's demeanor, was constantly yelling, and was very intense. He'd love to hear about this book. He was as old-school as you could possibly get. Smith and his people were all old-school guys. Their philosophy going into games was that it was a constant fight, and you just beat them down.

Away from football, our hangout was this legendary watering hole called the 502 Club. It was actually a restaurant called the California Pizza and Pasta Company, but the bar was called the "Five-O." It was at the corner of Jefferson and McLintock in the University Village, next to the Bank of America where a Yoshinoya Beef Bowl is now, and it was a part of USC for about 20 years. Kids at USC today don't have a place like that to go to. They cab to downtown clubs, or Westwood or the South Bay, but people at USC in those years had the Five-O. Even today, if you mention the 502 Club, people have this look in their eyes like it's a secret code or message, like, "Yeah, I remember the Five-O." Coach Smith tried to keep us out of there, but everybody was in there—baseball players, women athletes, fratties, locals, everyone.

I felt like I was one of the owners when I went in there. I felt like I knew everybody. Tony "Bruno" Caravalho, who did own the place, took care of

Matt Gee charges upfield against Ohio State during a September 1989 game in Los Angeles, which USC won 42–3.

us, and I smile when I hear of it. I almost got sick to my stomach when it closed. Most of the guys met there to blow off steam. Tony made us feel like family. When the 502 closed down from the 1992 riots, it changed USC. Now there's a glitzy corridor between Staples and the Galen Center. The neighborhood's cleaner, there's upscale housing for faculty, the air quality is greatly improved, and the academics are better. But there's no place to go on a Thursday night like the old 502 Club. The 901 Club is still around, but it never compared then or now.

I still stay in touch with Scott Ross. Mike Salmon is doing great, the Gibson brothers, Don and Craig. We've all taken care of Todd Marinovich at one time or another. He's trying to get well. He's a good guy. Matt Willig and Pat Harlow are good friends. I married a USC girl, Alana. I stayed in L.A. and went to the Raiders. I was on their practice squad in Los Angeles for one and a half years, and that prolonged my time here. Then I got married, and I'm sure glad I did stay in the area. I can't imagine living anywhere else.

I try to go to as many games as I can at home, but with three kids, it's hard on Saturdays. But my kids love it here. I go out to the practice field two or three times a year to keep in contact. I know Pete Carroll. We got set up at San Francisco when I was trying out with the 49ers. He was the DB coach there, so I knew him at San Francisco before he went to the New England Patriots. He's a people person. I wish I'd played for him.

It's really hard to explain what it means to be a Trojan. It's a great thing, and I'm very honored by it. People do not realize this until they're out of school. It's like having a gold medal. I hope I can get my kids in there. I got my start there and love it.

Matt Gee was a four-year letterman and team captain his senior year. He was in the Los Angeles Raiders organization before becoming a successful businessman in the L.A. area.

TASO PAPADAKIS

FULLBACK/INSIDE LINEBACKER

1994, 1996

LIKE MY FATHER BEFORE ME, I played at Rolling Hills High School. But when they combined it with Palos Verdes High, it became Peninsula High, which is what it was when my younger brothers went there. I was at USC from 1993 to 1998 and graduated with a degree in religious studies with an emphasis on Eastern thought.

I was involved in the football program from 1993 to the spring of 1997, but I stepped out of it when I had my fifth orthopedic surgery at the end of spring practice in '97. I just thought, *That's that!* I came in as a fullback until they changed me to a middle linebacker a year and a half into it, just as my dad had been a running back before they moved him to linebacker because they had running backs like Sam "Bam" Cunningham ahead of him.

To me, education is the most important part of what it means to be a Trojan. I studied in the religion school. When I was there, it was considered progressive. I got hooked into the subject from a class I took for general education. I was turned on by the rhetoric, the train of thought and analysis that coupled with emotions, and discovering deeper paths of spiritual thought. The teachers were progressive. One interesting professor was on a real "Jesus kick" with emphasis on the historical New Testament and the role of Easter. Professor Peter Nosco was the head of Eastern religious studies, which teaches many different courses on Eastern thought, including Zen Buddhism. I finished really strong with these classes.

Being Greek, I grew up not realizing the significance of my heritage until I could get some perspective. I look back at my father, who would read poetry, including the Beats—Allen Ginsberg, Richard Brautigan, Jack Kerouac—mind-bending stuff, meant to be read out loud like "Howl." Brautigan's *Dreamscape* was cool to hear. My father practiced his speeches in front of us. He was a motivational speaker with a through-line on Greek concepts, of the id, and Homer. His concepts and ideas about approaching people and relationships were always being espoused around the house. Food was also a big part of my upbringing, a celebration of life. Our religious emphasis was Lutheran, and in my high school memorial, I quoted verses from Isaiah. I was exposed to a lot of that.

I didn't choose this, to apply the cognition of philosophy, when I played. I did not address those issues at the time. It's demanding if you start thinking, it involves the opening of areas that create sensitivity, and that's not so hot about running into fullbacks. On a football team, you don't want to give anybody a reason to second-guess you. I didn't want to have real conflicts. There's not really a symbiosis between the two studies, football thinking and philosophical thinking. I was stuck in an area between the two and waited until I was out of football to expand my way of thinking.

The intellectual pursuit that I engaged in class helps me now. I think everything you learn in life can be used, whether it be writing or photography. People tuck away inside of themselves the things they learn. Perhaps these issues don't manifest themselves on the images I photograph, but it's present. I don't always know what it means, but my education enriches my work.

John Robinson was my coach. My experiences with him are easier to make sense of now that I'm outside of the game. I was hurt and worked myself back into playing shape. I had different experiences, but he was a wonderful speaker. He knew young people unbelievably well. The way he spoke to you was very emotional—very direct and personal. As a coach, he was a little scattered. Choosing assistants, he surrounded himself with people he trusted and relied on. But the way he chose kind of lacked specificity with his coaching. He gathered up on a conversation then walked over and talked to some alumni, then came back. He was entitled to his point of view and due the respect worthy of his accomplishments, but at that stage of his career, I don't know the levels of his motivation to come back after he'd been out of it a while. From my experience, he was like a father to me, but his focus was not as much as it should have been. He was a beautiful man but a bit disconnected, and even a bit jaded.

It always came back to academics at 'SC. I was in a special religious department and didn't stray too far from that. I was at USC at a time when Dr. Steven Sample was establishing himself and turning USC from a very good university to a world-class institution of higher learning. He insisted on higher entrance requirements, and there was a transition period.

A lot of alumni saw what was happening and came to the conclusion that there was a tradeoff—that Dr. Sample could preside over a great academic university or a great football school, but not both. I think toward the time I left and when my brother, Petros, was there, the alumni were satisfied that we were now a top academic school, and it was okay not to dominate in football as long as we were.

Dr. Sample had a lot of interaction with the football team. I knew him quite well. He was very energetic and passionate. As a football player, our role as student-athletes was clear. When Coach Pete Carroll came in, he had the challenge of restoring the football tradition while maintaining academics, and to have successfully accomplished that has been a huge achievement. I don't know too much about the program on a day-to-day basis, but I interact with Pete. He lives near my family in Rolling Hills Estates, and I see him at the pizza parlor with his family or down at the Hermosa pier. He loves the beach and interacts with fans there. They give him plays, and he takes them seriously.

277

Pete gives you his undivided attention and looks you in the eyes. He listens very intently and has a unique countenance with people. Anything he does is intense with results that are correct or successful. At that level, he's going to succeed and not just in football. It's not just the way he conducts practice. He's not preoccupied and lives in the moment.

Pete's son was at Peninsula High School, and my brother plays there. Pete likes the ocean, it's like a good church for him. Fans come up to him, and like any good director, he takes suggestions. He's open-minded, and the kids are open-minded with him. Every day he's your "god," so you mold yourself into that kind of mentality. He studies, and his football players see he's open-minded and grab onto his ideas. A coach gives you his personality, and if he's maniacal, then you feel constricted.

As far as my studies went, it's possible I was below par. I spent a lot of time slamming dominoes on a table in school and could have studied more, or managed my time better off the field. Some quarterbacks are premed. It's not easy, but I did well and loved it.

I spent 10 years as a Shakespearean actor in productions up and down the coast. I performed in some of the "sweat houses" in Hollywood and have the Shakespearean language. Petros also loves and reads Shakespeare, and would quote from the Bard at press conferences when he was playing, which perked up the ears of writers not used to hearing such things. When I got to *Hamlet*, it was the end of the line. *Macbeth* is a role that ruins your mentality for a while. I've never been to London to study with the Shakespearean masters, I but saw Ian McKellen play *King Lear*.

Taso Papadakis comes from the "royal family of USC." His father, John, and brother, Petros, played for Troy. His grandmother sat in on writing classes at the school before embarking on screenplays and daily missives she sends to the newspaper. Petros is a high-profile member of the L.A. media. The family restaurant, Papadakis Taverna in San Pedro, was the finest Greek eatery in the city and a destination for countless Trojans after games over the years. Taso is a photographer whose work can be viewed at www.tasophoto.com.

JOHN ROBINSON

HEAD COACH

1976–1982, 1993–1997

USC HAD ENJOYED SUCCESS IN 1962 with a national title team. And then in 1972 they had the greatest team of all time. Sam Cunningham was a catalyst in 1970, a great guy and a great athlete, but two men—John McKay and Paul "Bear" Bryant—by the nature of their relationship, bridged the gap and saw some of that change before it happened. We see this in the effect of the 1970 USC-Alabama game, and it was the experience of the sophomores of that year who formed the incredible 1972 champions.

Now if you think about the effect of the West Coast on society and how it plays out in sports, I think we're kind of wacky, anyway. A lot of civil rights things were happening, and California was part of that whole scene.

Up at the University of Oregon, we were like a radical Triple A ballclub. They sent you there for "training." There was a lot of unrest, new ground being opened in those areas. People in other parts of the country were reluctant, but there was a lot of new ground being opened up on the West Coast, not just in civil rights like in the South, but in the everyday expansion of things. In terms of athletics, it seems that so many talented African American kids got a chance to play in high school in L.A.—and you weren't going to succeed unless you recruited those players.

Over a 20-year period, from 1962 to 1982, USC was probably as strong in football as any college ever was. Our location was advantageous. We're right in the middle of the inner city, so many kids grew up wanting to play for 'SC.

280

John Robinson gestures from the sideline in the first half of the Trojans game against Texas Tech in the Cotton Bowl on January 2, 1995, in Dallas.

If they were basketball players, they wanted to go to UCLA. With all that going on, it was a major advantage. And, nationally, USC always benefited from the fact that African Americans felt welcome there.

There's no question that 'SC got it right. A lot of black kids looked at UCLA as being in the rich part of town, so we had this strange mixture of all things that linked us together. Maybe Miami was like that, during that stretch when they were so good. Miami and 'SC similarly did not have great facilities, but each had great weather, and athletes felt at home at these schools. Discipline was not a hallmark.

There's a coalition of people in the stands at an 'SC game that a politician would dream of. I'd drive through south-central L.A. and people would wave at you if you were from 'SC.

One other thing is that African American athletes became very socially adept at USC. Maybe this was because of the Hollywood connection, or because the school's located in a major city. There's always media around, and McKay was brilliant, he exposed his players to the media, to alumni groups, and so they became very comfortable and polished. Listen to Cunningham, Mike Garrett, Lynn Swann, Marcus Allen. They are savvy with the press, well spoken, and represent the school beautifully. Not all athletes, black or white, do this role well.

It's not just football players or black athletes. Look at John Naber, Pat Haden, Tom Seaver. Famous people go there. O.J. obviously flipped, but before he had his collapse, he was a star in Hollywood and sportscasting.

It's a major metropolitan area with four newspapers and a lot of TV coverage. It's different if you go to, say, Athens, Georgia, and the local guy is asking a player a question. Down there, it's "yes, sir," "no, sir," "proud to be here, sir," those kinds of answers.

USC and UCLA athletes were exposed to so much more. They were from a town with two pro football teams, two baseball teams, two basketball teams, and a broader social world. It's very interesting and ironic that in the 1980s and early 1990s, it kind of turned things the other way with the riots, and this made L.A. a negative place. USC basketball and football took a dip. It was not as attractive as it had been. But in recent years the city, the state, and USC have made a comeback.

It was fun to be there. A lot of those athletes were great friends of mine. In 1979 the only negative was that Anthony Munoz got hurt in the first game and only played again in the last game. Marcus Allen was a sophomore; we had a great secondary; and we were loaded from freshmen to seniors. The 1972 team was a veteran team—both were really good teams. I was an assistant, along with Marv Goux. We were both guys who were there with John McKay. It's sad that Marv passed on. That '72 year was magical, especially after I'd been at Oregon.

I was at USC for a number of years under McKay, then John Madden had me for a year in Oakland in order to broaden my range for head coaching, as USC had me in mind for replacing McKay. That happened. Sometimes the hardest thing is to be promoted from assistant to head coach, so my one year at Oakland kind of helped me to transition. If you go away, people think you're better. To be successful, I advise a coach to take on different jobs under different coaches and develop a range of experience.

That's what Pete Carroll's done, and now he's bringing all this back to USC. I had an easy transition and just said, "I don't want to change a thing." Certainly nothing major. I was hired over the phone. They just called me, I was at the airport, and they said, "Do you want the job?" I said, "Yes," and I was in.

282

John Robinson was an assistant coach for two national champions under John McKay (1972, 1974), then coached USC to the 1978 national championship, won three Rose Bowls, and had two players (Charles White, Marcus Allen) win Heisman Trophies. Between 1976 and 1982, his teams beat UCLA five times while beating Notre Dame five straight times (and six of seven). His first tenure completed the most dominant two-decade period any college has ever had. After a successful stint as head coach of the Los Angeles Rams, he returned to coach at Troy from 1993 to 1997. This included a 55–14 pasting of Texas Tech in the 1995 Cotton Bowl, the 1995 Pac-10 Conference title, and a 41–32 triumph over Northwestern in the Rose Bowl.

The
NEW
MILLENNIUM

CARSON PALMER

QUARTERBACK

1998, 2000–2002

I WORKED OUT WITH BOB JOHNSON at his camps. He provided lessons for quarterbacks in Orange County. I was the latest of this group (Todd Marinovich, Rob Johnson, among others) to play for the Trojans and in the NFL. I attended other quarterback camps in the area, as well. Jim Hartigan was my coach at Rancho Santa Margarita. He was a strict disciplinarian with a military background, and a very good high school coach.

I was highly recruited out of Santa Margarita in 1997. I started several games with success as a true freshman in 1998, but I sustained some injuries early in my time at USC. In 2000 we all thought we were in place for a national championship run. We beat Penn State in the Kickoff Classic and felt that we would be competing in the Orange Bowl or Rose Bowl at the end of the year.

I was a bundle of nervous energy getting ready for the season. I was working on my timing and rhythm with the receivers, and I watched a lot of film. I didn't have any restraints placed on me, except that I was under orders to duck out of bounds instead of lowering my shoulder. In high school, the DBs were 160 pounds, but in college they were my size.

Everything changed when Pete Carroll arrived. He has a different way of going about things. He was very inspirational, very positive. He makes it very easy to play for him—his attitude, the way he loves the game, the way he loves the university—so you really want to play for him.

Carson Palmer was a disappointment until Pete Carroll and Norm Chow unleashed his talents, leading to his winning the 2002 Heisman Trophy.

All the early attention, the Heisman hype, was crap. A lot of that stuff about me is false—the Golden Boy, Golden Arm—it's just the media talking. I think I know who I am. I really didn't pay attention to what all those other people were saying. Prior to the 2002 season, there were a lot of people on magazine covers, so it really didn't mean a whole lot. What matters is who's on the magazine covers at the end of the season.

I'd been on all the covers in my first four years at USC—*Street & Smith's*, *Athlon*—but the 2002 media guide cover was Troy Polamalu. After winning the Heisman, I was gracing the covers after the season!

After going 5–7 in 2000 and not playing in a bowl, people asked if I had some regrets about choosing USC before Carroll and Norm Chow, but I'd grown up with the tradition. It probably started when I was in the ninth grade and some of my friends' parents would take us to USC football games. I just fell in love with everything about their football games and the tradition. I always imagined myself running out of the Coliseum tunnel toward the field.

The first comment anybody made about me since I was a quarterback in the ninth grade, was how much poise I had. Don't misread me. I'm very competitive. I don't like to lose. But I've always been easygoing. What's going on inside is probably different. When I was young, if I threw an interception, I wouldn't get upset. I'd come right back and throw a touchdown.

Everything came together in 2002. We had a good team and beat Auburn in the opener, but it took a few weeks to get everything together. We lost at Kansas State and Washington State. We were driving late at K-State, but they held, then lost at Wazzoo mainly because we failed on extra points and field goals. Then Mike Williams found his game, and we became a juggernaut.

Down the stretch in 2002, I have to say that we were as strong offensively as any team Pete Carroll ever had. We were strong on the other side of the ball, too, with Troy just dominating. We killed Notre Dame and played as well as a team can play to beat UCLA at the Rose Bowl. They had a pretty good team. The Irish came in with a good record, and my performance against them apparently gave me the Heisman votes.

The UCLA game in 2002, my senior year, was very memorable. We had a really good group of seniors, but we'd lost to UCLA my freshman year, when they had Cade McNown and a really strong team. We made a vow not to lose to UCLA again. And the vow was not just to win, but to dominate them. We had won a nailbiter two years earlier when David Bell kicked a field goal, but after that we did dominate them. We ran the ball well, and I threw the ball well with great receivers. We had some defensive turnovers and turned it into a rout in their stadium. Their running back, Tyler Ebell, was talking trash in the media about our defense, and we just stuffed him. That put an exclamation point on the career of our seniors. We went out with a bang at the end.

Then we beat Iowa in the Orange Bowl, 38–17. That was a big game for us, but we didn't really know a lot about Iowa. They had a bunch of byes late in the season but had dominated the Big Ten early. Bob Sanders, who is now a great player with Indianapolis, was on that team, as was Eric Steinbach, who was Cincinnati's second pick the year I was drafted by the Bengals. Their quarterback, Brad Banks, was really efficient, and they had a bunch of really good players, so we didn't know what we were getting into.

Their return man ran the opening kick back 100 yards for a touchdown, and it set us back. Troy Polamalu could not play because the trainers screwed up on his medication and had numbed his nerves. We said as an offense that we'd better pull this together. I hit Kareem Kelly for about a 50-yard bomb, and we went down the field and scored. We only punted a couple times and ran them out of the stadium. We had a very physical team. We were supposed to be the "finesse" team, but we ran them out of there in a very physical manner.

People all said, had there been a playoff, we would have won the national title in 2002. Miami was injured at the end, and Ohio State was mainly a defensive team. We pounded Iowa in the Orange Bowl, and that game really showed the college football world that USC was back. It set the tone for all that happened since then.

287

I was fortunate to get that fifth year and make the most of it—the Heisman, the Orange Bowl, the first pick of the draft. I was able to come in to Cincinnati and get the handle on a good offensive system with some talented teammates.

It's been an honor to represent USC in the NFL, and to see the success of the guys who followed me there.

A fellow Orange County guy, Matt Leinart, followed me and won a Heisman, too.

He worked with Coach Johnson, as well. I've been on the sideline when USC won the national championship at the Orange Bowl in 2005, and it's been a joy to see Coach Carroll establish his mark.

Playing in Cincinnati, surrounded by Ohio State fans, is tough. All I want to see is the Pac-10, and it's Purdue versus Northwestern, or Illinois against Michigan State, and of course it's all Ohio State here. They're slow, a physical running team. I want to see people air it out and throw it. I don't get to see 'SC all the time, but I follow them.

It's very special to have been with Pete Carroll when he established what has since become so great at USC. Our whole group—Troy, Malaefou MacKenzie, Charlie Landrigan—these are the guys who saw the changes from the old regime to the Pete Carroll era. This guy is the best coach anywhere. I would have done anything for him, accepted any schemes he offered. He knows so much about the game and was firing on all cylinders all the time. He just seems to have a knack for the right timing and is great around football players. He's been around the game so long, his experience is just tremendous, and he's a guy who just doesn't want to lose. You don't want to let him down.

Every once in a while, I send him a text message, and we talk a couple times a year, but it's hard because he's busy and so am I. But I watch his interviews and pick up things. You can always learn from him, he's so knowledgeable. He's the best.

288

Carson Palmer was USC's fifth Heisman Trophy winner in his All-America senior year of 2002. The team captain that season, he also won the Johnny Unitas and Pop Warner Awards, was the Sporting News National Player of Year, was All–Pac-10, and the co–Offensive Player of Year. He played in the 2003 Senior Bowl after leading Troy to a resounding win over Iowa in the Orange Bowl (earning game MVP honors) and was elected to the USC Athletic Hall of Fame. Palmer became USC's fifth No. 1 draft choice before signing a multimillion-dollar bonus with the Cincinnati Bengals. He has since forged an All-Pro career.

KEVIN ARBET

CORNERBACK/SAFETY

1999–2001, 2003–2004

JEFF SIMMONS, WHO WAS A GREAT RECEIVER at USC, is my stepdad. Through him I rooted for Southern California. I fell in love with the band and the tradition. I just grew up rooting for USC. I was a running back, a corner-back, and a punt and kick returner at USC from 1999 to 2004. I came out of St. Mary's High School in Stockton.

I played for two national champions, and I wear the rings proudly. In the 2003 season, we beat Michigan in the Rose Bowl and won the national title. I was hurt halfway through that year. Growing up, I'd heard of USC's national title teams, but I never thought I'd be a part of it. In Los Angeles, you wear your 'SC gear, and it's incredible. People honk and smile and give you victory signs. We went back to Washington, D.C., and I met President Bush. We got a tour of the White House. I didn't know how much security there was at the White House, but this was not long after 9/11, and soldiers had machine guns. There are all these pictures and statues. We saw a statue of Martin Luther King and visited the Oval Office. We had lunch with the president and took pictures with him. I don't know if Pete Carroll had ever been at the White House before, maybe as an assistant coach in the NFL, but I think it was his first time. Coach Carroll had been an assistant coach at Ohio State. That team was denied the national championship in 1979 when USC beat them in the Rose Bowl. My stepdad was on the team that beat them. I just remember his being really happy and upbeat. Coach Carroll was fired up about how cool this was.

Kevin Arbet and Pete Carroll celebrate their team's 49–0 win over the Colorado State Rams on September 11, 2004. *Photo courtesy of Getty Images*

In 2002 we defeated the Bruins 52–21 at the Rose Bowl. In a lot of ways, that was the game that announced the Pete Carroll era was on, and we were a dynasty. It was one of the most total blowouts imaginable. To do that to our biggest rival—and they were pretty good, maybe 7–3 coming in—on their field in front of their fans, was one of the greatest dominations ever. I was hurt that whole year, but I remember Carson Palmer and everybody were fired up. It had been a long season. We lost early to Kansas State and Washington State, but then we went on a run. The 2002 Trojans in the second half could have beaten any team Pete Carroll has coached. We were the best team in the country by the end of the season.

We were all pumped up. Carson scored and jumped onto the pylon. Kareem Kelly was a senior, and we had a lot of seniors. It was their last regular-season game, so it was very emotional. The difference between the UCLA and Notre Dame rivalries is that I hated Notre Dame. I hated UCLA, too, but it was more about bragging rights. We're in the same city. With Notre Dame, it was hatred but also respect at the same time. Notre Dame went deeper, at least for me, but Coach said to treat every game the same. I remember losing to Notre Dame in

2001. We put a lot into it and got beat, and Coach said, "We'll never let that happen again." It made the game bigger than what it was. So there's hatred, but the respect runs very deep. With UCLA, we're in the same town and see the UCLA guys at the same parties.

The 2005 BCS Orange Bowl victory over Oklahoma, 55–19, was a game where we knew we were going to win. We knew they were good. But I remember sitting in a hot tub with Darnell Bing the night before, and somebody asked us how we felt. It was as though we felt sad for Oklahoma because we were going to kill them. Darnell said, "We're gonna kill 'em." We knew that the competition in the Big 12 was good, but we knew we could beat those guys. I was in awe of Adrian Peterson, but we had more confidence than the 2003 national champs. We were 90 percent confident in 2003 but 100 percent confident in 2004.

What does it mean to be a Trojan? When Carroll came in, he turned it all around. He's a great motivator and a great coach and instilled an attitude in all of us. We all wanted to play for him. We had to play for each other, too. And he made sure we stayed with the academics, as well. A lot changed when he came in, including academics. A couple of players had to leave for academic reasons. He was not playing around. He had us believe we could run through brick walls. We couldn't, but we'd try anyway. I was motivated so well, to this day, four years removed, it still seems like yesterday. I get some recognition as a Trojan. Not a lot, but it's just great to know I played, especially for Coach Carroll on some of the greatest teams in history.

What I learned at USC was to be a better man and to work hard. Carroll taught me, he pounded it in us every day, to compete at everything—your job, every day, never give up on anything. He always stressed competition and said it brings out the best in you. That's the number-one thing.

I made some great friends—Keary Colbert, Mike Patterson, Lofa Tatupu. We're all family.

291

Kevin Arbet is the stepson of Jeff Simmons, who was USC's career receiving leader when he left in 1982. A first-team All–Pac-10 special-teams player in 2001, Arbet was also selected as the top special-teams player of that season (an award now named after Mario Danelo). He was selected for the 2004 Hula Bowl.

MATT LEINART

QUARTERBACK

2002–2005

IN MY HIGH SCHOOL YEARS AT MATER DEI, there were other quarterbacks with big names in Southland prep football, like Matt Cassel, Brandon Hance, Kyle Boller, Kyle Matter, Chris Rix, John Sciarra, J.P. Losman, and David Koral. Matt Grootegoed was my teammate and was a huge star. We played De La Salle at "the Big A," Edison International Field. They were on an all-time winning streak and the best prep dynasty ever, but we played them close in a 31–28 loss. I had a big game, and it elevated my standing. Some people still call that the best high school football game ever played! Bruce Rollinson was our coach, and he had played at USC.

My father, Bob, is a big USC fan and was impressed when he heard that Norm Chow would be the offensive coordinator. Grootegoed committed to USC, and I decided to go, too. But my mind was not right my first two years there.

Riding pine was a major downer, but I'd overcome things in life. I'd been roly-poly as a child, and had vision problems. I was cross-eyed, wore glasses, and was kidded by classmates who called me "four eyes."

There was considerable competition in the spring of 2003. I knew that it was now or never. If I lost the starting job, the man who won it would probably hold it for the remainder of my career, and maybe beyond. I lifted and went from 215 to 225–230 pounds, which made an enormous difference mentally as much as physically.

Coach Rollinson showed a replay of the 2000 Mater Dei–De La Salle game to me in the spring of 2003. I was terrible, in danger of losing the job to John David Booty, Matt Cassel, Brandon Hance, or Billy Hart. I was actually third-string going in to the spring, and I just remember it being a battle. But I had worked very hard that whole off-season. My whole mindset miraculously shifted from March to the three months before the first game. I knew this was my opportunity, and my confidence kind of built as the practices went on because I could see the coaches gaining confidence in me, and I was gaining confidence in myself. From then on, I just took the reins and went with it. Then slowly the players started respecting me and gaining confidence in me, and that's when I knew it was my team and that I could actually play there and be successful.

In the first game at Auburn, I was 17-of-30 for 192 yards, mostly working short yardage in Chow's updated version of the West Coast offense. Mike Williams caught eight passes for 104 yards. Hershel Dennis rambled for 85.

At Arizona State, I was limping around. Pete Carroll just challenged me to play through it because he needed me to. "If you limp, you're not playing," he said to me. The Arizona State faithful were in a frenzy when the Sun Devils took a 17–10 lead early in the third quarter, as road crowds always are when they think the home team has a chance at an upset. I just gritted my teeth, put the pain up in my attic, and hit the first three passes in the second half. We scored 27 unanswered points and won 37–17. My teammates knew I was not a pretty boy, a Tinsel Town guy.

After the game, my teammates talked about my toughness and effort. The game was a turning point for me as well as the program. LenDale White rushed for 140 yards off the bench. Ryan Killeen kicked three field goals, and I hit on 13-of-23 attempts for 289 yards and two touchdowns. We scored 27-straight points in an ultimately convincing win.

In 2003 there were a lot of unanswered questions, but it was exciting. We were Rose Bowl champions, national champions. We savored it. *Sports Illustrated* featured me scoring on my touchdown reception, trumpeting the 2003 national championship with the headline, "USC's the One!" Five 2003 Trojans made All-America. They included wide receiver Mike Williams, offensive tackle Jacob Rogers, defensive end Kenechi Udeze, punter Tom Malone, and myself.

ESPN started calling USC a "Hollywood school," the "University of Sexy Chicks." My name started to get linked to Mandy Moore and Alyssa Milano,

293

but I had to stay focused when it came to football. I worked hard and was a leader. It was all about winning.

Bruce Feldman of *ESPN The Magazine* wrote an article that painted me as "the artist as a young quarterback," a guy with a mind that allowed me to see things—openings, defensive shifts, "vivid images"—that other players were clueless about. The coaches were really praising me. Chow said my mind was "perfect." My mother said I had a photographic memory.

The game just slowed down. Some people have it, and some people don't. I guess I just process stuff differently. But really, it's never been something I've worked on. My dad talks about a Mustang League World Series duel between me and a kid from Puerto Rico. He described the Puerto Rican as "a guy who looks like Cerrano from *Major League*." After 15 pitches, I won the match-up by taking "just a touch off it," which describes many of my passes. I struck out "Cerrano" to win the game.

My father "died" on a hospital operating table when I was young. I prayed and stayed strong for my mother, and he came back. Every Wednesday at USC he made the drive from Santa Ana to L.A. to have lunch with me. We only missed one lunch—the week of the Cal loss in 2003. We didn't miss one after that.

294

In 2004 I struggled against Virginia Tech, and they led 10–7 at the half. We struggled at times, but Reggie Bush, being the big player he is, made big plays. I just kind of got in a groove. We were off our timing a little but in the first half. I remember it being super loud. About 80,000 or 90,000 people were there for Virginia Tech, so it was definitely a hostile environment. I really believe that that game prepared us for the whole season to do what we did. Playing a team like that early, battling back from halftime against a championship-caliber team that only had two losses the whole year definitely helped us the rest of the year, and we won.

Against Cal in 2004, obviously, there was a lot of hype going into that game.

It was kind of a revenge game for us. I wasn't really thinking like that, but inside of everyone else, including the coaches, we just wanted that game bad. It was a battle from the get-go. We got up on them early, 10–0 or something like that, and the defense was playing well. But they held onto the ball, kept the defense on the field so long, and we kept going three-and-out, four-and-out. So the defense was getting tired, and it came down to the last series of the game. Back and forth, back and forth. And then four plays on the 9-yard

Matt Leinart leads the USC band in playing "Conquest," after earning MVP honors in beating Michigan at the 2004 Rose Bowl to capture the first of two straight national titles.

line. With a potent, smart offense like that, it was going to be tough. I remember just sitting on the sideline, thinking, *Get ready for a two-minute drill and try to score*. But our defense, on the two biggest plays of the year, they stopped them.

In the national championship win over Oklahoma, Lee Corso went on record saying that it was the greatest single performance in a game that he ever saw. I was the game MVP after passing 18-of-35 for 332 yards and five touchdowns. We left no doubt. I think we proved we were the No. 1 team in the country—without a doubt.

Then I decided to return for my senior year because the things I valued at school were more important to me than money. I realize the money I could have made if I had gone to the NFL, but I wanted to stay in school. I wanted to be with all my friends and teammates, living the college life and going through the graduation process. All those things made up my college experience, and I didn't want to give that up.

Being in college was the best time of my life. There was something special going on at USC that I didn't want to give up. I was having fun there. It's all a part of growing up, all part of being a kid, and I wasn't ready to pass that up. A lot of people said they didn't envy my being in that situation. In a way, it was a great position to be in, but on the other hand, it was one of the biggest decisions of my life. There was still a lot of motivation for me to play college football. I realized that some said there's really not much more I could accomplish, but I got a lot stronger physically and mentally. Another year of experience helped. It's not about the awards. It's not about trying to win another Heisman. It was really about trying to win a third national championship and getting better as a player.

The next level is business. I was playing for passion and for the love of the game. Sometimes I just kind of looked around and thought, *It's cool being in the position I'm in. Yeah, life is pretty cool.*

As for my celebrity status, it was crazy. I got linked with people because they're celebrities I've hung out with. It was kind of sad that I couldn't go hang with them without getting my name in the paper. I just wanted to hang out.

I don't want to be in all the magazines. That's not who I am. When I go out, it's all over the TV. That's the thing about celebrity life. You never know who's watching you. You just have to be really secure in what you're doing.

I'm a normal guy, just like any other young guy. Really, there's nothing special about me. It's hard to trust a lot of people and know what they're after.

At one party, I tagged along and Nick Lachey was there. Introductions were made and then it was cameras, paparazzi. A cop asked me for my autograph. I just thought, *Yeah, I can live the life of an NFL player right here in L.A.* I was partying with Jessica Simpson and Lindsay Lohan. I was shooting for *Esquire* and *GQ*, was a guest on Kimmel, had my own Internet TV show, and was hanging out with Maria Sharapova, Wayne Gretzky, and Adam Sandler.

I remember when Carson Palmer won the Heisman, he said his heart was beating out of his chest. Mine was about to do the same thing. I just kind of dropped.

My legs were weak. My heart was beating 20 beats a second. It was probably one of the greatest feelings I've ever had in my life. I was a fat kid, cross-eyed, and other people made fun of me. So I was extremely honored.

But when I got home, I put the trophy away and acted like nothing had happened. I was still the same guy. I let my team know that I thanked them. Then I continued to work hard. I feel like I still have so much more to accomplish. I'm still the same person and act the same. All my friends treat me the same, as a goofball. They still could care less. I remember talking to Jason White after he won, and he said how winning the Heisman changes your life completely. My life changed drastically. A few years ago I was a nobody. To me, I'm still a nobody, but in the eyes of a lot of people, I'm a role model, which I take pride in. It's been an incredible journey so far.

I love having pressure on my shoulders. I've had pressure my whole life. That was the spot where we wanted to be as a team. We liked being on the national stage where everybody's watching us. I had great players around me.

Our system worked, obviously. We recruited the best players every year. We had backups who were awesome.

I'm not the most physically gifted kid. I'm not going to scare anybody with my arm or with my running ability. But I felt like my mind set me apart. And my accuracy.

I'm laid back. But I expect perfection. I'm very hard on myself. On the field, I have a cool confidence. I've never been arrogant. I could care less about awards. I just want to win. I don't like being in the spotlight. I just like playing. Obviously, you're going to be the hero or the goat when you're the quarterback. But I'm more of a roll-with-things kind of person. As a person, I'm pretty boring. I play video games. That's my favorite hobby.

If you told me when the 2003 season started that I'd do what I did, I never would have believed it. The season I had, the team had, I think no one really expected that. It was a dream come true. It was kind of surreal. I learned a lot from Carson Palmer on how to lead a team. He was the same all the time, never nervous, always calm under pressure. And that's kind of how I was.

The way Carson carried himself, even when he was getting ripped by everybody, I really admired that. I tried to be the same way. And with all the talent around me, it would have been hard not to be successful.

Mike Williams had my back from day one. He was constantly in the newspapers saying I was the man. When one of the best players in the country is saying, "This is our guy. He's going to lead us wherever we go," that gives you great confidence.

The toughest game of my career was the 2005 Notre Dame game. I was in shock. I didn't want to celebrate 'til the clock hit zero, because who knows what can happen in three seconds? It was just a great game, and I'm still really speechless. I would imagine it will go down as one of the greatest games ever played.

They played exactly how we thought they would. They did pressure us a little more than we thought, and that can get you off rhythm a little bit. But they did what we thought, and I missed some easy throws that would have been big plays.

On fourth-and-nine during the final drive, Dwayne Jarrett made a great move on the defensive back, and the ball just fit in there perfectly. Then he just took off and did the rest. I actually thought I underthrew the ball. The camera caught me doing a little sign of the cross before that last drive. I needed all the help I could get.

Of the rollout to set up the winning score, we were trying to throw it low and get a quick hit, but it is tough to hit those, and they covered it well. I probably could have got in the end zone on that play, but the ball got popped out.

I was off all day. I don't really know what was wrong. I threw two bad interceptions. But what matters is how we finished the game.

Against UCLA in my last game at the Coliseum, I was a mess, an emotional wreck, but Reggie carried the day. Getting to the national championship game in 2005 at Pasadena was a great way to end my whole career: in L.A., in front of our home fans, family, and friends.

It was crazy; it was intense. It was an honor to play in that game. Some called it the best game ever played. Texas was up to the challenge, and Vince Young was great. I felt we had the best team, but all the credit has to go to Texas.

Matt Leinart may be the greatest college football player who ever lived. He made All-America three years (2003–2005), was the runaway winner of the 2004 Heisman Trophy, and was a New York finalist behind teammate Reggie Bush (2005). Leinart was three times All–Pac-10 and twice the conference Offensive Player of the Year. He won the Columbus Touchdown Club's Archie Griffin Award (2003–2004), the Walter Camp Award (2004), was the AP Player of the Year, the Manning Award winner, and Victor Award College Player of the Year. He won the Johnny Unitas Award (2005), the Pop Warner Award (2005), was the Sporting News Sportsman of the Year (2005), and, along with Bush, was one of *Sports Illustrated*'s co–Sportsmen of the Year. He was elected to the USC Athletic Hall of Fame and was twice team captain (2004–2005). In 2003 he led the Trojans to victory over Michigan in the Rose Bowl (earning the Player of the Game Award) and a national championship. The 2004 unbeaten national champion Trojans are one of the finest teams in history. Leinart was the MVP of USC's 55–19 win over Oklahoma in the 2005 BCS Orange Bowl national championship game. Drafted in the first round by Arizona, Leinart became the Cardinals' starting quarterback.

BRANDON HANCOCK

FULLBACK

2002–2003, 2005

Was USC everything that I thought it would be? I think without a doubt it was. But to be frank, they were 6–6 in my senior year of high school. Obviously, it was USC, but it was a gut decision to come here. Academics was my thing, so I took a three-tiered approach to how much a degree from here means. I looked at the social environment, the weather, and the demographics. I have family in Southern California, which played in its favor. But basically I wanted the chance to win a national title. It was between Stanford and USC. Stanford's an academic juggernaut on the West Coast, but they've never assembled a team that could win a national title or a BCS bowl game. Maybe 20 years ago, I would have made a different decision, but in the last 15 years under Dr. Sample, USC has narrowed the academic gap with Stanford so much that it's the best of both worlds now.

I graduated from Clovis West High in Fresno a semester early. USC went from 6–6 the season before I enrolled to 11–2 in my freshman year; then 12–1, 13–0, and 12–1 my senior year. Three Heisman winners, BCS bowl wins. Wow. Are you kidding me? That said, with two national titles and five Pac-10 championship rings, the way the school lived up to the hype for me was the fact I got my bachelor's degree, my secondary minor, and a master's paid for by my scholarship. Academically, the school provided me everything and more. With no NFL team in Los Angeles, we're a big-ticket atmosphere. The college life, the quality of the school, the weather, beautiful girls,

Brandon Hancock heads for a fourth-quarter touchdown against Stanford on November 5, 2005. USC defeated Stanford 51–21.

Photo courtesy of Getty Images

business opportunities—USC provided me all I could dream of and beyond. It's a good time to be Trojan!

Dallas Sartz was my teammate and good friend. The *Los Angeles Times* ran a funny human-interest story about how Dallas lived in a place with four good-looking girls, how they'd model their clothes for him and ask for his opinion before they went out. "Is this too suggestive, Dallas?" "Do guys like this, Dallas?" It was like that old sitcom *Three's Company*.

I had a chance to live with a couple of attractive girls. Sunny Byrd was like 25 or 26 years old, a senior, and a wiser man than me. He said, "Chicks can be crazy." They're cleaner, yeah, but you have to put up with so much stuff. You don't want to make a mess where you eat, so to speak. But Dallas, he got in touch with his feminine side. He's a ladies' man and was like the queen bee in reverse. Besides, he had his buddies living across the hall, so anytime he wanted a break from that, he could just walk over there for the chips and beer.

What they say about Pete Carroll is all true. Coach has an incredible gift for powerful rhetoric. He understands the power of words and conveys a message that is readily perceived. He's persuasive. He comes to your house, sits in your living room, and gets your attention. He thinks about things you say, he listens, and the next thing is, *Wow, what just happened there?* I was committed to Stanford, but after I went to USC and met him, I changed my mind—and he didn't even have his record then. He's a great storyteller and can go to a house in inner-city L.A., Compton, or a house next to a golf course in the suburbs of Marin County. Carroll can identify with any audience. He's like a politician or an attorney. He studies this stuff. I walked into his office once, and he was watching tape of himself. I said, "What are you doing, Coach?" He said he was going over this again. It was always, "How can I do this better?"

Guys from every state come to USC because Carroll conveys what it means to be a Trojan, and guys want to be a part of it. He has a keen memory and doesn't operate some run-of-the-mill meat market. He embraces our families and makes us feel like important people. I sat with Lloyd Carr of Michigan, and it was *booorring*.

Pete Carroll possesses the kind of charisma that gets guys to want to compete. A Mitch Mustain wants to be a part of it with no guarantee he'll start. Pete recruits players who are competitive. These guys are competitive athletes who think that, with proper mentoring, they can beat anybody out. We had seven tailbacks, all five-star, blue-chip kids, and none of those guys was thinking, *I'm not good enough.* Chris Carlisle works those guys hard. You work hard at football and at school, and guys learn to be model Trojans, to earn their stripes on the field. Sometimes they fade away, but others embrace it and make the most out of it. Stafon Johnson was almost ready to hang it up and go someplace else, but he stuck it out.

The guys who have what it takes to be Trojans are the ones who look at this situation, and it fuels their fire. *I'll be the best.* Matt Cassel was phenomenal, plus a pitcher on the baseball team. He was drafted without playing much baseball. A Matt Cassel stays in the program, a *great* quarterback who never played but still had a legitimate shot with the New England Patriots. He had a good preseason with New England and ran some good offensive series. When Tom Brady went down, he had a chance to shine. Our system's crazy, but it prepares you. We're stockpiled with talent, but Carroll allows freshmen to play. He guarantees them a shot. Some schools don't play freshmen, but 80 percent of our incoming freshmen play. I don't know how he does it. I'd coach myself if I knew how to sell this idea that you can be part of something big.

Sometimes we have guys who get hurt because of the way we practice, which is unique in its intensity and tempo. We pretty much scrimmage every day, one-on-one at full speed, double-sword, go hard, compete at a *high* level. On Saturday you almost slow down after the week. There's a risk of injury. Every fall camp there's 13 or 14 hamstring pulls. At one practice, guys were dropping like flies. But he recruits with the philosophy that the depth chart is etched in sand, and there's not a lot of drop-off. I was the starting fullback, but it was no big deal when I tore my ACL. Ryan Powdrell just came in and kicked butt. When he got hurt, Stanley Havili was an incredible athlete until he broke his leg. It's like what former assistant coach Ed Orgeron said: "When you're on the firing line and the guy next to you takes a bullet in the chest, you just pick up his musket and keep on marching."

Ex-coach John Robinson used to talk about how the fan base at USC was a "politician's dream." I was attracted by the school's demographics. I took my first recruiting trip to UCLA with Bob Toledo. The school's surrounded by Westwood. It's pristine, it's so nice with Brentwood, Bel Air, Beverly Hills, Santa Monica beach—heck, the Hugh Hefner mansion's a couple blocks away. That experience, though, feels soft, like a country club. It's too nice. It's not roughneck, hardcore football.

USC is an island in the ghetto. They've brought it up to speed along with downtown L.A., "L.A. Alive," the building of Staples and Galen Center, new condos, businesses, restaurants, and nightlife. We've expanded student housing, faculty housing, cleaned the streets, decreased crime, even cleaned up the smog a lot.

303

Downtown was a ghost town when I first got there. Back then you didn't cross Exposition Boulevard, but now you have a cross-section of demographics, of all kinds of people. They call it the "University of Spoiled Children," but that's a fallacy. There's a diversity of contact with all kinds of people, and you enjoy the academic experience. It's a diverse pool of people, and I thoroughly enjoyed that facet of it. Our fans are a wide-ranging group, from the super-elite, wealthy, old-school alumni to your more hardcore crowd.

We had a lot of fun at USC. There's a couple of choices, as at any college. You have your "animal house" fraternities. During the fall, nightlife is the best. That's when a college becomes a social arena, what with concerts on campus, on Thursday nights the frats would blow up, and there's rush. But if you're a football player, you kind of lock it down and miss that experience. In the spring there's some of that, but you never really know until your last year what the experience of game day is like—the barbecues, the tailgating.

Most of the guys had fun, but it was so much different when USC became a Hollywood-type environment with Matt Leinart. He was hanging with Paris Hilton and all these beautiful models and starlets, and we were all a part of that. We'd go to these Hollywood blowouts, rolling it out with Reggie Bush or someone, and I'm telling you, we were the biggest thing in town. A lot of guys would lock it down during the season, but after the 1990s, when Pete Carroll got here and the pro teams were gone, USC football became a celebrity scene. Some of the stuff that went on is still infamous. You take your licks on Thursday, then get in a plane Friday, or stay in the team hotel, and play on Saturday. Then the rest of the week is practice. During the season, people kept it close to home.

Some guys don't like being gawked at by chicks. Most want to get away and concentrate on being a starter. That walk from the locker room to practice could be a gauntlet of autographs, cameramen, and reporters. You'd be late to class because a camera crew wanted a quick interview. Most players live with each other. In the off-season we'd get around to L.A., the South Bay, Manhattan and Hermosa Beach—maybe a quick trip to Vegas.

I live in Manhattan Beach, and there's a lot of cardinal and gold down there. The Trojans are huge. It's a great place to live your senior year and then after you graduate, but you like that roughneck situation near campus. There were kids with no clue, they'd never been exposed to that lifestyle. Don't get me wrong, Westwood's nice, and you can't say it's not an advantage for UCLA, but I honestly mean it when I say the neighborhood surrounding USC was part of the broader educational experience, and I was glad to have it.

Brandon Hancock was one of the most popular Trojans of the Pete Carroll era, a hard-nosed fullback who sacrificed for the good of the team. Hancock was part of two national champions, two Rose Bowl teams, and the 2003 Orange Bowl champions. He won the Howard Jones Football/Alumni Club Award for the highest GPA, and the John Wayne Memorial Scholarship given to the player aspiring to postgraduate education, who does not go into pro football. After injuries ended his career, Brandon became a respected radio football analyst.

TOM MALONE

PUNTER

2002–2005

I WAS REALLY LUCKY TO GO TO USC. As a freshman and sophomore at Temescal Canyon High School in Lake Elsinore, California, we had a guy named Nate Goodson who was a big recruit. USC had recruiters looking at him, and consequently I came to their attention. I wasn't going to go to USC, but Coach Paul Hackett and his coaches saw me a lot. I never heard much from them until Ed Orgeron called. I grew up rooting for the Washington Huskies and had no interest in USC, but they called me back. I thought about it and saw the campus, and I was impressed. Orgeron offered me a scholarship. I checked Arizona out, a couple other schools, but committed within a week. It was my junior year at Temescal Canyon. I got everything ready to graduate early, so I could come in for spring practice. I wanted to have spring practice and summer training under my belt in order to get a head start. I graduated from Temescal Canyon in December 2001, and enrolled at USC in January 2002, right after the Vegas Bowl. I started as a true freshman in 2002.

Quarterback Carson Palmer was great, and so was that team. I hadn't realized the team was down a little before I got there, but with Pete Carroll you just knew we were going to be really good. Carroll said we were a couple years from competing for a national title, but we were there that year. Troy Polamalu, Malaefou MacKenzie, Carson—we had a fantastic team, as good as anybody in the nation. But it was hard getting used to college and the big stage.

Receiver Mike Williams was incredible, so athletic. He was a basketball player, and we played basketball a lot. He was so tall and so big that anything that was coming up, he came down with. Keary Colbert and Kareem Kelly were phenomenal, as well. That was one of the funnest years I ever had. We started fairly well, but not great. We lost a couple games, then just took off, and by season's end we were the best. Then the next year it carried over.

Defensive back Troy Polamalu was incredible, one of the best I ever played with. He had a great work ethic. I picked up his work ethic, in the weight room and on the practice field. We'd still be working with the punt-return team for half an hour after practice was over, and we got that from Troy. He was an All-American and one of the all-time best Trojans. We wanted to do all we could to make it work. We knew we had All-Americans and first-round draft picks, and wanted to make the most of the talent we had. It helped me out a lot.

In 2003 sophomore quarterback Matt Leinart took over. At first we thought there would be a transition from Carson to Matt, but he was another one of those guys who just came in with that winning attitude, and he worked hard in the weight room. He did everything he could to be the best. So did Matt Cassel. He had been around, and there was a lot of competition for starting quarterback. But that was the good thing about USC—there was always somebody who could take your spot. Matt was calm, and we always had the feeling it was going to be good when he was out there.

Reggie Bush was a guy I knew from the start, every day in practice. I felt bad for other teams that had to kick to that guy. He was ridiculous. He had unreal talent and was freakish about working out. He was so fast, and everything we did, he took over, doing it really well. In 2003 that was probably the most fun overall I had. The team had a good year. We had a loss but battled back and we were able to be in a position to win the national championship at the 2004 Rose Bowl.

Against Michigan, I think we were really confident going in. By that time in the season, the way we were playing, nobody doubted how the game would turn out. Plus it was at "home" in the Rose Bowl. Winning the national title was on the line. It was like winning against Iowa in the Orange Bowl the previous year. Now we knew we'd be good, and we were confident.

Tom Malone (14) congratulates kicker Ryan Killeen as Killeen celebrates his second field goal against UCLA on December 4, 2004, at the Rose Bowl. *Photo courtesy of Getty Images*

We beat UCLA every year. In 2002, 2003, and 2005 we just crushed them. Beating UCLA's so big, it's awesome to do that. We never had to worry about the outcome. We were messing around on the sideline, but we'd take care of business against them. We always prepared hard, but there was a little difference against them. There are bragging rights, and you knew or watched so many guys from Southern California, it's a lot of fun and great to play in.

There's a difference between the Notre Dame and UCLA rivalries. UCLA is more for bragging rights, and you know so many players in L.A. You've got the bands, and there's so much going on in the stadium. But with Notre Dame, you feel the tradition of that game. Personally, Notre Dame is bigger as far as what the rivalry meant. I hated USC growing up and watched that game, rooting against them. For the fans, there's no tradition like it, and there's so much hype when you go back to South Bend. It's a lot of fun to be part of. The Notre Dame game is a great college tradition.

Against Oklahoma in the 2005 BCS Orange Bowl national championship game, everybody had a great game across the board that night. We were prepared and had been unbeaten during the season, but there was a feeling of being a slight underdog. We practiced hard for all our games and had the same approach, but our practices were a lot of fun before that game. We worked hard but still had a great time going out in Miami. Some people said we didn't take it seriously because we'd go out and see the city, and Oklahoma got there early. They never wanted to do all the bowl stuff, but Coach Carroll said for us to just have fun. It was a reward for a good season, and we didn't change anything. We went at it as hard as we could in practice and got it done. Then we'd have a good time. But we came out right away, jumped on them, and never let up. We finished every game.

In 2005 I was never on the field. I was hurt, but I wouldn't have gotten to punt much because we were unstoppable. People said we were the best team in college football history. In that UCLA game, the last game at the Coliseum, I ran out on the field for the last time as a senior, but I never punted once. It was a fitting end, to not play against UCLA, because our offense was ridiculous. We never got held to a fourth down. It was awesome. LenDale White was a Heisman-caliber player in his own right. He was just a football player who never went down. He'd do what he had to do to get a first down or a touchdown. He was a great football player, a great athlete, but he never touched his true potential on that team. As a punter, I could watch a lot of the game, sit back on the side, and watch them break runs.

Being down on the field against Texas in the 2006 BCS Rose Bowl national championship game was awesome, right until the last few seconds. We'd worked so hard, and Matt had come back for his senior year. We worked hard all off-season, and it was a great season, maybe the best any team ever had. We were confident and felt good, but Texas played a great game. It was definitely not the feeling we wanted to leave with after four years, and it wasn't what we expected. But it was a fun game, it was so close. You want those games—it's the most fun to play well at the end in close games. That was an awesome game, some say the best ever played. Vince Young was very good and had a great game that night. I don't think, without him, they'd have had the same game. He had the majority to do with that win, but there were a lot of great players on the field that night for both sides. The fans had a great game, and it was a thrill to be a part of it. For a long time, I felt like I wanted another year. We'd worked so hard to have a great season, and I tried and remember that.

Pete Carroll is the best, period. I know of a lot of guys at a lot of colleges and hear what they say about their coaches. I can't imagine playing for another coach. Practice was 100 percent all the time. If you were tired or not into it, he got up to it every day, and that makes you practice hard. We always had a great time, and the team got along so well. We'd sing and dance. We all went out together, and we worked hard. We were prepared, but we had more fun than any team and hung out as a team. Carroll brought us together. He just turned on and knew how to prepare us, how to play football, not just all on the football field but in life. It carries over: be early; pay attention; whether in class or on the job, you always do your best. There's always somebody working harder than you, so you have to compete against yourself more than others on the team. It was awesome.

I don't know what his secret is. Coach Carroll loves football. He never tires. Every game he does as good a job as anybody. He says anybody can beat you; no game is bigger than any other game. So we never do anything special versus a particular opponent. We'd just go out every day and work hard. It carried over. He did a good job, and we all bought in. We just had so much fun. During games he runs around; at meetings he's enthusiastic. On Tuesday practice he runs around and never gets burned out. We never realized how hard we were working because he made it fun. Other players on teams were ready for a vacation, but we were ready every week.

Tom Malone is the greatest punter (and first All-American at the position) in USC football history. A 2003 All-American, he played for two national champions (2003 and 2004), two Orange Bowl champions (2003 and 2005) and a Rose Bowl champion (2004). Tom was twice all-conference (2003–2004) and a two-time Playboy Preseason All-American (2004–2005). He would have led the nation in punting in 2004, but the Trojans scored so much he did not get enough tries to qualify. He played in the 2006 East-West Shrine Game, but injuries sustained in his senior year impeded a professional career.

MARIO DANELO

PLACE-KICKER

2003–2006

When Mario Danelo passed away, former Trojan football player Tim Lavin wrote about his funeral. Eventually, Tim's missive made its way onto the Internet, eliciting a thousand responses. Here is the essay.

★ ★ ★

Trojan in the Sky
Mario Danelo #19 PK
USC Trojans Football 2003–2006
Friday, January 12, 2007

Today, I attended the funeral services of a young man I did not know personally, yet we are part of the same family: the Trojan football alumni family. Today, I witnessed families, friends, and teammates coming together to pay tribute to a young man who touched the lives of thousands of people. I was not planning on writing about my experience but was inspired to do so.

When I got to the San Pedro church, there was a crowd of hundreds, maybe over 1,000 people gathered around the front entrance spilling onto the blocked-off streets. All roads surrounding Mary Star of the Sea Catholic Church were barricaded by the police department. At 10:30 AM, the casket, flanked by eight young men in the prime of their lives, was carried from the hearse, parked directly in front of the church, up the steps to the front doors. With more than 100 USC football players and coaches in coat and tie surrounding the front of the church, they slowly followed the casket in a procession that proceeded inside and down the center aisle to the altar.

From the outside looking in, a funnel of ominous young men disappeared into the wide-open doors that welcomed their entrance. Swallowed up by the flow of their wake, patrons began to file in side by side. Mary Star seats some 1,500 people. Its high ceilings cast the sunlight through scores of stained-glass windows. The pews are split down the center with a wide middle aisle. Three-quarters of the way down the center aisle is a cross aisle, creating a "t" or a "cross," if you will. With standing-room only, both of the side aisles were jam-packed, making the cross aisle completely full, and the center aisle filled up. When it was time for the crowd to sit down, those that couldn't inadvertently created a standing human cross.

In the rear of the church, the vestibule was shoulder to shoulder, chest to back, 20 people deep. People continued to arrive only to find out there was no place left inside. Hundreds of mourners remained standing on the steps outside the church, spilling onto the sidewalk and into the street between parked limos and police motorcycles. They were forced to listen to the outside loudspeaker of what was being said on the inside.

Mario Danelo was just 21 years old when he left this earth six days ago. He was the place-kicker for the USC Trojans. When officials cleaned out his locker, amidst the socks, cleats, T-shirts, and shorts, was Mario's Bible. That Bible lay on top of his casket during the entire service. During the homily, the priest spoke of doing mass services for the Trojan football team before games. He spoke of the tough loss at the end of the regular season being a tragedy. And then later, on January 1, the victorious Rose Bowl game that turned into glory. He spoke of the tragedy last week that took Mario away from us here on earth. And then, the victorious ascension into Heaven that has turned into glory. And he spoke of remembering the great big smile on Mario Danelo's face.

When the mass had ended, four people got up to face the overflowing congregation, inside and out, of more than 2,500 people. First to speak was Joey Danelo, Mario's older brother. For some 10 minutes, Joey captivated us with moments of sadness along with outbreaks of laughter. Fighting back the tears, he actually told several humorous stories of Mario's aggressive behavior from his childhood days. He said Mario was the first five-year-old

Mario Danelo gets ready to kick off during a game against the Arizona State Sun Devils in October 2005 at Sun Devil Stadium in Tempe, Arizona. USC won 38–28. *Photo courtesy Getty Images*

basketball player to foul out of a game in the first 11 seconds of the first quarter. Later on, in Little League baseball, he was the first pitcher to hit four batters in the same inning. Regardless of what he and his brothers did together, they were constantly having fun, living the life, and always smiling. Joey said that Mario once told him you can tell the content of a man's character by how many people attend his funeral. He looked up from his written script to glance around the church through his watery eyes. It was beyond a chilling moment.

As they got older, they became even closer. In the past couple of years, they hung out with each other's friends and became even tighter. Joey finished his eulogy by saying, "Thank you, I love you, buddy," and walked over and gave his brother one last little pat on the shoulder as his hand came down on the casket. Brian, his friend of 20 years, took the podium. He too had several stories that created moments of laughter and sadness at the same time.

Whatever happened while they were growing up, he could always remember Mario laughing and smiling. Next to speak was from Mario's San Pedro High School football team, Coach Walsh. During the coach's 26-year reign at the school, only three players were ever named to the All-Academic Scholar Athlete Team of Los Angeles, and Mario was one of them. On the field, he was an outstanding young football player who carried himself with grace, dignity, and pride. Off the field, he was an exemplary student with the highest grades. On or off the field, Coach Walsh always saw Mario having fun, and always smiling.

Lastly, Coach Pete Carroll came to the microphone. He reiterated what the priest talked about earlier of this being a glorious day, and actually a time not to mourn Mario's passing, but to celebrate his life. And, oh man, how he did live. He was living the dream. Coach Carroll, not surprisingly, talked of that "Mario Danelo smile" that we had heard so much about from all the others. And then, for the first time in my life, I experienced something that I had never experienced before at a funeral service. Coach Carroll talked about the NCAA scoring records that Mario has. He said, "Most of you don't know that Mario has the highest scoring record for college football. I think that is something to cheer about!" Carroll went on: "...now when I say Mario has the scoring record, I want to hear you!" Nervous laughter seemed to fill the church. And then Coach Carroll yelled out for all to hear: "MARIO IS THE SCORING RECORD-HOLDER IN COLLEGE FOOTBALL!" The seated patrons rose to their feet in an eruption of thunderous applause, cheers, yelling, screaming, and whistling. It was like being at the Coliseum and USC's Mario Danelo just kicked the winning field goal and the place is going wild!!!

For nearly two minutes, the church was going berserk with deafening cheers on the inside, absolutely booming roars that filled the daytime sky on the outside and the entire building was shaking. People, blocks away, must have been thinking, "I thought there was a funeral going on at Mary Star????"

As the noise slowly started to subside, Carroll stepped away from the microphone, pointed at his 100-plus players in the front 15 rows, and said, "COME ON, LET ME HEAR YOU!" The football players let out even louder cheers and cries that had to have echoed through the Coliseum tunnel. The crowd went nuts again for another two minutes of constant clapping, cheering, and whistling led by the Trojan team. It was one of the most amazing things I have ever seen.

Shortly thereafter, the priest gave his final blessing, and the exodus of 2,000-plus began to overrun the streets and join those hundreds of others who had been out there for nearly two hours. On my lapel I wore a Trojan football alumni pin. In my pocket, I had another lapel pin still in its package. I wanted the Danelo family to have it. But, not knowing them, it was certainly not appropriate for me to approach them at this time. So I wondered what to do as I stood on the grass on the side of the church. Not more than 10 seconds elapsed when Coach Pete Carroll walked by, saw an opening on the sidewalk, and stood alone only a few feet away from me. Questioning my own thoughts of the right thing to do, I nervously approached Coach Carroll. With the pin in my hand, I reached out so he could see it. As he looked down at the pin in the palm of my hand, I said, "Coach, perhaps you can give this pin to Mario's parents. When Mario walked on the field, he was a Trojan football player. When he walked off the field for the last time, he became a Trojan football alumnus. He will always be part of the Trojan Football Alumni Club." With that, Coach Carroll took the pin out of my hand, looked me in the eyes, and said, "Thank you. I will give it to them."

Today I witnessed what the Trojan family is truly all about. Regardless if we know each other personally or not, we are always family. You may not know us personally, but if you need us, we are here for you.

May God bless Mario, his family, friends, and teammates during this most difficult time. FIGHT ON!

—Tim Lavin
Trojan Football Alumni '88–'91
Club Secretary

Shortly after the Trojans defeated Michigan in the 2007 Rose Bowl, Mario Danelo walked to the rocky shores of his native San Pedro, California, to contemplate things. He slipped and fell, apparently hitting his head and dying. Since then, the special-teams award has been renamed in his honor: the Mario Danelo Special Teams Player of the Year Award (given to Thomas Williams and Clay Matthews in 2007). Mario's funeral was a well-attended, emotional affair, and when Troy came out for their first extra point of the 2007 season against Idaho, Coach Pete Carroll sent the team out with only 10 men—no kicker—taking the penalty in his honor. Mario always said he was "living the dream" playing for USC, and the goal posts at the Coliseum are draped with those words in his memory.

AN BING · AMBROSE SCHINDLER · BILL GRAY · JIM HARDY · GO
LAKIS · MARV GOUX · JON ARNETT · C.R. ROBERTS · MONTE CL
M ROSSOVICH · RON YARY · ADRIAN YOUNG · MIKE BATTLE · ST
McNEILL · MANFRED MOORE · J.K. McKAY · RICHARD WOOD ·
FOSTER · JEFF BROWN · MICHAEL HARPER · TIM GREEN · STEV
MARINOVICH · SCOTT ROSS · DERRICK DEESE · MATT GEE · TA
RT · BRANDON HANCOCK · TOM MALONE · MARIO DANELO · N
FRANK GIFFORD · AL CARMICHAEL · TOM NICKOLOFF · SAM
IX · HAL BEDSOLE · WILLIE BROWN · CRAIG FERTIG · BILL FISK
E · JOHN McKAY · JOHN VELLA · SAM CUNNINGHAM · ALLAN GR
HEWS · FRANK JORDAN · PAUL McDONALD · KEITH VAN HORN
JEFF BREGEL · REX MOORE · MARK CARRIER · JOHN JACKSON
AKIS · JOHN ROBINSON · CARSON PALMER · KEVIN ARBET · MA
BING · AMBROSE SCHINDLER · BILL GRAY · JIM HARDY · GOR
LAKIS · MARV GOUX · JON ARNETT · C.R. ROBERTS · MONTE CL
M ROSSOVICH · RON YARY · ADRIAN YOUNG · MIKE BATTLE · ST
McNEILL · MANFRED MOORE · J.K. McKAY · RICHARD WOOD ·
FOSTER · JEFF BROWN · MICHAEL HARPER · TIM GREEN · STEV
MARINOVICH · SCOTT ROSS · DERRICK DEESE · MATT GEE · TA